Praise for Innovation and Entrepreneurship

Fascinating to see that the early learnings of the European Institute of Innovation and Technology (EIT) now hit the public in a book that is the most comprehensive and understandable description of the role of (networked) entrepreneurship in the Knowledge Triangle. Following the author, I sincerely hope that in Education, in Business firms and in Research Institutes, Innovation in Europe returns to its entrepreneurial roots in search of new prosperity.

Professor Martin Schuurmans
Founding Chairman of the European Institute of Innovation and
Technology, former Vice President of Philips

In an increasingly research and technology rich world, Daria Tataj explores the growing importance of 'technology push' - in place of demand pull - in driving innovation and growth. She identifies the critical role of the entrepreneur as the integrator of the innovation process from idea to funding to market. Based on extensive research, this book will help shape policy and thinking for a new model of innovation-driven economic growth.

Professor Dame Julia King
Vice Chancellor, Aston University, Birmingham

Innovation
and
entrepreneurship

A Growth Model for Europe
Beyond the Crisis

ISBN-10: 0-692-41980-2
ISBN-13: 978-0-692-41980-9

Book Reviewer: João Caraça
Book Reviewer: Manuel Castells
Book Editor: Melody VanWanzeele

Cover Designer: Miguel Trindade
Book Designer: Miguel Trindade
Development Editor: Alexander Lindroth, www.targetmktng.com

To
Darek, Misia
Tosia and Helena

Table of Contents

Preface

Understanding Innovation in the Real Economy – At Last!

by
Manuel
Castells

Innovation and entrepreneurship are the key sources of productivity, competitiveness, and economic growth in the knowledge economy. Thus, in recent years there has been a flurry of theory and research on the processes conducive to enhancing the generation of innovation and entrepreneurship, two distinct but intertwined components of economic growth in our time. Yet, most of the current literature is either based on formal neo-classical theory, with little connection to the real world, or on empirical observation limited to a particular context, thus making it difficult to replicate the findings for companies, regions, or nations in search of a new path of development. However, we may be able to better design innovation policies and entrepreneurship strategies by reflecting on a major experience undertaken by the European Commission in 2008: the European Institute of Innovation and Technology (EIT). This is not a new academic institution, although it is an organization of sorts, built on a pan-European network of companies, universities, and government agencies.

The significance of the EIT is that it proposes a new model of innovation, entrepreneurship, and economic growth, and that it has supported the proposition with a multi-billion euro, multi-year program that is transforming the European landscape of innovation. This is a real life experiment that is testing some of the most audacious ideas about the theory and practice of innovation.

This book aims to elucidate the key factors accounting for a synergistic relationship between universities, businesses, and entrepreneurs in the innovation process. It relies on an extensive review of the literature on innovation and entrepreneurship, constructs an analytical framework, and proceeds with an empirical analysis of the experience of the knowledge and innovation communities created by the EIT. It considers the implications of this experience for a new model of growth for Europe and beyond, as the developed world still struggles to leave behind the consequences of the financial crisis of 2008. The analysis presented here pays careful attention to the specificity of each economic and institutional context, so that the global innovation model is only an analytical reference that needs to be adapted to each country and to each domain of activity where the innovation process takes place.

The book is timely and highly relevant because, as the author points out, the West has suffered a major financial crisis since 2008, with dire consequences on growth and employment in many countries, including most of Europe and the United States, in spite of recent upward trends in job creation in the US. Austerity policies and responsible fiscal policy are only some of the components of the strategy to overcome the crisis. But restarting the growth engine is the only sustainable policy in the long term. Under the stricter conditions of private lending and public spending, the only possibility for recovering the path of economic growth in a sustainable form is a substantial increase in productivity and competitiveness in the business sector as a result of superior innovation and entrepreneurship. Innovation and entrepreneurship are the drivers of the economic recovery. However, where are the sources of innovation and entrepreneurship in the current context of a shaky world economy? This is where this book provides empirically grounded answers with theoretical meaning and policy relevance.

Looking at the recent international experience, particularly in the United States, the author proposes the notion of networks of innovation. In a fully networked world, based on relentless flows of information and management supported by telecommunicated computer networks, innovation is no longer the result of an individual firm or of a sole innovator, but a networked process between the producers of knowledge, the entrepreneurs that transform ideas into business projects, and the institutional environment that may be conducive to the surge of innovation or, instead, to the limitation of its potential because of lack of entrepreneurship or excessive bureaucracy. Networks are the operating system of the economy in the age of digital communication and information processing. But networks are specific and organized around certain goals, and when innovation is the goal, the networks of collaboration must be geared toward this purpose. This is what the author shows, using a variety of examples in the international experience, with particular emphasis on the United States, birthplace of the new, innovative economy associated with the information technology revolution and the rise of new forms of entrepreneurship. The author has conducted interviews and has observed entrepreneurial processes in Silicon Valley, Michigan, and other seedbeds of innovation in the United States. And this is apparent in the fine grain analysis through which she explains the formation and dynamics of the networks of innovation that are at the source of dynamism in today's economy. She has been able to integrate these insights in the analytical scheme on which she bases her research.

The book draws on extensive observations from the author's experience as a founding executive committee member of the European Institute of Innovation and Technology, and particularly from the actual performance of the first three Knowledge and Innovation Communities (KICs) launched by the EIT under the auspices of the European Commission. Because of her leading role at the EIT, the author has had access to highly relevant data from these KICs. These data are used to conduct research on the experience and to draw lessons of general analytical value. This book is not an evaluation of the EIT's performance, nor a defense of the EIT's activity. Rather, the study of the EIT experience is a testing ground for the hypotheses on the generation of innovation and entrepreneurship that the author formulates on the basis of the literature review and on the observation and interviews she conducted in the United States and in Europe on different models of innovation.

The "Knowledge and Innovation Communities" are networks of universities, research centers, business firms, and small and medium enterprises co-located in a given metropolitan area, then networked with other co-localized networks in several metropolitan areas in Europe, managed by a governing agency that is largely self-reliant in terms of its own budget, though initially supported by the European Union. It is an original model of innovation that results from ideas that emerged in the international practice and that have been articulated in a coherent manner for the first time in this pathbreaking book by Dr. Tataj.

The key model proposed in the book is what Dr. Tataj calls "the knowledge triangle." It refers to the synergy resulting from the interaction between education, research, and innovation. It is in the interaction between knowledge produced in research, educational resources that allow both research and the implementation of its findings, and the application of this knowledge to the creation of wealth in the business world, that a synergistic relationship emerges, leading to growth in productivity and competitiveness: a new growth model that results from supply factors, rather than from stimuli from demand, be it public spending or consumer demand. Yet, perhaps the most original approach in Dr. Tataj's contribution is her emphasis on entrepreneurship as the vector that operates the transition from knowledge and education to business performance and economic growth. This is because the historical record of innovation in all contexts shows that the uses of new knowledge to create business projects most often comes from the action of entrepreneurs who have the ability to understand the opportunity of a potentially successful project, and who have the drive to risk their investment and their livelihood in the creation of new enterprises and new lines of innovation in process and in product.

The missing link in the process of innovation, as Dr. Tataj explains, is the entrepreneur that brings together all of the components of the innovation process and creates a business firm out of his/her project. In this process he/she requires access to venture capital under its different forms (including business angels): without capital that accepts the risk of investing in innovation, there is little chance that new knowledge results in innovative business. The experience of high technology industries and advanced business services in the last three decades shows that venture capital is an essential factor to induce entrepreneurship, the source of innovation in the new, global economy.

However, the diversity of institutional contexts matters, as innovation results from different models, as the author shows by contrasting the experiences of Silicon Valley, Finland, and a number of European innovation systems. The relative weight of government, educational institutions, and venture capitalists varies in each context, but in all cases, the knowledge triangle is present and the role of entrepreneurship is essential. This attention to institutional variation of the innovation process is one of the great strengths of this book, which can be read with benefit in many different countries without having to comply with the ethnocentric biases of some studies of innovation.

Furthermore, the author analyzes the processes and institutions of innovation governance, and shows that governance is a key factor in guiding innovation toward successful business practices and socially useful innovation. The analysis of the complex interplay between the structural components of innovation and the institutional and individual actors who intervene in the process is a truly original contribution of this study, and one that will be most helpful to business executives, academic researchers, and policymakers learning the theoretical and practical lessons of innovation from this book. This is a fundamental, innovative book on innovation that will reshape the way we think about innovation and may yield the most needed policy lessons for a new model of growth in the aftermath of the economic crisis.

Manuel Castells

Professor Emeritus of Planning and Sociology, University of California-Berkeley
Fellow of the British Academy, and Fellow of the American Academy of Political and Social Science

Introduction

Is There Growth After the Crisis?

This book is about innovation and entrepreneurship, and how nations and regions can embrace innovation-driven entrepreneurship to integrate and exploit its knowledge, technology, human capital, and industrial base, and thus boost economic growth and job creation.

A global financial crisis, triggered by the bankruptcy of Lehman Brothers in 2008, has had a detrimental effect on the European economy. In 2009 alone it shrunk by 4.3% (Eurostat). After two years of anemic growth, it shrunk again in 2012. Over the four years of struggle, the financial crisis forced lending institutions to severely tighten credit for companies and households. Without financial backing, businesses reduced investment, cut salaries, and laid off workers in many countries, which led to social unrest and political instability (Thompson 2012; Engelen 2011).

As a result of these measures, consumption sharply fell, along with domestic demand, which accounts for about three quarters of GDP growth in the European economy. Governments came to the rescue, bailing out banks with public money and stimulating demand with public spending in infrastructure and social subsidies. Given the already high level of indebtedness of most governments, sovereign debt rose substantially, and financial markets elevated the risk premium and interest rates of sovereign debt to unsustainable levels.[1] The European Commission, supported by the IMF, intervened to rescue countries in exchange for imposing strict policies of economic austerity. These measures helped deal with short-term solvency issues. But what is needed in the mid-term is a new model to help Europe return to a path of growth beyond the crisis.

In Europe, productivity growth and exports are the lighthouses guiding the way toward new prosperity in the darkness of the economic crisis. Indeed, one of the main causes of the crisis in the Euro zone was the artificial integration of economies with vast differences in productivity,

---

(1) There are some exceptions to this trend, most notably Poland. The country has had positive GDP growth throughout the crisis peaking at 4.5% in 2011 (Eurostat). The reasons why Poland has been coping well with the crisis are multifold and synergistic. They surely include the inflow of structural funds from the European Union, as well as a relatively high level of entrepreneurial activity, and a young, well-educated work force.

culture, and institutions, without a fiscal union and without a regulated, integrated banking system. While the crisis induced the EU to set up the foundations of a common banking system and a common fiscal policy, under the aegis of Germany, the question remained of how to steer all economies toward higher productivity and higher competitiveness.

Economic theory and recent historical experience show that productivity growth is largely a function of innovation and entrepreneurship: innovation because it creates wealth out of the synergy generated by combining production factors in the production process (growth of multi-factor productivity in traditional econometric terms); entrepreneurship because once innovation is generated, there is a need for economic actors to finance and to bring new products and processes into the market, often assuming a high risk for their investment in expectation of high returns.

However, knowing that innovation and entrepreneurship are the sources of productivity and competitiveness does not solve the problem. The next question is how innovation and entrepreneurship are generated in our current global networked, knowledge-driven economy, and in the specific context of European economies. One question immediately leads to other queries: What environments are conducive to innovation? What accelerates this process? Why do certain collaborative partnerships or ventures fail to create value when innovating, while others succeed? Why do certain spots attract resources—knowledge, talent, and capital—while other regions are deserted despite efforts to revitalize clusters through public investment in research infrastructure, education, venture capital industry, and subsidizing R&D activities of local industry?

The answers may lie in the theory and practice of innovation in the knowledge-driven economy. In order to propose such a theory, to understand how value is created in a networked environment, this book examines a number of settings in which innovation takes place. The scrutiny of these settings allows one to understand how, where, and when knowledge is produced, disseminated, and translated. It inspects structures, dynamics, architecture, and management practices of various types of innovation networks comprising institutional actors from research, education, and industry and focuses on understanding emerging business models as mechanisms of value creation.

Scrutinizing a number of environments in mature and emerging markets, innovation appears as an ever-present, self-perpetuating system of information exchange and knowledge sharing. In the information age, formal education and its institutions exist in parallel with a myriad of ad hoc emergent learning environments where people learn by "hanging out, messing around, and geeking out" on the Web. Innovating becomes a collective distributed open learning process and this is an essence of the capacity to innovate in a world constantly in flux.

The main idea of the conceptual framework proposed in this book includes four components critical to the operational success of innovation networks: research, education, innovation itself, and entrepreneurship—all of these in relation to business strategy and policy-making. The outcome of this analysis is locked in a simple model for investigating collaborative partnerships and the way these partnership networks are capable of creating value in economic and social terms.

The author has based the whole analytical premise of this undertaking on an assumption that in order to enable collective capacity to develop new products and processes and to bring them to markets and to society in a timely fashion, it is necessary to understand networked environments that are conducive to innovation. In this context, the author has defined innovation as a social process of knowledge production and dissemination, during which human creativity leads to translation of knowledge into shared and enriched capacities.

Effectiveness of collaborative partnerships is largely a function of both innovation and entrepreneurship in university-industry collaboration: innovation because it creates wealth out of the synergy generated by recombining knowledge; entrepreneurship because once innovation is generated, there is a need to manage and finance the process of bringing new products and processes into the market. Evidence shows that bridging the gap between innovation and markets can be done through a diverse set of entrepreneurial entities starting with small innovative firms and ending with large multinationals, through not-for-profit organizations as well as public institutions including universities, and through single individuals: creative, self-employed professionals and micro-multinational entrepreneurs.

Subsequently, I contend that there are three components: research, education, and innovation, which form the Knowledge Triangle, conceptualized initially as a network of institutions engaged in knowledge production and dissemination representing either industry or academia.

I recognize, however, that production and diffusion of innovation occur within institutional settings, such as research institutes, universities, and industry, but they also take place beyond the institutional boundaries of academia and business. Evidence shows that knowledge production, dissemination, and translation also occur in the public sector as well as in the non-government sector. They are driven by individual or collective users (user-driven innovation) as well as by the society-at-large (social innovation, cultural innovation).

If so, innovation happens in more settings than initially assumed, and in fact there is no hierarchy between these settings, although innovation process participants tend to believe there is, for example in the case of academics disregarding industrial applied research and industry innovators discrediting academic research on account of its inapplicability. What is observed in the Knowledge Triangle is a shift from transaction cultures driven by exchanges and the logic of "zero-sum game" to collaborative, relational, trust-based organizational cultures typical of open innovation environments.

I derived the next critical issue from the following question: Is there any specificity of different kinds of flows in such a network as the Knowledge Triangle? The proposition put forward is that there are flows of a specific kind of knowledge, a specific sort of people, and a specific type of capital. It is the flow of codified knowledge, which takes place across and within innovation settings, institutions, and actors in an innovation network. What makes it different from other similar flows is that it is shared in an open innovation environment.

While codified knowledge is transmitted with tangible carriers, often through formal partnership arrangements and intellectual property regimes, the non-codified knowledge is carried by individual people and is disseminated solely upon their decision to share it or not to share it, which is a derivative of a shift from transaction to collaborative culture. For innovation to take place, these flows of talent are critical since they carry unique capability to frame the codified knowledge, connect different pieces of it, reframe it in a changing context, and give it a new meaning.

These continuous flows of talent enable a translation culture, that is a culture of constant learning. The ever-present, self-perpetuating system of knowledge sharing becomes one of the key ingredients of innovation in a world of relentless change. In this context, the Knowledge Triangle is a specific form of an innovation network comprising research, education, and innovation itself. These activities form part of interlinked social processes occurring within diverse institutional settings, which create national or transnational innovation systems, in a myriad of ad hoc, emergent learning environments.

The question then arises: What keeps this particular type of a transnational, trans-institutional, trans-sector, and trans-disciplinary innovation network together? It has been shown that there are a wide variety of models for structuring formal contractual collaboration, linkages, and alliances. But there is evidence that a number of innovation networks tend to cease to exist or operate once public funding is withdrawn since there is not enough of a structural model for the network to generate value to participants.

The answer may lie in emerging new types of organizations, such as those presented in this book.

The analysis moves toward distilling value creation mechanisms epitomized by various business models in a new paradigm of a network enterprise, defined as a unit, with or without legal structure, time-limited, and organized in order to accomplish a particular goal, for which diverse actors allocate resources and create a project, which is a business plan or social innovation.

The search for a constituent that holds together the Knowledge Triangle leads to entrepreneurship being the integrative component, the glue of the Knowledge Triangle. It is proven that entrepreneurship is critical for integrating networks in diverse settings where the components of the innovation process take place, and that entrepreneurship acts as a catalyst for value creation not only by integrating the network but also by creating synergies between the three remaining components.

Therefore, what was initially presented as the Knowledge Triangle is re-conceptualized as a multidimensional network, in which three components of the process—research, education, and innovation—happen simultaneously in a synergistic interaction in a variety of settings. This marks a conceptual shift diverting from thinking of innovation as bilateral or multilateral forms of collaboration between actors in academia and industry with a varying degree of government involvement.

The new paradigm conceptualizes the innovation process of knowledge production, dissemination, and translation (commercialization or application) within a non-hierarchical, dynamic, open environment where different kinds of knowledge flows take place carried by entrepreneurial talent and by entrepreneurial capital. The Knowledge Triangle becomes a multidimensional dynamic and emerging construct "in-the-making." And as a result of the analysis, the components of the Knowledge Triangle are characterized by a shift: from intellectual property-based research to open innovation; from university education to learning environments with a strong peer-to-peer learning component; from innovation within industry to innovation in different kinds of social, creative, and process networks.

These environments conducive to innovation are interlinked and codependent in a context of the global network of innovation networks, which imposes its logic, dynamics, and structures on management practices and business models. What has long been observed is that knowledge, talent, and capital flow freely across the borders and that these resources are accumulated in certain metropolitan areas. The process of industry clustering dates back to the early stages of the industrial revolution.

However, the emergent business models of global and local network enterprises change modalities of value creation. Certain regions or cities emerge as mega nodes and gain access to the global pool of resources: they become magnets attracting excellent knowledge, entrepreneurial people, and smart capital. What is observed in certain cases more prone to success is a shift in the Knowledge Triangle from transaction cultures driven by exchanges and the logic of "zero-sum game" to collaborative, relational, trust-based organizational cultures typical of open innovation environments. Still, there is no answer as to why certain collaborative partnerships fail to generate innovation and entrepreneurship in this networked global environment.

This is the intellectual landscape of this book, leading ultimately to a redefinition of the policy debate on the sources of new growth in Europe and beyond. These issues will be tackled in three sequential analytical operations: the theory of innovation; the practice of entrepreneurship in the knowledge-driven economy, in a comparative perspective; and the reflection of an innovative policy experience in which this author has taken a leadership role: the European Institute of Innovation and Technology, established in 2008 by the European Commission, precisely to create a new model of innovation by bringing together leading companies, research universities, and entrepreneurs, in local networks of innovation connected in pan-European networks under the organizational arrangement of Knowledge and Innovation Communities.

The theoretical references, the observation of international experiences of innovation, particularly in the United States, informed the design and practice of the EIT. And the experience of the EIT, as lived and documented by this author, may inspire a broader reflection on the conditions under which knowledge, innovation, and entrepreneurship may rekindle the European economy, thus reversing the process of decline that, under the current conditions of merciless competition in a global economy populated by new economic actors, could transform the Old Continent into a historic museum of its glorious past—for others to visit and enjoy.

The argument presented here is constructed in a sequence of analytical steps that inform the chapters of the book as follows:

Introduction subchapter "Innovation Blowback" presents the evidence for how innovation and entrepreneurship are induced in a number of environments. It entices the discussion of the essence of innovation and entrepreneurship as driving forces of economic growth and societal development. The starting point for this deliberation is the situation at the beginning of the twenty-first century when two trends collided. Knowledge spillovers allowed companies originating in emerging markets to challenge Western incumbents. Crises in Europe and shrinking domestic markets undermined their position and eroded profits. In this situation, understanding where innovation comes from and how to exploit it rises to the top of the agenda of business leaders and policy makers in Europe. To face this challenge, I offer examples of learning, coming from both the emerging markets and emerging industries.

Chapter "Innovation Networks" is divided into three parts. The first, "Structure, Modalities, and Drivers," focuses on the analysis of different types of innovation networks. The analysis distills a number of features, drivers, and mechanisms that make innovation networks evolve. The process of evolution of network nodes leads to an explanation of why certain nodes change, attracting the flows of knowledge, talent, and capital. Accumulation of these resources changes the status of a node in the global architecture of innovation networks. It appears as an innovation hotspot. Structure, local and global architecture, dynamics of flows between the nodes and the peripheries uncover the underlying drivers and catalysts of accelerating the velocity of flows and wealth generation and accumulation.

The second part of the chapter "Innovation Networks" is entitled "Toward New Business Models." It aims to explain how value is created in innovation networks through different types of business models— business models being a proxy for value creation models. It presents the conceptual framework of a network enterprise to understand the specificity of an organizational unit in a network economy. The emerging business models in the global innovation network draw upon this new paradigm of a network enterprise in order to understand and interpret such phenomena as social networks and open innovation, as well as process networks and creation networks. The concept of a network enterprise is used to explain how and why certain types of networks create value, while others fail to do so.

The third part of the chapter entitled "Meaning and Power in the Global Innovation Network" depicts the fundamental contradiction between the mechanisms for knowledge and wealth accumulation that are dominant in the network society. The dynamics of flows across innovation networks induce a new geography of social, economic, and technological inequality and draft a map of exclusion from the global mega nodes that attract the most competitive resources. The role of this subchapter is to prepare ground for a reflection on what governments should do to prevent brain drain, capital outflow, and knowledge waste.

The next chapter, "A Growth Model for Knowledge-Based Economies," introduces a new conceptual model of networked innovation: the Knowledge Triangle. The model depicts a particular type of innovation network, which includes three components: research, education, and innovation. The scrutiny of the Knowledge Triangle takes the analysis starting with the "cluster model" of innovation milieus and proposes a new paradigm of a global network of clusters, which is defined in a dynamic, overlapping distributed model as a network of innovation networks. The observations of the nature of collaborative relationships between business and academia in the innovation process point to the changing paradigm of institutions involved. It is demonstrated that research–education–innovation enter into dynamic exchanges through three types of flows: flows of knowledge, flows of talent, and flows of capital, which generate new capacity to innovate and ultimately create value, defined in different ways by the institutional and individual agents of the process.

The next chapter is entitled "Knowledge and Innovation Communities." It discusses the experimental application of the Knowledge Triangle model on three novel organizations called Knowledge and Innovation Communities, established by the European Institute of Innovation and Technology in 2010 as legally and financially structured collaborative partnerships between industry and academia.

The chapter encompasses three case studies of these pioneering organizations: Climate-KIC, KIC InnoEnergy, and EIT ICT Labs, which are to bring a qualitative change to operational innovation processes in the areas of climate mitigation and adaptation, sustainable energy, and future information and communication society, respectively. It compares the three KICs' legal setup and governance, their specific network architecture, and three emerging business models. It analyzes how each of the KICs introduces entrepreneurship into the integration of the components of the Knowledge Triangle, to accelerate the velocity of flows in the network and ultimately generate value in its economic and social dimensions.

The last chapter, "Innovation Policies Beyond the Crisis," highlights the role of entrepreneurship as the missing link in the knowledge-driven economies of Europe. It fine-tunes the model introducing entrepreneurship as a missing link in the Knowledge Triangle and implies a multidimensional shift. I discuss entrepreneurship in the context of policy making. Policy can substantially increase probability of success of university-industry collaborative partnership and support or hinder a strategic shift toward a new kind of academic institution, open innovation, and creation of high growth business ventures supported by venture capital. The chapter illustrates this with the observation of the practices induced by the EIT in the context of European innovation policy. The limitations of the EIT experience are discussed, and a set of policy recommendations is proposed.

The argument put forward in this book suggests that at the core of the renewal of the European economy there is a need for a structural and cultural transformation and the crisis is an opportunity to accomplish such a transformation. The creative destruction prompted by the "invisible hand" phases out obsolete and inefficient models of business practice. The emerging model of value creation rises from the dynamics of the flows of knowledge, talent, and capital in the global innovation network.

In the end, it is a question of identity: Will the young generation of Europeans choose to be entrepreneurs rather than employees? And if so, will they be able to innovate?

Chapter 1

INNOVATION BLOWBACK

The Silicon Valley, Boston Route 128, and Austin, Texas in the US, as well as innovation hubs in Europe spreading between Oxford and Cambridge, or clustered in metropolitan areas of London, Northern Brabant, Paris, Grenoble, Munich, Helsinki, and Stockholm, are still at the forefront of technology development, design, and innovation. However, the pool of innovation hotbeds has been broadened.

Many countries including China, India, and Brazil have overcome their initial stage as cheap global outsourcing sites and have become innovators in their own right and scope, building growth not necessarily on cutting-edge technology (Porter 1998; Hamel Prahalad 1996; Prahalad and Krishnan 2008; Breznitz and Murphree 2011). Western companies entering markets such as China or India often assume that superior technology remains their sustainable competitive advantage (Lieberthal and Prahalad 1998). Their "imperialistic approach" to both customers and labor in many developing countries was demonstrated by an underlying assumption in their business strategy that while consumers may become increasingly prosperous, the labor market will remain low-cost. John Seely Brown and John Hagel III call this phenomenon "innovation blowback" (2005).

The presence of Western multinationals has changed the markets in transition in the economic and social sense. It has also surged the local capacity to innovate by knowledge spillovers, better-educated work force, and a vast number of consumers who aspire to become the middle class. As of 2009, 1.8 billion people belonged to the middle class in Europe (664 million), Asia (525 million), and North America (338 million) (OECD 2010). The size of the "global middle class" is expected to increase dramatically from 1.8 billion to 3.2 billion by 2020 and to 4.9 billion by 2030. This social change will be a driver for economic growth. It is projected that by 2020 Asia Pacific will represent 54% of the global middle-class population and 42% of middle-class consumption, as compared to 28% and 23% respectively in 2009 (Kharas 2010).[2]

Contrary to the general conviction, these emerging middle class consumers look not only for the best price but also for the best price to quality ratio. They are by necessity extremely price-conscious. It does not mean, however, that they are not value-conscious or brand-conscious. On the contrary, they are in fact more demanding as they weigh the price-to-value ratio with more sensitivity.

For example, South American "digital Latinos" or African women entrepreneurs are ready to pay a premium for access to the Internet, and for the quality of mobile connectivity, as well as for the brand.[3] Owning a mobile device like a mobile phone or a smartphone often allows these consumers to fulfill the basic human needs of survival such as earning a living, but also other needs such as belonging to a certain high status social group. Moreover, the demographics of mass consumers in emerging markets show that they are much younger and demonstrate different spending patterns than mass consumers in the developed world. They are also less loyal, more open to trying new things, and very brand-conscious. Companies that choose to serve the segment of low or middle income customers have no choice but to

---

(2) Middle class is defined by the OECD as those living in households with daily expenditures between USD 10 and USD 100 per person in PPP terms.

(3) I discussed emerging middle class customer behaviors in the telecom industry with the members of Telefonica Disruptive Council during a meeting in Sao Paulo, Brazil, 2011.

learn how to innovate in the most creative ways to deliver more quality with less investment in infrastructure and lower operating costs.

Major economic and social shifts occurring in the markets in transition are an environment offering superior learning opportunities both for local entrepreneurial firms as well as for multinationals (Lieberthal and Prahalad 2001; Radiou, Prabhu, Ahuja, and Roberts 2012). Local firms are known for their low-cost leadership, yet some are moving increasingly into the higher margins with indigenous product and process innovation. They often cater to the mass market of the emerging middle class as well as to the communities "at the bottom of the pyramid." In the first case, they build unique core competences and innovate with business models. In the latter case they often develop and deploy frugal innovations at a mass scale that are low-cost solutions to tackle pressing needs of underprivileged communities.

On the other hand, Western corporations operating in these markets still often deploy expansion strategies defined as "reaching for the low hanging fruit," or focus on the most affluent market segment. Strong engineering culture and over-engineered innovation processes often turn out to be barriers to innovation and impact. In the emerging markets innovation is sometimes low-cost and non-technological yet entrepreneurial and meaningful (Radiou, Prabhu, Ahuja, and Roberts 2012). There are a number of studies documenting business failures of Western companies in the emerging markets resulting from their inability to deal successfully with innovation challenges (Henderson and Clark 1990; Chesbrough 2005 and 2011).

The home markets of Western companies are no longer the only or even primary places where innovation takes place. This is increasingly true for research-based and technology-driven innovations with the trend to open offshore research labs as in the case of Nokia Research Center in India (Bangalore), Philips Research Asia in China (Shanghai) or ABB Corporate Research Center in Poland (Kraków). And local market leaders compete for markets and for talent, developing quality innovation in emerging hotspots, which go far beyond product reengineering or simple copying (Ketels and Memedovic 2008; Breznitz and Murphree 2011).

This is even more evident in the case of process optimization and global value chain management (Pavitt 2005; Salter and Tether 2006). The principles of scientific management and the analysis of massive data used for improving the efficiency of business processes are but one source of process innovation, corporate culture being another. Observing management practices of market leaders serving low-income consumers in the emerging markets, successful strategies are based on management of innovation networks rather than optimizing global value chains.[4]

European companies often outsource production or services in Central and Eastern European countries, which has been a convenient location and resource of well-educated workforce. IKEA, which started collaboration with subcontractors in Poland back in 1961, is but one of many examples proliferating over the last twenty years in automotive industry or agriculture. Known for the high quality of European products, manufacturers make system control their priority. With an ultimate goal of preserving the conditions for the highest quality, Western companies insist on deploying identical processes as in the counties of origin, despite the fact that some of them turn out to be over-engineered and obsolete.[5]

For example, a German manufacturer outsourced its production to a mid-sized Polish enterprise. The condition for collaboration was importing both the production line from Germany but also

(4) I interviewed John Seely Brown in Palo Alto, California in April 2010. He strongly emphasized that Western companies are not aware of nor understand the invisible social processes underlying offshore practices of local subcontractors.

(5) This was the point made by Jeffrey Liker, a professor at the University of Michigan, global expert on lean manufacturing, and author of numerous books on Toyota production processes and operations. I interviewed him in March 2011, where he described the given example.

implementing all production procedures and system control in the Polish factory.

A scrutiny of production facilities for optimization and the introduction of lean manufacturing processes showed that floor workers at the Polish factory developed alternative practices. Managers implemented ad hoc innovation to prevent interruption in production in case of a breakdown of a minor part in the fully automated molding process. In case of a breakdown, the missing mold was cast by hand, by a skilled worker.

The contracted lean manufacturing expert recommended implementing this factory floor practice as an integrated part of the whole automated process in case of costly stopover, giving a sound rationale. First, the handmade manufacturing did not compromise quality. Second, production was cheaper as it did not require high maintenance cost of the production line. Third, the workers were not interrupted by training, which required traveling to the company headquarters in Germany and generated additional costs.

The client company decided to forbid this practice and revert to the casts molded in the fully automated process even at the price of higher costs. The innovation driven by necessity and ingenuity of floor workers could be implemented at a larger scale as a backup solution in other production facilities. However, the engineering culture was not receptive to learning from the emerging markets. Full automation remained the preferred manufacturing option.

Innovation often results from "bridging" ideas from different domains and creative collaborations, which are characteristic of practice-driven, interdisciplinary and trans-disciplinary teams, at the crossroads of culture, both national and corporate, in the space of indeterminacy, complexity, and connectivity of global innovation networks. A manifestation of this concept is Edison's innovation strategy, which relied to a great extent on exploiting the past by harnessing the knowledge and efficiencies that reside in elements of existing technologies (Hargadon 2003). Bridging ideas from different domains is not trivial and often counterintuitive, especially when structured innovation processes dominate individual creativity. Understanding the essence and origin of innovation is vital.

Innovation Is More Than Invention

Since the beginning of the industrial revolution, applying science and implementing both incremental improvements and breakthrough technology has played a vital role as a driving force behind innovation. There is still a prevailing conviction in Europe that innovation means technology, technology comes out of science, science is critical for innovation, and knowledge is produced in research labs.[6] Forbes and Wield outline these myths in their studies related to innovation, listing typical misconceptions: technological self-reliance as the key to breaking from technological dependency; more technology is always good, high tech is the best tech, action should be focused on gaining more blueprints, not learning and adapting; Research and Development (R&D) is key to innovation and is led by the former (Forbes and Wield 2002).

In this context it is of critical importance to underline the difference between an invention and an innovation.

At the origin of invention is culture with its individual and collective capacity to create—that is, creativity. Creativity materializes in an invention. Invention is an idea, a concept, a prototype. Science may lie at the source of an invention as it enhances human knowledge and the

---

(6) This is the case in academia, in industry, and in policy making and has been often demonstrated in discussions I witnessed in each of these environments as well as during their interactions.

knowledge-making capacity enabling insights into the nature of things, properties of organisms, and dynamics of processes.

Invention is transformed into innovation in a creative process of bridging the gap between the world of ideas and market or societal reality. Innovation is usually associated with a material quality such as a product, a service, or a process. Innovation can also be empirically immaterial, symbolized as a body of knowledge or an experience.

An innovation can be a focused attempt to carry out an invention into practice. However, an invention can also occur without major scientific discovery or investment into research. An innovation may happen without an invention in an effort to bring an existing concept or body of knowledge to the users and customers. Science is important for invention and innovation, but it is one of numerous underlying factors of the ingenious process of creating value.

There are numerous approaches to catching the essence of innovation, which originate both in economic and in organizational research. Schumpeter (1934) defined innovation as the introduction of:

- a new good or quality;

- a new method of production;

- opening of a new market;

- the conquest of a new source of supply, new materials, or parts;

- carrying out a new organization of an industry.

Schumpeter linked innovation with entrepreneurship in that entrepreneurs were actors carrying out innovation in order to create value by reallocating resources to the areas of higher productivity in a process he called a "creative destruction."

Fagerberg (2005) and Mokyr (1990) followed Schumpeter's distinction between an invention and an innovation, and defined the former as the first occurrence of an idea. Within the research stream of organizational studies, Higgins (1995) distinguished four types of innovation, extending Schumpeter's original definition by categorizing innovation into product innovation, process innovation, marketing innovation, and management innovation. Frambach (1993) and Edler, Meyer-Krahmer, and Reger (2001) tagged organizational innovation from the perspective of new product development, competition, and the process of innovation adoption by users and customers, especially in the context of the emergence of new technology (Frambach 1993; Edler, Meyer-Krahmer, and Reger 2001). The significance of user-driven innovation, yet another perspective on innovation, was theorized by Von Hippel (1988). Through these convergent perspectives, West and Rickard (1999) defined organizational innovation as the intentional introduction and application of new ideas, processes, products, and procedures within the work context of an organization (West and Rickard 1999).

Christensen (1997) made a significant distinction between incremental and radical innovation and argued that the latter causes major disruption in established business models and discontinuity of industries. Estrin (2009) added the third element to this classification: orthogonal innovation. It refers to reframing the problems and reintegrating things in a different way. Henderson and Clark (1990) proposed a more nuanced model that categorizes innovation into four groups: radical, incremental, architectural, and modular innovation. It takes into account linkages between core concepts and component changes.

Ernst and Naughton (2004) applied their model to information technology and provided a systematic typology of innovation. They used axes of architecture and component changes to demonstrate that incremental innovation takes dominant component design for granted, but improves cost efficiency, time-to-market, and performance, while modular innovation plugs new components into a fundamentally unchanged system architecture. On the other hand, architectural innovation leaves existing components unchanged, but modifies the way they are integrated. Finally, radical innovation induces the use of new components and changes in architectural design simultaneously.

Brian Arthur (2009) developed a singular approach to scrutinize development of new technology. He concluded that technology and technology-driven innovation have self-perpetuating and self-recreating attributes. He analyzed the evolution of technology, applying Darwin's concepts of variation and selection to the physical or virtual artifacts. This specificity of the nature of technology is expressed, among other things, by filing for families of patents, which displays both the heritage of, and interrelations with, other technologies. He concluded that these evolutionary processes in technology lead to larger, more complex, self-creating structures and architectures. Technology came to be more of a morphing organism than an outcome of a rational engineering process.

He argued that the process of reinventing technology is derived from a human creative capacity to imagine new things, from a kind of intellectual entrepreneurship, often necessitated by a pragmatic need to solve a problem. He pointed out that technology is in essence an assemblage of practices and components of different technologies and that innovation resides in this compilation ability, which creates a pool of devices and engineering practices. He used a jet engine as an example of a situation in which an assembly of different pieces of technology is brought together in such a way as to deliver a new technology.

A qualitative change to a society does not always require a qualitative increase in science or technology. Since the interdependencies between cycles of scientific and technological research, and between the applied research and innovation processes, are multilateral and dynamic, then both technology and innovation come out of human ingenuity and creative reinterpretation of the surrounding world of the tangibles and the intangibles. As Arthur pointed out, technology co-defines and co-creates culture and thus helps fulfill the purpose of human existence (Arthur 2009).

Following Arthur's intellectual divagations, indeed technology should not be taken as a proxy for innovation. The question then arises: What is innovation and what is its origin?

Creativity and Innovation

What is the origin of invention and innovation? The creative ability to design a world of ideas and a world of things seems to reside in the human capacity to interpret in a different way data perceived or apprehended from the external environment. This happens through a synthesis of new ideas and concepts and by a process of restructuring and re-associating existing knowledge enabled by an individual's ability to reinterpret the world and to reframe its elements (Heap 1989; Simonton 2000).

Creativity is a mental process, an act of ideation, an act of developing new ideas (Csikszentmihalyi 1996). Csikszentmihalyi describes and analyzes this ideation process in terms of a state of flow, a state of concentration, of complete absorption, of mindfulness (1999). The state of flow is a mode of pure intrinsic motivation, resulting in a feeling of fulfillment and a forgetting of mundane constraints such as time and space. He claims that a state of flow can occur only in a situation of the right sort of balance between the difficulty of a challenge and the skills of a problem solver. If the task is too easy or too difficult or the skills are insufficient, this state of flow does not occur. Looking at a skills level and a challenge level on two axes, both must be high and parallel. The flow state implies a kind of focused attention and could be described as a state where motivation and reality meet, resulting in a creative harmony.

But is creativity an act of genius or rather an outcome of a more or less rigorous structured process of examination and discovery through which ideas are identified and developed? To what extent is it an individual, inborn predisposition to come up with novel ideas and in what part is it an outcome of a cognitive process?

The god's-like narrative of the creative process is obviously a myth. Creativity is the interaction among aptitude, knowledge, process, and environment which allows combining, recombining, organizing, contextualizing, framing, and giving a new meaning to the external world and its phenomena, creating products and processes which are novel in the given context (Plucker et al. 2004; Castells 2008). Reference to novelty underlies all tangible and intangible human-designed artifacts against the stock of existing knowledge in a society (Amabile 1983; Castells 2008).

Creativity entails multitude approaches and different levels of analysis. It has been discussed on individual, team, and organizational levels. The individual-level approach suggests that individual creativity is a function of individual characteristics, social influences, and contextual influences.

The group-level analysis suggests that creativity is a function of the individual creativity of group members, and of group and contextual characteristics. As a group process, creativity is staged in phases that are managed by drawing on various resources and capabilities. The process usually consists of a number of stages such as preparation, idea incubation, illumination, and evaluation of the quality of the generated ideas (Bakhshi and McVittie 2009; Coyne et al. 2007; Fernandes et al. 2009).

For example, design thinking is an example of a process approach to manage a collective creative act into an effective process (Brown 2009). It is a human-centered approach to problem solving that puts people at the core of problems and is conducive to enhancing innovation and creativity among organizations in different industries. While the process may be structured, the outcome and impact of new idea generation is undetermined and may lead to unintended consequences for individuals, organizations, and society.

Ford and Sullivan suggested that the idea generation process is essential when teams are still looking for measures to bridge the outcome of their ideation and boundary conditions and specification of an innovation project. Continuity of the same dynamics of new idea generation may be disruptive at a later process and potentially lead to negative consequences in lower project quality, decreased team member satisfaction, reduced team member learning, and inability to meet time requirements (Ford and Sullivan 2004).

The organizational-level study points out that creativity is a function of group creativity and organizational characteristics (Agars, Kaufman, and Locke 2008). A specific line of studies focuses on analyzing creativity in companies (Amabile 1996). Other approaches take into account different kinds of organizational aspects, labeled as creative knowledge environments (Hemlin, Allwood, and Martin 2008), creative cities, creative regions, and networks (Florida 2002; Scott 2006). At a policy level, creativity is explored in the context of national innovation systems (Furman, Porter, and Stern 2002; Lundvall, Johnson, Anderson, and Dalum 2002; Patel and Pavitt 1994).

Interestingly, the distinction between creativity and innovation seems to collide around the concept of novelty in the term creative imitation. It can be used as an oxymoron but it actually captures the essence of certain practices where existing knowledge is copied, and this imitation process as such requires creativity. This is, for example, the case of Chinese social networking sites. Their founders imitate the existing model and business concept of such companies as Google, eBay, or Facebook and derive their prominence in the internal market, not from the novelty of their creative act but from the way they translate creativity into innovation in the specific context of China (Dong 2012).

The research on creativity tackles the continuum of creativity invention/ innovation. Differentiation between these concepts is based on the distinction between idea generation (a mental process) and implementation (a social process). Some argue that as a mental process, creativity always involves linear and often illogical personal expressions but innovation involves a calculated social process in which novelty is driven by extrinsic incentives and motivation (Clydesdale 2006; Howkins 2006). At the initial phase of the creative process, when teams develop new ideas in response to a perceived need, creativity may seem more salient (Hoelscher 2010). As the process of innovation moves into the stage of adapting ideas into the organizational context, less creativity is required (West 2002).

High-Tech, Low-Tech, Non-Tech

Numerous breakthrough innovations have been developed thanks to available technology. There are cases when existing technology is only an enabler, while the low-tech or non-tech aspects of innovation create real impact and value, complementing existing technology or relying on it only to a very basic degree.

Such a former case is illustrated by the Internet. Obviously, the Internet uses technology, which enables it to offer a new sort of human and social experience through mass, real-time networking. It is actually based on a computer network technology developed in the mid-1960s in the laboratories of the Advanced Research Projects Agency (ARPA, later DARPA), as the US military communication solution know as ARPANET. It was a relatively old technology when the technological opportunity opened for a civil application.

In 1989, while working at the European Organization for Nuclear Research (CERN), Tim Berners-Lee came up with a concept of the World Wide Web (WWW)—a virtual environment based on hypertext. He designed it originally as a communication tool between scientists in universities and research organizations. Berners-Lee did not patent his invention. He opened the sourceware, demonstrating thus a set of idealistic values that making a difference in the world was more important than accumulating personal wealth (Berners-Lee 2000).

As a result, the Internet and the WWW rapidly evolved into an inclusive, open, global environment, in which users developed radical new ways of communicating, interacting, learning, and innovating. As a consequence of its global reach and scale, a new virtual economy has emerged with novel products, services, and systems. It triggered changes in the organizational and institutional set up of the global market as well as enabled the emergence of a new social form theorized as a network society (Castells 1996, 2000, 2010).

There are many other examples where existing technology along with social and cultural innovation have created unprecedented value, as for example in the case of Google and Facebook. Taking the analysis one step further, by scrutinizing innovation that does not really require a technological component, brings the discussion into the cultural and social aspects of innovation.

Indeed, innovation induced by art and design contributes to a significant portion of the innovation actions performed by firms as well as by individual actors. Creative industries generate economic value but also social value in that, for example, they facilitate communication between technology and society (Jacobs 2007). Social innovation delivered often within the context of the non-profit sector and by social entrepreneurs brings economic and social impact. For instance, it develops new sustainability models and new business models to cater to underprivileged communities.

The Heidelberg Project is an example of both cultural and social innovation. It is a non-profit organization built around the artwork of Tyree Guyton, an artist from Detroit. Returning to the neighborhood of his childhood in 1984, he found his city destroyed and his community disintegrated, most of which he attributed to the racial riots of 1967. As a political protest and a call for a solution to the deteriorated urban space, he began transforming abandoned houses into large-scale art installations—a modern structure fashioned in large bright polka dots.

For over twenty-six years this initial art gesture transformed the quarter by appropriating the street and other abandoned houses. The artist covered them with his paintings and with ready-made discarded objects of everyday urban life such as shoes, toys, cars, shopping carts, and refrigerators. The area was transformed into a creative learning environment for children with a rich program of hands-on art classes. The impact of these creative engagements is also social education in the power of an individual to transform the surrounding reality rather than surrender. On two occasions, in 1991 and in 1999, the Heidelberg Project faced partial destruction by the City of Detroit. In 2012, it was visited by over 200,000 people from over 140 countries.[7]

(7) I visited the Heidelberg Project in 2011 and 2013 and met with Tyree Guyton and Jenenne Whitfield, the managing director of the Heidelberg Project, and their friend and supporter Tom Porter. Tyree explained that initially the polka dots that he painted on his house reminded him of the happy moments of his childhood, when his grandfather, a self-made artist, shared jelly beans. When we met for the second time, one of the houses decorated by Tyree had been recently destroyed by a fire of undetermined cause. Seeing the house half-burnt and half-decorated in a neighborhood of many half-burnt houses and empty building plots made me acutely aware of the symbolic meaning of this work in the never-ending conflict between the forces of renewal and destruction.

Analyzing high-Tech, low-Tech, and non-Tech aspects of innovation in various environments leads toward a better understanding of what innovation is. As discussed, innovation originates in creativity, which is both a mental and a social process of ideation.

Innovation can be a tangible outcome of creativity such as a product (service), a process, or a system. In the former case, it is demonstrated, for example, by electric cars or e-commerce. In the latter, it is embodied, for instance, by novel production methods as in the case of the "just-on-time" manufacturing model of the Japanese automobile industry, which eliminated inventories, permitted constant quality improvement, and reduced operating costs (Bar et al. 2001). As a system, innovation refers, for example, to the evolution of technology as in the case of software architecture built of components and modules (Arthur 2007).

Innovation can also deliver intangible results. The non-technical aspects of technical innovation can be tightly connected to the technical ones, and for example bring social change by increasing the speed of technology adoption. A product (service) innovation cycle depends on the capacity to manage the dynamics of the process of innovating, which depends on organizational aspects and on contextual ones such as features and structure of an industry sector. But the intangible outcomes of the innovation process can also be new concepts, user experiences, or creative environments as in the case of the Internet or the Heidelberg Project discussed above.

In sum, innovation is both a tangible as well as an intangible outcome of a process originating in ideation demonstrated by high-tech, low-tech, and non-tech artifacts, ideas, experiences, and environments. It can rely on technology to a various degree, as well as the innovation process. The question that comes next concerns the process, which results in these diverse outcomes.

Innovation as a Learning Process

"Innovation is a learning process and not a pedigree idea."[8]

The process of managing innovation involves multiple reiterations. The initial idea is to transform by adopting and incorporating information and knowledge provided by the team members, potential users, and customers. Through feedback loops, an innovator affects a change and the change affects an innovator in the way the innovation matures.

The feedback loops are essential in moving forward. They allow inventions and innovation to mature. The whole innovation process is all about the speed of learning. Ability to give, get, and absorb feedback is a key driver that accelerates the pace of innovation.

Companies increasingly rely on innovation outside the firm to develop new products, services, and processes, claims the 2008 report of the Organisation for Economic Co-operation and Development (OECD). Innovation is based to a greater degree on knowledge assets that lie beyond the firm's boundaries:

> Co-operation has become an important way to source knowledge, accelerate learning, and get new ideas quickly to the market (outside-in). At the same time, companies spin out technologies and intellectual property developed internally. The intellectual assets, which lie beyond the core business, are more and more often commercialized by others (inside-out) (OECD 2008).

Brainstorming for "the idea" is a learning process in itself. Quite often this is true for non-breakthrough technological innovations, which

---

(8) The quote comes from Regis McKenna, a Silicon Valley icon, whom I interviewed at Santa Clara University, San Jose, California in 2010.

bring value to the customer in quite a different manner and scope when initially conceived by innovators and entrepreneurs. Even the founders and investors of Facebook and Google did not initially think of what their ideas could become when they turned them into multibillion-dollar opportunities.

Google did not start on the Internet. It started by connecting people, and its first product was not a search engine. The first Google product was to be a Dutch auction, and so the founders conceptualized a financial tool that would allow people to barter online using the Internet. As they interacted with people, the idea and the concept changed. Their idea went through several cycles of customer feedback that led to creating and developing a value proposition to its users and customers. With each round of financing, there was a lot of uncertainty and a lot of risk. Ultimately, they got it right, and the the number of users took off. They got it right. The consumer value resides where the consumer, not the public or private investors, place a lot of value. The basic idea, along with the proof that the idea has a value, is demonstrated while testing the prototype in a controlled setting. The test leads toward the first generation of the commercial product. In trying to develop the second, third, and subsequent generations of the product, engineers work each time to decrease costs while improving the value for the customer. When Apple engineers were designing the iPad1, they already knew that they would design an iPad2 and an iPad3. The space of competition was not with other products but actually with themselves in the sense of the speed with which they could get subsequent versions of iPad to the market. What they were learning with each model was what customers really liked and disliked. They were improving the product and driving the cost down in order to scale it up. The speed with which they could move along the learning curve was the ultimate measure of their competitiveness— that is, the fervor of their learning process. In the meantime, they often simultaneously create infrastructure and the supply base to enable scaling up toward a more mass market. The basic rationale for this process remains unchanged: the value has to exceed the price, the price has to exceed the cost, and the product has to rise up in the market to justify investment. This is how technology develops and this is how venture capital finances it.

The way to advise companies on how to innovate in a creative way is to look at the areas where there has been no market or no analogy for a product: for example, no first integrated circuit, no first microprocessor, no first semiconductor memory or first commercial laser, no first personal computer. Marketing through key people in a given domain—media stars, or role models in a society—is needed for the adoption, referencing, and diffusion of innovation. When Apple introduced Macintosh, the company gave hundreds of its computers to key people in the IT industry. These key influencers came from across the spectrum, yet they belonged to the 10% of the industry who were watched by the remaining 90% of industry participants. The key is then to influence the influencers. The key 10% is an entity itself, consisting of the key leaders within it. Then, depending on the nature of a business, the rest of the participants would be software manufacturers for a computer company (Bill Gates, for example), and then key industry analysts; in some areas of the world it must be the government and politicians. The media is low-priority, and the reason for this is that once the media is contacted, the media will go directly to the influencers and ask them if the product is real. If there is no forward movement and no infrastructure and knowledge pool in place, a new product will not be likely to succeed in the marketplace. The company should then invest time in how to define its architecture and define those hundreds of people in different segments so that a message would be spread by word of mouth that such and such people are using the product. These people could include scientists, politicians, and businesspeople who would become a sort of social reference model who would say, "it's cool for you to use this product." Would they be today's young people? Not necessarily. They would be the more popular people in terms of their personal branding in a given market space. This group would certainly include more young people than before, because young people have become more recognized than before, but it would depend on the market the company is after.

Chapter 2

ENTREPRENEURSHIP AND ENTREPRENEURIALISM

In public policy and economy, entrepreneurship is referred to as a sector of small and medium-sized companies. The specificity of this sector is based on four converging factors: employment, revenues, assets, and ownership. The EUROSTAT defines small and medium-sized enterprises (SMEs) as "businesses with less than 250 employees, with total turnover not exceeding EUR 50 million or a balance sheet total not exceeding EUR 43 million, and that are independent (i.e. not owned by more than a third of their capital by non-SMEs)." In exceptional cases, the size of work-intensive industry firms with more than 250 employees can be considered an SME.

Since the crisis erupted, a shift in attitude toward entrepreneurship took place across societies, and entrepreneurial activity rates reflect both changing demographics and availability of opportunities. Global Entrepreneurship Monitor traces these trends by collecting data on total early stage entrepreneurial activity, presented as a percentage of the 18-64 year old population who are either nascent entrepreneurs or owner-managers of new businesses (GEM 2014). Over the period of 2008 to 2013, the trends demonstrate that the level of new business owners increased in the United States from 10.8% to 12.7%, in the Netherlands from 5.2% to 9.3%, in Germany from 3.8% to 5%, and in the United Kingdom from 5.9% to 7.1%. On the contrary, it decreased

in Finland from 7.3% to 5.3%, in France from 5.6% to 4.6%, and in
Spain from 7% to 5.2%.

The number of people in the population who are "risk-preferers" is
small and unevenly distributed. Media have created a myth around
star-entrepreneurs. The fact is that there are few highly successful
entrepreneurs and most businesses remain small, if they survive the
"valley of death," the time between when a start-up firm receives an initial
capital contribution and when it begins generating revenues sufficient
to cover its costs. Potential payoffs of becoming an entrepreneur are
enormous, but the likelihood that, for example, great engineers who
are also "risk-preferers" will be ultimately very successful in creating
market value is quite low.

Fear of failure is one of the key factors hindering entrepreneurship. It was
qualified in GEM data as a percentage of the 18-64 year old population
with positive perceived opportunities who indicated that fear of
failure would prevent them from starting a business. Interestingly, the
countries with the highest fear of failure rates are Poland (47%), France
(41%), and Germany (39%), compared to merely 31% in the United
States and 36% in the United Kingdom, which is one of the lowest rates
in Europe (GEM 2014).

In the United States, an archetype of an entrepreneurial nation, one
third of would-be entrepreneurs state that the fear of failure is strong
enough to prevent them from exploring business opportunities. In
Europe, known for its more risk–averse culture, numbers historically
have always been much higher as in the case of, for example, France,
Spain, or Germany.

Interestingly, the crisis in Europe has had a quite diverse impact on
attitude toward risk among would-be entrepreneurs. Between 2008
and 2013, the percentage of the population disinclined to pursue

entrepreneurial opportunity because of fear of failure increased from 23% to 37% in Finland, and from 29% to 37% in the Netherlands, but it dropped in France from 52% to 41%, and in Spain from 47% to 37%. A conclusion could be drawn that the crisis has created an opportunity to reinvent Europe's growth model.

The crisis created a push toward entrepreneurship, not necessarily because of targeted policy actions or visionaries' desires to build global businesses, but because of the lack of alternatives offered by the job market. This is demonstrated by the GEM data on necessity-driven entrepreneurial activity, expressed as a percentage of those who start a business as a consequence of having no other option for work. This was an evident case in Spain where necessity-driven entrepreneurship increased from 15% in 2008 to 29% in 2013, as well as in the United States, where it jumped from 12% to 21%. It is worth noting that over this period risk aversion decreased from 26% to 19% in Germany, indicating a robust job market despite the crisis (GEM 2014).

The impact of the crisis usually means that the number of those with no other career choice increases, as in the case of Spain, where the number doubled. But data also shows an interesting case of the German economy where the percentage of entrepreneurs by necessity has dropped since 2008 from 26% to 19%. Whatever the motivation of entrepreneurs, the SME sector in Europe has been generating more jobs than large enterprises, and innovation-driven SMEs are engines of growth and job creation (EUROSTAT). European SMEs have offset to some extent the pains of the crisis. Since creating new companies is so important for economy and society, what is the relationship between creativity, innovation, and entrepreneurship? How do entrepreneurial ventures create and add value?

Innovation and Entrepreneurship: Creating Value

Creativity is considered a precondition for innovation. Jeffcutt and Pratt (2002) warned, however, against the perception that creativity acts as a kind of "magic dust" which can turn metal into gold. Levitt pointed out that so-called creative individuals often pass off onto others the responsibility for getting work done. They get stuck on generating ideas but fail to make an effort and follow through in a business-like manner (Levitt 2003). Creativity can be translated into innovation through implementation. It has been argued that creativity refers to the development of novel, potentially useful ideas and creative collaboration at the team level.

However, although employees might share their ideas with others, only when the ideas are successfully implemented at the organizational level can they be considered innovation (Shalley et al. 2004; Amabile 1996; Mumford and Gustafson 1988). What is the essence of these "implementation activities?" What is the relation between innovation and entrepreneurship? Who are the implementers of innovations and why are some individuals, teams, and organizations more successful than others? Where do new ventures come from? How is value created in the entrepreneurial process of implementation? Is entrepreneurship a for-profit activity by definition? Does it only concern micro, small, and medium-sized businesses? Are entrepreneurs driven mainly by moneymaking?

The most prominent approaches in research on entrepreneurship emphasize environmental determinants of venture creation and performance (Shane 2000; Yates 2000). The team-level analysis focuses on understanding the process of creating and growing new ventures (Heath and Sitkin 2001). This process could be considered a "pure" form of organizational activity focused on allocation of available resources.

For example, Schumpeter and Drucker stated that "entrepreneurship refers not to an enterprise's size or age but to a certain kind of activity."

At the heart of that activity is innovation, which is the specific tool of entrepreneurs who shift resources from areas of low productivity and yield to areas of higher productivity and yield (Schumpeter 1934; Drucker 1986). Drucker specified four areas of entrepreneurial opportunities originating inside a company or inside an industry, and three induced from the outside. The former include: unexpected occurrences, incongruities, process needs, and industry and market changes. The latter originate in the social and intellectual environment and comprise demographic changes, changes in perception, and new knowledge (Drucker 2003).

The link between innovation and entrepreneurship is focused on a number of major themes, such as the theory of individualism, knowledge transfer, technology adoption and diffusion, product design, and—in particular—entrepreneurship. The research on entrepreneurship evolves around four streams: decision making, strategy and performance, organizational design, and venture finance (Shane and Ulrich 2004). A psychological tradition of entrepreneurship research deals with some of these questions and analyzes founder traits or personality in association with venture performance (Shaver and Scott 1991; Shook, Priem, and McGee 2003).

Lines of inquiry at the individual level address the issue of how processes related to the founder's functional background and identity play a role in the interpretation of the uncertainty in the environment (Jaussi 2008). Bennis studied highly successful teams and pointed to the creative collaboration process as the origin of their success, independent of the sector of activity both in economic and political or historical settings (Bennis 1997). Mueller and Thomas found that the national culture had a substantial impact on entrepreneurial predispositions (Mueller and Thomas 2000). They used Hofstede's cultural model to point out that innovativeness is more widely spread in cultures displaying individualistic rather than collectivistic features. Cultures scoring high on internal locus of control rather than external orientation are often combined with low uncertainty avoidance (that is, cultures in which people are more prone to risk-taking and more resistant in case of a failure), while cultures ranking high on uncertainty avoidance orientation are more characteristic for collectivistic cultures.

The American culture is an example of national culture with dominant orientations: high individualism, internal locus of control, low uncertainty avoidance, and masculinity orientations (Hofstede 1984). Indeed, the United States is high in the rankings of innovativeness and competitiveness (WEF 2011). Part of this culture is a high regard for entrepreneurship. For example, William Shockley, a Stanford professor, Nobel Prize laureate, and the inventor of the silicon chip at Bell Labs, had been considered a failure in the Silicon Valley. He never made any money, and was remembered as a terrible man and a poor manager. His team of collaborators at Shockley Semiconductor Laboratory left him to start Fairchild Semiconductor, a company that is considered to have initiated the silicon chip revolution and given birth to the semiconductor industry in the Silicon Valley.

The studies of the Silicon Valley phenomenon and its entrepreneurs found that the only common differentiating feature is a certain degree of marginalization characteristic of the immigrant population, along with the openness of the Valley culture (Bennis 1997; Saxenian 1996). Creativity is a precondition for both the innovative and entrepreneurial activities. However, since innovation has been discussed in a broad sense beyond the technological and non-technological regimes, what implications does it bring to the concept of entrepreneurship, especially in the context of non-economic returns?

Entrepreneurship can be defined as a project-oriented activity during which an entrepreneur, or rather an entrepreneurial team, organizes limited resources under time constraints to create superior value by reallocating them to areas of higher productivity, which results in increased competitiveness of a venture. In the competitive business environment, value creation during this process is defined as the value to shareholders and expressed by economic indicators and ratios, such as: EBITDA (Earnings Before Interest Depreciation Added), ROI (Return on Investment), or ROA (Return on Assets). Capital investment decisions are made using NPV (Net Present Value) and valuations are based on DCF (Discounted Cash Flows), that is, expected cash generating capacity of a venture.

However, the value created is economic and also social. The former is expressed as new jobs, prosperity for people, stability for societies, and in some cases more freedom and empowerment, especially for women; the latter, as the only way to overcome structural poverty and, as a result, limit crime and increase wellbeing of communities. This social value may also mean higher quality jobs and better work conditions, which increase the level of prosperity, balance, and public health. It can be expressed in satisfying the needs of users and customers, bringing technological progress to underserved communities, tackling challenges of global scope, and dealing with failures of the complex system of the globalized world.

Thus, the concept of entrepreneurship, while being indeed a project-oriented activity with the pragmatic attitude of actors and focus on operational aspects of launching, growing, and managing a venture, cannot be limited only to economic returns and subdued to the logic of profit-making, although it is true for the overwhelming majority of ventures.

Whatever the value, social and economic, created or destroyed, entrepreneurship is inherently linked with innovation. Firstly because innovation needs entrepreneurs to take it to the markets and societies. And secondly because entrepreneurship requires innovation in that entrepreneurs reallocate resources in a more competitive manner.

Some studies of entrepreneurial dynamics have taken a process-driven approach (Shane 2006; Jaussi 2008). Shane defines entrepreneurship as "an activity that involves the discovery, evaluation and exploitation of opportunities to introduce new goods and services, ways of organizing, markets, processes, and raw materials through organizing efforts that previously had not existed" (Shane 2003). Ford and Sullivan accept Shane's definition and develop their enactment-selection-retention theory. They split the entrepreneurial process into variation (opportunity discovery), selection (opportunity evaluation), and retention (opportunity exploitation) (Ford and Sullivan 2008). They argue that at each of these three phases, the probability of performance success is a function of environment uncertainty, founder organizing, and cognitive qualities. At the team and venture levels, these three elements become key evaluation tools on high growth and value creation.

Additionally, Hoelscher has proposed a process-based approach to analyzing entrepreneurship. He distinguished four phases of the entrepreneurial development of a new venture: budding, developing, transition, and maturity (Hoelscher 2010). He linked the phases in a sequential order and argued that a higher-level proposition incorporates the predictions of the preceding propositions and adds contextual influences (Hoelscher 2010).

Different streams of entrepreneurship research have not integrated multi-level theories capable of capturing the complexity of interplay among founders, founding management teams, new ventures, and their value networks (Ford and Sullivan 2008). The key question that the existing approaches to studying entrepreneurship do not answer is: Where do new ventures come from? (Ireland, Reutzel, and Webb 2005). They also do not provide a sufficient explanation in a satisfactory way of how value is created—or destroyed—at different phases of venture development in the networked context of our globalized economy.

Smart Investors

Embraced by the world "in-the-making," high risk capital investors— venture capital and business angels—represent particular types of "mavens" who acquire knowledge from learning-by-doing. There is a limited understanding of the specificity of this industry and especially of the learning process during which they acquire experience, which has earned them a nickname of "smart capital." They display various attitudes toward uncertainty as a general condition, and failure in particular. This culturally preconditioned mindset either stiffens creativity or becomes a catalyst for a rewarding learning experience in the face of adversity and technical, business, social, or environmental challenge.

This is in particular true in the highly competitive context of venture capital (VC) and business angels. Venture capital is a risk capital co-invested by fund managers on behalf of limited partners, along with entrepreneurs who are often founders of an investee company. Business angels are high net worth individuals, usually serial entrepreneurs themselves, who invest their own capital in entrepreneurial firms. Both venture capital and business angels invest in early-stage businesses either at seed, start-up, or the first stage of expansion.

The "smartness" of the smart capital comes from the hands-on experience acquired in the contextual learning-by-doing process. While access to funding is critically important for a start-up since it allows it to bridge the liquidity gap until a company achieves a break-even point, it is ultimately the know-how that is the real value as compared to the anonymous sources of funding such as grants, subsidies, or bank loans.

Venture capitalists and business angels are good at asking the right sort of questions to accelerate innovation in start-ups and high-potential growth ventures. Klonowski proposed a multi-stage capital investment model based on practices of institutional investors in the emerging markets. The process includes nine stages starting with deal origination, initial screening, feedback from the investment committee and due diligence Phase I, pre-approval completions, formal approvals and due diligence Phase II, deal completion, monitoring, and closing with an investment exit or write-off (Klonowski 2007).

Steve Blank, based on his experience as a serial entrepreneur and Silicon Valley investor, specified "four steps to epiphany," a process of structured inquiry for understanding the market opportunity, the value proposition, the business model, and the team who are to deliver on the plan (Blank 2005; Blank and Dorf 2012). The team is a go-or-no-go factor in the investment decision. Unless the team represents a creative and reliable group of individuals who display the learning capability, venture capital will not make the investment decisions. Only if the entrepreneurial team is accepted will the VC look into the potential of the industry sector, competitive landscape, growth potential, and political, macroeconomic, technological, environmental, and legal risks. Once the investment is closed, VCs spend the rest of their time helping the company succeed.

This is where VC creates value. It is not only the capital that they bring to the table, but the business skills, particularly in the area of guiding an early stage company through the fast growth stage, validating technology, getting the first paying customer, building the team and the customer base, and scaling up operations and sales internationally. These entrepreneurial skills can be learned by doing. The lack of access to VC know-how prevents firms from ultimately converting business ideas into credible business plans, and, then, into viable enterprises. Newly created enterprises with entrepreneurs inexperienced in a commercial environment usually have shortcomings in their managerial skills and abilities.

There are two key areas where assistance is required. Firstly, in the early stages, beginner enterprises are often "virtual" in their development. The key problem for these enterprises is survival. Secondly, more mature enterprises require different assistance, as the key concern is management of growth, raising the next round of financing, and the existence of the investment.

In 2011, over 50% of global venture capital industry was concentrated in the San Francisco Bay Area in the United States, which is a unique learning environment in particular for all types of technology innovators and entrepreneurs. VC is the only industry in the world that invests money to try new things in the market and then moves on quickly when they fail. Failing defines learning and in the Valley having experienced business failures is a badge of honor and a credit in the sense that in the perception of peers it increases the probability of success with the next venture.

Venture capitalists and the investors in VC funds expect that, in general, half of the investee companies fail to achieve above average returns, yet they do not know which half. Their tactic is to introduce to the market as many ventures as possible and fail them as fast as possible if they underperform. According to the rule of thumb in the industry, two out of ten investments fail, one or two might achieve outstanding valuation over a period of two to three years, and the returns on the remaining six might pay back the investment. This spread epitomizes both the upside potential as well as the consequences of entering into the zone where macroeconomic risk, market risk, technology risk, and management risk coincide at their extreme in the business opportunity.

Quarterly reports of the top 150 companies in the Silicon Valley show that almost all of them were born during the last 30 years. The second tranche of 25 to 50 largest companies have revenues between USD 250 million and one billion. The majority of the remaining companies that are lower in the ranking incur losses. Some of the large companies who are present in the Silicon Valley do not have their headquarters there and so are not present in the ranking. The point is that the innovation model of growing value comes from big companies acquiring smaller companies that struggle during an economic downturn.

Thus, the economic stability of Silicon Valley as well as the knowledge flow and the learning comes from the buzz around the Valley start-ups that attract top global talent and innovators in the established industry. So it is both the large industry and small entrepreneurial ventures that make the Valley such a valuable area for learning.

A degree of marginalization is a common characteristic of a Silicon Valley entrepreneur (Bennis 1997). Bennis claims that immigrants search for identity and legitimacy in the American society, in which anxiety is one of the key drivers. This search is the most fundamental human experiences. Defining their identity through their behavior as risk-takers, Silicon Valley entrepreneurs are also motivated by the joy of collaboration in what Bennis defines as the "Great Group" (Bennis 1997). Saxenian demonstrated that in the mid-1990s one third of companies in the Silicon Valley had an Indian or Chinese CEO while 10% were led by Slavs, Israelis, and Brazilians. Forty percent of companies were created or headed by immigrants. As a society, Americans have been gifted at attracting immigrants who have created an archetype of a Silicon Valley entrepreneur.

However, a lot of Americans have successfully innovated. Evidence shows that while there are many descriptions of great leaders, the derivative of the analysis of their activities is that great leaders are those who have inspired followers. The key question is then what makes followers inspired. The collaborators of many outstanding leaders, such as Walt Disney, Warren Buffet, and Jack Welch, acknowledge that "one knows one works for one of the best" (Bennis 1997). The great leaders spell out a vision in a way that creates excitement in a group of people. Margaret Thatcher said, "it is a small group of committed people who can change the world." As Bennis points out, the "Great Man hypothesis" has been substituted by the "Great Team" hypothesis. The history of the discovery of cubism demonstrates that this breakthrough was the result of a creative collaboration of Picasso and Braque, who shared an atelier and for seven years worked side by side, co-signing their work. In a peer-to-peer learning process, they created a new avant-garde art—cubism.

Marginalization stimulates learning. If we look at innovation in companies, the person contributing creative solutions is quite often somebody who is not necessarily an exile, but somebody who is not entirely in the profession or business, who has not done a lot of work in the area, who is an outsider, able to gain a fresh perspective to see the obvious that others had stopped seeing because they were inside of the process too long.

The collective learning in undertaking the creation of an enterprise is often also about customers with empathy as a driver. For example, children were the original target audience for Apple computers. Apple wanted to help them use technology for learning. This demanding clientele required Apple products to be intuitive. This key feature, still underlying all products designed by Apple in California, is a leading factor in the Silicon Valley measure of success—making money. For many entrepreneurs, undertaking a venture is about making money as well as making a difference. They declare that they want to create their own opportunities, be creative, solve problems, be part of high performance teams, and think big.

Money is a significant motivator for Silicon Valley entrepreneurs, although they may not openly admit it. In the majority of cases, the magnitude of problems solved by entrepreneurs thanks to their "smartness" is modest and mundane. For example, Netflix, the movie rental business that destroyed the international chain Blockbuster, is incredibly creative and problem-focused. Netflix understood clients who did not want to leave home to rent movies. The company proposed a new way for solving this problem and helped organize home entertainment in a way that is to a certain degree counterintuitive. Customers sign up for up to four movies per month. They can keep the four DVDs as long as they wish, and then send them back to Netflix, which pays for shipping.

What is the nature of the problems that entrepreneurial companies like Netflix solve? They identify potentially paying customers, take a partner, build a business, solicit a myriad of little daily problems, and take calculated risks. What distinguishes their always steep learning curve is a mixture of a desire to be smart and show it to the world and a longing for success, since these companies have an inherent drive to compete and to achieve.

Availability of entrepreneurial talent and risk financing are critical elements of driving innovations to the markets. There is evidence that venture capital and business angels play a critical role in the process of financing and managing fast-growing enterprises. Venture capital as an industry is highly concentrated globally in few locations. In 2011, the United Kingdom, Nordic countries, and France, with Benelux, managed more than 83% of the VC amount raised in Europe. Because of the hands-on approach in providing strategic guidance, venture capitalists tend to operate globally and co-invest in consortia so that one of the fund managers is located in the proximity of the portfolio companies, with proximity defined casually as half a day's trip. Business angels choose to operate in proximity to the location of their portfolio investments, as it is their know-how as well as capital that help the companies manage fast growth.

Both VC and business angels operate under specific legal structures: their nature is transactional and the main success criteria are the return on investment in the case of the former, and both financial returns and some motivating, less tangible returns for the latter, such as sharing knowledge, giving back, or caring to solve a problem.

Beyond Profit-Making

What about innovation that is neither new in its essence, nor pragmatic, with no immediate application, that is not patentable and has no potential commercial value, and is not based on a novel technology? What if innovation is in principle a human experience, a cultural immersion, or even an existential insight? If culture is considered the essence of innovation, how can it be defined and statistically quantified?

A systematic approach to measuring creativity and design as enablers of innovation is presented by Hollanders and van Cruysen based on the scoreboard approach (Hollanders and van Cruysen 2009). They have derived a set of concrete measures covering both long-term and short-term indicators that cover the creativity and design enablers from widely different but still relevant directions. The Internet can be analyzed as a technological innovation, but at the same time it can be viewed from a social or cultural perspective. The Internet was already old technology in the 1980s when it went beyond the military or scientific use. It enabled a new way of communication, yet at the time when it started to spread, it had no immediate business application, was not patented, and had no commercial value.

The degree of uncertainty and complexity in dealing with global challenges such as climate change, sustainability of energy, efficient transportation, or urban mobility exceeds any innovation technology driven paradigms of the product and service economies (DG Research 2007). Technology is fundamental but definitely not enough to solve these cross-societal, global, and urgent issues (EC 2008). For example, sustainability in its broadest sense, encompassing both environmental and economic aspects, is a long-term, multidisciplinary undertaking involving a wide range of stakeholders.

While sustainability-driven research addresses the long-term horizon, at the same time, it requires immediate actions to be taken. They include, among other things, changing the patterns of consumer behavior and social impact evaluation. The definition of these new processes assigns the research university and innovation forces unexplored issues to be tackled. Other non-technological research also adopts interdisciplinary approaches. It elaborates on new remuneration schemes; process critical success factors; role of incentives; taxes and regulation; system, network, and knowledge economics; and complex process control and modeling.

Dealing with complexity requires a changed mindset. It relies on a redefinition of open and co-operative architectures, and use of network connectivity as an amplifying factor of product-service diffusion in the market and optimization of global process rather than any single component, measured by aggregate performance metrics. Creativity of individual innovators and creative collaboration of teams through open innovation networks are key characteristics of non-R&D innovation.

Interdisciplinary research is conducive to breakthrough innovations. The origins and early development of ubiquitous computing is a good example (Weiser, Gold, and Brown 1999)[9]. The term ubiquitous computing was coined by Marc Weiser at Xerox PARC to describe a new post-desktop paradigm of computer presence and human-computer interaction. Initially, Weiser, the Chief Technologist at PARC, and his team collaborated with the division of anthropologists of the Work Practices and Technology area within PARC to understand how humans really interact with computers.

The observations of the situational use of the technology pointed to specific ways computers were embedded into the complex social framework of daily life, especially at the interface with the real world of physical environment. The team at PARC analyzed these converging forces "from atoms to culture" and came up with a radical answer to issues obscuring the seamless use of computers. They wanted to make computers less complex, easy to use, less absorbing, less isolated, and less dominating over human physical space and lives.

The core idea was to reposition computers from human-to-computer interface to human-to-human interface by redefining the entire spectrum of relationships between humans and machines for the post PC area. Three non-desktop devices were conceived: a large wall-display program known as the LiveBoard, which was later used in high schools; book-sized ParcPad precursors of tablets; and the palm-sized ParcTab, a milestone toward a future smartphone. PARC researchers, supported by a three year DARPA grant, used the Active Badge system originally developed for Olivetti, an Italian office equipment manufacturer, and combined it with a flexible computational infrastructure that recognized the location, situation, usage, connectivity, and ownership of the device.

---

(9) Insights on PARC come from literature as well as an interview the author of this book conducted with John Seely Brown, former Chief Scientist of Xerox Corporation and the director of its Palo Alto Research Center, Palo Alto, May 17th, 2010.

PARC was the first ground where this ubi-comp infrastructure was deployed and tested in 1994. It created a new paradigm of seamless interaction between computers and humans in their daily work and life, as a new infrastructure based on continued connectivity and continuous network with invisibly interwoven sensors, actuators, displays, and computational elements. A new era of Internet-of-Things started raising a number of fundamental questions concerning individual privacy, individual freedom, and control systems.

Insights into the innovation coming from the emerging economies such as China put reverse innovation on the radar of innovation activities, which is based on an ability to recover knowledge from existing products, services, and processes, and cost innovation, which aims to produce the same quality product at a significantly lower cost. India is a fertile ground for implementing frugal innovation, which means using low-tech methods suitable for underdeveloped or unreliable infrastructures such as electricity grids or road transport, to deliver solutions to millions of underserved users in rural areas. Rugged innovation develops solutions to be used in extreme conditions with little if any technical support and service. Finally, innovation also happens in public administration and there have been interesting attempts in the sphere of public policy innovation and social innovation.

As innovation happens in different dimensions, not only in technological progress, entrepreneurship does not only take place in for-profit activity but in other realms, creating new aspects of this concept, such as social entrepreneurship or institutional entrepreneurship. There are specific types of entrepreneurial activities since they involve specific kinds of capital, labor, and knowledge, and engage in a specific process of production.

Social entrepreneurship can be defined as a specific kind of entrepreneurial activity. Social entrepreneurs care to bring impact rather than make profits, although sustainability of a social enterprise is one of their concerns. However, social entrepreneurship is not a specific form of entrepreneurship limited to the two billion people living below the poverty line.

It is indeed an emerging model of development for underserved communities. New business models that emerged at the "bottom of the pyramid" became drives for development (Prahalad and Hammond 2002; Prahalad 2005; Hartigan and Elkington 2008; London, T. and Anupindi 2011). Karnani challenged this approach. He proposed keeping entrepreneurship as a concept solely limited to the domain of the for-profit companies. He also dismissed their corporate social activities (CSR), since the key function of the private sector is maximizing value for the shareholders (Karnani 2011). However, based on data from the Silicon Valley's Tech Awards and the Global Social Benefit Incubator at Santa Clara University (Castells and Koch 2009), social entrepreneurship develops a new model for growth, because it leads to a convergence of the specific features, namely:

- An organizational form based on radically redesigned value chains and business model innovation;

- The integration of social metrics with financial criteria and its convergence with increased accountability for externalities in the macro-environment;

- The growth of social capital as a new asset class that aligns with longer development and market creation cycles for serving marginalized populations;

- Empathy as a methodology for ground "truthing" product design;

- The proliferation of mobile devices, applications, and social media;

- The use of logic models and new ways of thinking about "scale."

The social enterprise model is the antithesis of "trickle down" economic theory and top-down models of economic development. It is animated by individual and collective agency. In contrast to the dilution of benefits in top-down development models, social enterprise investments and bottom-up change induces multiplier effects that can be measured in sustainable social and economic benefits. Focused efforts in vertical market sectors and elements of regional advantage can amplify these effects (Castells and Koch 2009).

Since the very early stage of human civilization, creativity, innovation, and entrepreneurial activities should be interpreted not only through the lenses of technical or technological progress and science but as a complex system, exhibiting both technological as well as cultural and social aspects and components and touching upon philosophical and ethical issues.

Globalization and increased market competitiveness in the context of the persistent economic and financial crisis in Europe challenges its advanced economies, multinationals, small enterprises, and citizens, especially students, who find little—if any—opportunities for satisfying work and meaningful life in the existing political and economic system. While integrated, linear sequential processes of innovation were suited to the knowledge economy, the science-based technological innovation processes are not the most efficient response in the fragmented world composed of networks of networked global value chains, and a search for new meaning.

Chapter 3

LEARNING IN A WORLD OF CONSTANT FLUX

The interlinking of the physical reality and the virtual reality enabled by information and communication technology creates a multidimensional world of constant flux. Learning in the world-in-the-constant-making challenges the established models of education focused on acquisition of knowledge and skills. The shifts in learning patterns linked to the new reality shaped by information and communication technology have been explored in an interesting fashion by Douglas Thomas and John Seely Brown (Thomas and Brown 2010).

Douglas Thomas and John Seely Brown describe two shifts that occurred over the last decades in the area of education. This is a transition from learning-about to learning-to-be, and from learning-to-be to learning-to-become.[10] They search for cultural values, which underlie educational models, and point to the relation between the approach to education and the conceptualization of time. A linear or cyclical perception of time in Western cultures makes these societies more prone to the first two modes, which focus on the outcome rather than on the experience as such. The notion of time apprehended by Eastern societies merges experience and awareness, being simultaneously immersed in the external world and in the internal consciousness of an observer, the self. The latter approach puts the emphasis on the process of becoming rather than on reaching an expected learning outcome.

(10) This chapter is inspired by the interview I conducted with John Seely Brown in Palo Alto, 2010.

Their explorations on the new nature of learning are based on the concepts of codified and tacit knowledge developed by Polanyi. Navigating the complexities of the multidimensional world-in-the-making shifts the emphasis from codified knowledge to tacit knowledge with the latter becoming a dominant component of learning. Polanyi introduced a distinction between explicit and tacit knowledge, both integral dimensions of the very nature of knowledge as such (Polanyi 1967, 1974). The tacit dimension of knowledge is acquired by experiencing, that is "learning-to-become," during a collective act of co-creation of a social context. It is not objectified and thus cannot be transferred.

Thomas and Brown build further on the work of Polanyi. They refer to the three broader perceptions of human beings in the context of learning in the world-in-the-making: first, Homo Sapiens (human as a knower), then Homo Faber (human as a creator) (Thomas and Brown 2010). Homo Sapiens values factual knowledge. It is explicit and codified in social and cultural artifacts. Its reliability depends on the trustworthiness of sources validating its authenticity and on the knowledge production process. Homo Faber uses tools available in the networked world, such as social media, to experiment and thus learn. Polanyi's concept of indwelling, that is immersion, reflects this learning experience.

Thomas and Brown also dwell on the concept of Homo Ludens developed by Mimi Ito. They claim that it is the most overlooked element of learning in the twentieth century theories and that this aspect of human predisposition is given a new and prominent role in the learning process, which occurs in the space created by new media. A typology of the learning modes in the context of play-and-learn, offered by Mimi Ito, includes "hanging out," "messing around," and "geeking out" (Ito 2009).

"Hanging out" in the space of new media includes participation in social networking sites such as Facebook, chatting, and instant messaging. Through exchange of information while engaging in meaningful social interaction, the young generation constructs new social norms and forms of media literacy in networked public space. It touches upon the Polanyi concept of "indwelling" since it goes beyond immersion in an experience toward internalization of social norms, roles, and values (Polanyi 1974). "Hanging out" helps answer one of the most fundamental questions—that of defining relationships with others.

"Messing around" occurs when young people start to look into the technology itself, and explore its properties and functionalities. This leads toward the development of another dimension of learning into a better understanding of the relationship between themselves and the environment. These sorts of explorations, facilitated by the tools of the digital environment, result in production of personal videos, blogs, pictures, and websites. The digital media become an extension of oneself in a virtual space and thus interplay with the development of personal identity, of who we are and who we want to become in opposition to or in accordance with our environment. "Messing around" is not instrumental or purposeful. It is a playful part of our search for identity in both the virtual and real world.

"Geeking out" is enabled by free access to broadband connectivity to the Internet. This unlimited access to the abundance of resources, interest communities, and support groups allows one to learn by exploring the traffic and indulging in the flow of information, becoming "a flaneur" of the virtual space created by new media. This is an experiential model of learning, contextual, with immediate feedback loops, and peer-to-peer interaction. "Geeking out," through first-hand experience and direct communication both peer-to-peer and peer-to-community, leads to a purely tacit form of knowledge or rather knowing how a community of knowledge functions. The learning takes place as a result of indwelling, embodiment, and agency, creating a radically different learning environment where knowing, making, and playing create and decode the tacit dimension of knowledge.

The change in the nature of reality, in which the network society is immersed, gives new opportunities for learning which have yet to be embraced by Western educational systems. Social media is a new learning lab offering a new space for deepening understanding (acquiring knowledge), experiencing content (acquiring skills), and collectively co-creating learning spaces with others (making of virtual reality).

This third element happens often in a mode of a child-like experience of playing with peers and offers a fundamentally different experience of participation from that of reading, writing, lecturing, debating, or even action learning, mentoring, or coaching. The new media with their virtual social spaces as new informal learning environments challenge dominant educational paradigms for learning. They offer tools that are becoming standard for making inquiries and enabling process-based learning. They also shift the emphasis on the tacit dimension of knowing and leave out the accumulation of codified knowledge and skills to the agents deprived of the access to the learning environment of the knowledge community in the "world-in-the-making." This world is co-created by the new interactive media. Learning in this environment is a collective, participatory, interactive, and multidimensional process. Accumulation of knowledge is no longer the purpose of learning. Its main goal is knowing and becoming as a process of learning.

Innovation
Networks

Around the end of the last millennium, a convergence of social, technological, economic, and cultural transformations triggered the emergence of a network society (Castells 1996, 2000). The network society is a social structure made of interlinked, local and global networks, which continuously communicate using ubiquitous microelectronic, fixed, and wireless informational technologies. It depicts the social reality powered by digital information and communication technologies, where the flow of information is continuous and ubiquitous and knowledge production takes place at exponential speed in innovation networks. While networks are a natural organizational form of life in general and have always been a fabric of human societies, they have gained a new dimension under a new technological paradigm characteristic of the information age.

This new social paradigm surfaced along with the semiconductor industry in the 40s and 50s of the last century, consolidated predominantly in the United States and spread across the globe in the 1970s with the Internet and the World Wide Web. This new form of social organization was characterized from its naissance by formation of a global networked structure composed of uncountable, interrelated, multilayered, and multidimensional social networks. The emergence of this networked global society marked a transition between two separate forms of social organization: the industrial society and the network society. It was enabled by the networking capacity, which came from the combination of an old organizational form—networks, with new digital networking technologies that allowed speed, volume, complexity, and real-time interaction.

The network society has emerged as a network of networks. The materialization of this new, partially real, partially virtual structure liquidated hierarchy in the sense of linear interdependencies between the power holders and the subordinates contained within formal institutional or organizational constructs. The existence of additional leverages on top of clear lines of direct or indirect relations became in itself a mighty source of empowerment. Complex relations between agents in networks blurred the borders between organizations and eroded formal and institutional power, shifting the command from one to many and multiple, simultaneous, geographically distributed, often informal influence sources at individual, group, organizational, or network levels.

As a consequence, there was increased indeterminacy, volatility, and unpredictability in the system. The consequences of a failure are embedded in the system, as explained by the complex system theory; radical and abrupt transformations are often triggered by a seemingly minor event at the periphery of a network. The first decade of the twenty-first century was abundant in examples of unexpected consequences of the new, networked social structure.

The scope, strength, and impact of transformations were illustrated by the spiral of the financial crisis started in 2008; by the dramatic, "instant" revolutions of the Arab Spring erupting in 2010; as well as by the emergence of multimillion user and multibillion value social networking and e-commerce websites in the span of merely a few years, such as Facebook, Skype, and Groupon. Complexity, volatility, unpredictability, contradictions, and indeterminacy are some of the characteristics of the network society. They induced new forms of work organization and novel mechanisms for wealth creation and distribution.

The transition from the industrial society to the network society was marked by increasing turbulences and discontinuities in the existing structures of social, economic, and political power and control. The new form of social organization was composed of a network of networks, as a new source of power and control introduced into the system. While a network has been a fundamental unit in human evolution and history, proliferating in the industrial society by extensive travel, the telegraph, and the telephone, a network of networks has never been an equivalent or dominant social structure. Networks of individuals, groups, and organizations were used to preserve or challenge the status quo but never before had they created among them a central form of social organization as an alternative or supplement to all other existing structures.

The rise of the industrial society was the consequence of the industrial revolution, which fueled mass industrialization and created a mass labor market. The formation and internationalization of a corporate organization generated the need for new management practices to control widespread manufacturing facilities and optimize global value chains.

The perception of humans as labor machines was expressed in Taylorist rationale to measure work productivity in terms of labor output per unit of time. With the increasing complexity of industrial organizations reaching the ultimate convolution of a matrix structure, all sorts of leadership theories linking management to a value system were deployed in order to raise human performance and productivity.

The proliferation of the protestant work ethic based on a set of values such as wealth accumulation as a goal in itself, high work performance, and the supremacy of working over living, helped implement corporate cultures as the basis for successful deployment of multinational corporations across the globe. The logic of this industrial society was taken to the dystopian extreme by artists showing the futility of the modernist approach and the destruction of our planet, with humans squared into multi-dwelling habitats located in an unending landscape of highways and city suburbs. The post-modernist societies questioned these values and ways of living. The experimentation with alternative forms of social organization in some cases succeeded in creating more inclusive and fair societies such as Finland or Sweden.

The lack of two-dimensional hierarchical structure eroded established values and norms and affected all aspects of individual and collective behavioral patterns. Thanks to digital networking technologies, the networking experience has overcome limitations of time, space, and scale. Virtual social networking has overcome the traditional boundaries of personal or professional communities, neighborhoods, cities, and states.

Networks of networks created a structure of the network society, which became a global networked social system powered by endless, self-perpetuating, and morphing social networking and social networking sites. People have gained access to a wider than ever base of information and knowledge stored as virtual equivalents of traditional repositories such as libraries, publications, and statistics, as well as direct contact with peers, experts, and mavens.

The interaction between development of technology and work resulted in erasing the need for some types of skills, and giving rise to technology savvy, migrating professionals: the "creative class" (Florida 2004). The fundamental difference between the industrial and network societies is in the real-time dimension and "virtuality" of human interaction. Simultaneously, people live and multitask in multimodal dimensions, communicating via the Internet, mobile phone, and fixed line telephony in parallel to face-to-face interaction. The virtual existence has become an integral part of being and not only of a way of living.

The information and telecommunication infrastructures are the backbone of the network society. By the mid-1990s, the Internet reached a critical level of penetration across the globe. With the expansion of the Internet, the World Wide Web became the most powerful open resource for information searching, sourcing, sharing, and exchange. Wireless telecommunication infrastructure, financed at a large scale over the last two decades of the twentieth century, enabled global use of mobile telephony. Since GSM masts covered even most distant and developing parts of the world, it changed the patterns of how people live, learn, work, and entertain, not only in the richest areas of the globe, but also in the poorest metropolitan suburbs as well as in underdeveloped regions of Africa, Asia, or South America.

By the end of the century, the convergence between wireless telecommunication infrastructure and mobile applications multiplying the points of access to the Internet became the prime mode of communication, with wireless subscribers exceeding fixed-line subscribers in 2002. During the next decade, the introduction of new mobile devices, and in particular the proliferation of smart phones and tablets, created new user-friendly standards for interaction designed by Apple with its novel iPhone, iPod, and iPad product lines.

This convergent potent information and communication infrastructure and software enabled the dissemination of the Internet and the spread of the network society model but was not the origin of this process (Castells 1996, 2000, 2010). Global communication infrastructures, vital components of new social processes, developed because there was a need to increase the communication and management capacity of all sorts of networked organizations. More demand for better communication and management led to higher investment in transport and telecommunication infrastructure. Better infrastructure increased connectivity and work productivity, attracting the creative class and its dependents to old and new metropolitan areas in search for superior work opportunities and better life.

The Internet, the World Wide Web, and wireless devices converge and form an interactive communication infrastructure enabling interaction between members of innovation networks. These multimodal communication channels hold innovation networks together by means, mechanisms, and practices characteristic of the network society. The World Wide Web is a communication network used for posting, sharing, and exchanging all sorts of digital content including text, audio, video, and software applications.

The Internet has also increased access to traditional forms of mass media such as radio, television, and newspapers. It has become an online library for books, magazines, journals, music, films, and all sorts of data. It transforms traditional mass media by the on-demand availability of content also on portable devices, and by integrating virtuality into their real life presence. E-mail, blogging, social networking sites, online news, reservoirs of personal photos and vlogs, and Really Simple Syndication (RSS) feeds created a multichannel, multimodal system of digital communication. These systems enable mass-self communication across horizontal networks of interactive virtual, real-time exchange of ideas and information at local and global levels simultaneously.

The theory of the network society helps one to understand ultimately different forms of social organization, interrelations, drivers, mechanisms, and behaviors. It can also be used as an analytical framework facilitating deconstruction and interpretation of determinants and consequences of social activities such as innovation. The conceptualization of the network society as a network of networks yields a more thorough interpretation of new modes of innovating than other existing analytical frameworks. The application of this framework will structure and lead the analysis of the networked phenomena in the space of innovation over the first decade of the twenty-first century. The analysis will be focused on the trends and modes referring to the structural analysis of the network society and in particular on the issue of openness, the articulation of innovation networks and new networked models of innovating, spaces where innovation happens, and the relation of these new networked modes of innovating to the existing innovation systems designed to support innovation models characteristic of the industrial society.

Chapter 4

STRUCTURE, MODALITIES, DRIVERS

In the network society, innovation as the learning process has gained different dynamics under the new social structure—innovation networks. An innovation network can be conceptualized as a manifestation of a specific type of social organization characteristic of the network society and functioning within the context of innovation and innovating as one of the social activities of this society. This organizational form emerged along other social transformations taking place in the complex process of social evolution in the sphere where science, innovation, and technology meet with markets and societies.

Innovation has always been a social phenomenon and different sorts of innovation networks existed also in the industrial area, defined and sponsored by academic and corporate organizations and institutions. However, under the new regime of the network society, innovation as such gained a new dimension of openness and escaped institutional barriers. An innovation network became—like other networks—a network of networks and in particular a network other than innovation networks with synchronically interlinked micro and macro dimensions.

There are different kinds of innovation networks, though all of them share common features. They are composed of interconnected nodes, which have different importance and functionality and a temporary status. The node's status is undermined by its current capacity to absorb, process, and share information, which is relevant and useful for accomplishing a purpose of the network. If a node does not contribute to processing the flow of information, it becomes redundant, in which case a network reconfigures itself by deleting useless nodes and adding new ones.

An innovation network has no single center of control and command. It is governed by a program that is made up of codes defining the goal of a network, thus giving it a meaning and specifying a set of rules of performance and criteria to assess success or failure. It is managed by programming—that is, a set of pre-agreed or emerging ad hoc, simultaneous, and consecutive activities—which together lead to accomplishing the raison d'etre of a network. Unless there is a new program, the network will continue to produce a similar output in terms of quality and a largely unchanged pace in terms of quantity.

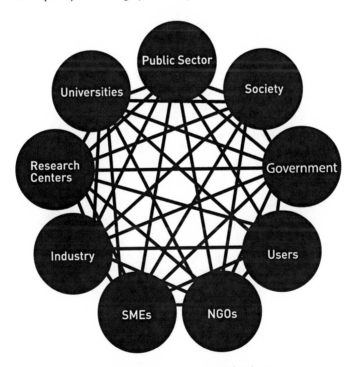

Figure 1. Diversity of Innovation Actors and Settings

Different sorts of innovation networks can collaborate with each other if they have a common capacity to communicate. This means that they possess common codes of translation and inter-operability (protocols of communication) and switches (connection points). Innovation networks can also compete. It is the case when some are more efficient and achieve certain goals faster than other networks in a competitive environment, especially in industries where advantage resides in developing time-sensitive technologies and the "shelf-life" of a product or service tends to zero.

The superiority of networked organization of innovation processes over linear, chain-like models lies in their flexibility, scalability, and inherent capacity to reproduce themselves. These features are enabled by digital communication technologies and lead to unique features of innovation networks, giving them sustainable advantage over other organizational forms. Flexibility means that an innovation network can adapt to a volatile environment through its capacity to self-reconfigure the nodes. Scalability entices the network's operational stability while expanding or shrinking. The capacity to reproduce itself comes with the DNA encoded in each and every node, enabling it to reproduce the program and programming of the entire network unless connecting points are physically eliminated, breaking the network as a unit.

The characteristics of innovation networks depend on a number of converging attributes that define their potential impact and relevance. The value of a network can be defined as a sum of the values of its members in two dimensions. One aspect is increasing the relative value of its members as elements of the original network by developing their capacity to become linking agents to other networks. This can be called networking value.

The second factor is increasing the value of the network as such by creating multiple, overlapping, and multi-layered connection points with other relevant networks and including members of the original, through projects leading to adding value and their status as connectors at the crossroads of networks. This is a relational value since relations and not only contacts drive this feature.

The relevance of innovation networks depends on an added subjective value that members can provide to other members in achieving their objectives and also in building their capacity to change both their status in a network by becoming a connector, and the network in itself as an element in the global innovation system of complex interlinked innovation webs. The impact of an innovation network is then multiplied if there is a mechanism for leveraging its potential by interlinking with other networks and thus adding value to an innovation system in which a network functions. Taking into consideration potential impact and relevance, innovation networks can be characterized based on four key characteristics, which are distinct.

Firstly, geographical spread dividing networks into global, regional, and local. Global networks spread across the planet linking focal points, which attract most quality traffic and resources since they are highly regarded by the mavens of a given innovation sphere. Regional networks are limited to a certain extent by natural barriers and to some extent by political and economic boundaries of an innovation system. An example could be an innovation network existing only in Europe or in North America. Local innovation networks can include national networks; for example, a network of national universities of science and technology.

Secondly, networks differ in their structure, which can be horizontal, vertical, or octagonal. An example of a horizontal innovation network is an industry network of innovation-driven sectors, such as information and communication technology, media, or climate and energy. Another case would be specialist networks within an industry relevant for innovation, such as a venture capital network or business angels network.

Yet another type would be networks that attract members because of a particular feature, such as businesswomen's networks in finance industry or inventors' networks. Vertical innovation networks include all sorts of organizations integrating members across value chains of an innovation process, such as research networks for climate change or business networks for vertically integrated multinationals. Octagonal innovation networks cross sectors and disciplines such as, for example, networks between industry and academia.

Thirdly, networks can be divided according to their connectivity in the overall system. Some are closed, and there is some sort of protocol or formal procedure to become a member. LinkedIn, a social networking site for professionals, is a good example since it consists of a number of closed yet interlinked networks. Entering any of them requires a recommendation and consent of the author of a particular profile. Other networks are by definition open to anyone who is interested in joining, such as some Internet fora and crowdsourcing sites. The value of some networks lies in their connecting function as their principal raison d'etre since they were established to facilitate networking between members and to link them with other networks. Chambers of commerce or student associations are illustrations of these types of networks.

Fourthly, networks can be classified according to their potential in bringing changes to the innovation system at a local, regional, or global scale. The example would be networks organized within national or regional innovation systems changing existing patterns and mechanisms of public funding for innovation. For example, this category would include networks sponsored by the European Commission aiming to integrate the innovation potential across the European Union and thus increase Europe's innovativeness and competitiveness. Another example would be networks integrating Chinese researchers and scientists within re-immigration policies of the Chinese government, which change the global system of innovation by stimulating the outflow of talent, in particular from North America back to China.

Innovation networks have proliferated along with the spread of the new technological paradigm characteristic of the network society. Under this regime, innovation networks, while existing always as part of the social structure, have been sublimated from the science and industry-driven networks typical of the industrial era into a wide variety of diverse, overlapping structures with new features.

Under the new technological paradigm, digital information and communication technologies, enabling exchange of information and knowledge production, tend to diminish the time lag between feedback loops to zero. The two-way, real-time communication powers innovation as a learning process, and knowledge grows exponentially, feeding in return more and more precise information and thus facilitating the learning process of the members of the network. With the increasing number and diversity of network participants, and with the acceleration of the information exchange between them, feedback loops change not only the amount of knowledge produced but also its quality.

This is the reason why knowledge grows exponentially in more open innovation environments, becoming ultimately a crowdsourcing phenomenon, bringing in information from an unlimited number of sources of knowledge from the networks of networks. Open innovation communities are the ultimate effective social structures for knowledge production because the feedback to the community is given with added-value information, turning it more relevant for knowledge creation within the network. This brings to the surface latent or emergent properties of codified and latent knowledge along with digital communication technologies, which go beyond established frontiers, discontinue evolution tracks, and restart processes with innovation breakthroughs (Himanen 2001).

Analyzing innovation in the context of the network society and the information age becomes in fact a scrutiny of the global innovation system and the networked model of innovation. Innovation and innovation models in the network society are determined by a number of convergent processes.

First, the technological transformation and application of scientific discoveries to industrial or commercial use beyond and above the origin of their conception, often at a global scale from day one. Second, the limitation of nation-state regulators to monitor, tax, and control the free flow of knowledge, capital, and talent across borders. Third, the seemingly unlimited financial resources for investment and global expansion underwritten by artificially low cost of capital and easily accessible debt financing. Furthermore, public investment into research and private investment into venture capital fueling the inertia of the national innovation systems and blowing the prices of high tech companies to the point of investment bubbles. Fourth, the financial and economic crises of the developed economies accompanied by a resilience of the newly industrializing innovation economies of Brazil, Russia, India, China, and South Africa, which leads to reallocation of resources and shifting knowledge, talent, and capital globally. Fifth, the new nature of management and coordination dissociates the centers of decision-making cumulated in the nodes with the process of its implementation, driven by specific sorts of power and power sources exercised in the innovation networks.

Network Spaces

In the network society, there are two parallel communication realms creating its networked fabric: a "space of places" and a "space of flows" (Castells 2010). They co-exist, supplement each other and, in certain cases, enter the space of one another. The "space of flows" is a global macro electronic network of decision implementation. The "space of places" is a micro network of power and decision-making based on direct interpersonal contact.

The space of places, the local dimension of a network, is epitomized in the emergence of ever-expanding metropolitan areas. They are not self-contained independent global cities but elements of a networked system of exchange and value creation. The connectivity to other nodes in the global networks is the driving factor transforming selected areas of these urban structures and increasing their innovativeness, competitiveness, and attractiveness, or just the opposite—depriving them of a better future at the pace of the brain drain. The importance of a node in the global constellation of innovation networks is measured by its ability to attract, maintain, and grow talent and investment. The node gains in importance if it becomes a meeting point, a point of connection, and a switching port rather than merely a port of transit, through which people and capital pass but no value is added.

To become a major node though, a location has to rely on multidimensional transport infrastructure and both physical and virtual connectivity including airports, highways, and sometimes shipping facilities, as well as broadband telecommunication backbone infrastructure and computer networks. It also must possess the infrastructure of supplementary services for the support of the development and management of the node in its role of a connector in the global innovation network of networks. For this, the node needs to be functionally served by skilled professionals, who require support services in return to be able to combine work and life and thus give employment to service workers.

During the evolutionary process of node formation, it attracts progressively more wealth and power, and becomes an environment stimulating more innovation in its technological and cultural dimensions. As a consequence, the node spreads spatially as a metropolitan region by integrating into a common urban structure surrounding municipalities and villages, and becomes a diverse urban area with migrating centers of creative activities.

The space of flows in the global network is the space of decision implementation. It is manifested, for example, by management practices in administering the global value chains and by the emergence of global markets. In both cases, the management processes and practices required to administer and supervise these globally distributed systems are based on computer networks, information systems, and telecommunication infrastructure.

Human ability to conceive and design systems that exercise control over these complex networked processes in the mode of 24/7 (that is, constantly) means that the decisions made at a local level in corporate headquarters or regional offices are being implemented globally in real time if needed. This management capacity over global processes gave rise to global markets. For example, the global financial market is managed out of a few centers such as London, Tokyo, Shanghai, and New York. However, these cities have not created the global financial market. They were empowered as a consequence of the arguable ability to manage millions of transactions at the speed of milliseconds across the planet.

If there is such a gap between the space of places and the space of flows, is there any sort of relationship between the two kinds of spaces? First, there are flows in the space of places. Decisions are implemented also at the local level. Communication takes place via e-mail, text messages, or Skype conferencing, even between two adjacent office rooms. There are also places in the space of flows. Instant, real time, peer-to-peer, one-to-many, or many-to-many interactions via chats, tweeting, blogging, and videoconferencing create virtual space of online networking as the social space for real life power and decision-making.

If the two kinds of spaces are to some extent embedded in each other, what are the dynamics explaining the interaction between the two modalities? Can they exist without one another? Can the virtual interaction totally substitute physical contact?

Local and Global Architecture

Manuel Castells proposes a theory of special dynamics of the Information Age. In the structural sense, he claims the innovation landscape in the network society and the knowledge economy gains a new meaning derived from the logic of two kinds of space: the space of places and the space of flows, and "the global architecture of innovation networks connects places selectively, according to their relative value for the network" (Castells 1996, 2000, 2010). In this process, certain regions are becoming vital points for knowledge creation and for learning.

As a consequence, they become learning regions. They provide an underlying infrastructure for knowledge creation and accumulation as well as for the connectivity with other learning regions across the globe. The infrastructure facilitates learning and attracts creative talent, turning them into learning environments for innovation networks. With time, and along the innovation process characteristic of networked models of innovation, they gain importance and change the geography of the global innovation landscape. Despite continued predictions of the end of geography and the shift of innovation into the virtual space, creative learning environments remain important nodes or clusters of economic and technological organization on a global scale (Florida 1995; Thrift 1992, 2002).

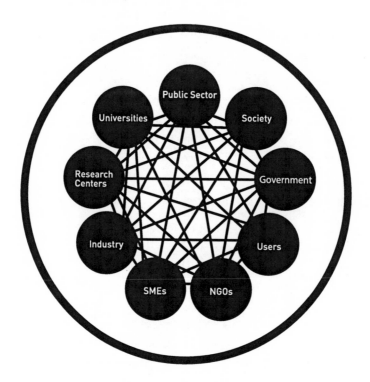

Figure 2. Local Dimension of an Innovation Network

A key characteristic brought with the emergence of the network society is that innovation happens not only in physical locations that attract talent and capital (industrial clusters) but also in the virtual space. The theory of innovation clusters uses knowledge spillover as an example of positive externality to explain why concentration of multiple actors leads to accelerated growth.

A degree of connectivity of actors with stakeholders from other innovation networks (dimensions of how tightly knit versus how loosely coupled with how many other nodes) brings events from the periphery of a network to trigger disruptive innovations, which result in discontinuities. The concentration of actors in a physical location and the dynamics of exchange within the networks both lead to cross-fertilization, serendipity, and spillover effects.

Thus, innovation milieus have become living and morphing organisms. Physical mobility of people and data altered the number of interrelations between local and global innovation networks. A node of an innovation network gathers traffic: physical traffic at the airports and on the roads, and virtual traffic such as telecommunication and data transfer, voice, and image streaming. The effectiveness of interaction within a node multiplied by the number of loosely coupled connections with other nodes accelerates the outcome of innovating: economic growth and societal impact. Tracing the traffic of people and data in the "corridors of space" reveals that the stronger the correlation between the importance of innovation milieus, the more they are interwoven in the global innovation network.

Paradoxically, in a networked "flat" world, more scientific activity, technology development, and innovation happens in these global networks than in select geographic locations. The world is not flat. It is networked. Access to the global networked innovation system is critical. The system consists of a complex network of interconnected local innovation networks, and interconnections with diverse networks are as important as exposure to a leading innovation spike. The structure of this open innovation system consists of nodes, or spikes, which cumulate talent, knowledge, and capital, as well connections between spikes in different geographical locations. Its participants keep tightly coupled local connections with the innovation ecosystem and are at the same time loosely coupled with other networks and other innovation spikes.

A local innovation ecosystem can be looked upon as a network of multiple stakeholders ranging from businesses to universities and research organizations, government agencies, and not-for-profits. Innovation can start anywhere in this web: in research, in education, or in any of the organizational settings. However, innovation is not only local, it is also global, linking up innovation milieus and research centers with other nodes through a network of innovation.

If innovation networks are manifestations of the new social architecture of the network society, they should mirror it also in its spatial articulation. The key geographic characteristic of the network society is the networked connection between the local and the global. The nodes in networks have the ability to interact globally, in real-time, at necessity or for fun, in chosen intervals throughout all time zones.

However, global interaction carries different functionality than interaction at the local level when face-to-face personal contact is possible. The interaction at the local level is part of the decision-making process, making politics, exercising power, and developing new initiatives and projects. The interaction at the global level is, to a large extent, a management exercise in the implementation of ideas and the execution of power generated through the local interaction. Thus, innovation networks coexist in the "space of places" and the "space of flows."

In the process of restructuring the global innovation landscape, certain regions have become mega nodes in the global meta-network. Mega node status is a consequence of concentration of superior resources as well as power over global assets. The changing global landscape of innovation hotspots poses a question as to why certain places become major nodes of innovation networks, while other places lose their importance, and yet other locations remain insignificant despite political efforts and public investment.

Figure 3. Local versus Global Dimension of Innovation Networks

The analysis of spatial articulation of innovation networks demonstrates that they do not have the same geography. A network of information and communication technology, of cleantech or biotech, has different nodes. The map of innovation networks may differ from the map of other types of networks or in some cases it can overlap.

For example, the global financial network operates from a few places, such as London, Tokyo, and New York, which are also major nodes for the innovation network concentrating political power and wealth. Others accumulate innovation capacity expressed by concentration of academic institutions, industrial R&D labs, and creative talent, but are marginal for the global network of finance, like Michigan, Eindhoven, or Warsaw. The key questions for understanding the logic of the network of innovation networks concern the concentration of resources in certain metropolitan places and the diffusion of innovation networks.

Structured Chaos: Logic of Innovation Networks

The economic geography of the industrial era was determined by the availability of natural resources, transport infrastructure, and access to the networks of power and decision-making. The global landscape of the knowledge economy characteristic of the network society is conditioned by the availability of knowledge resources and connectivity to multiple global communication networks, as well as to the local network of power and decision-making.

This is a space of places and the space of flows where multiple networks overlap and create synergies from the co-existence of networks of high-technology industries, venture capital, business angels, and all sorts of ancillary services. The accumulation of resources at a given node leads to the economies of scale, which was one of the critical competitive factors for the industrial economy. In the networked knowledge economy, these economies of scale also matter, but the economies of synergy provide a necessary leverage for the growth of the innovation networks and through them also innovation regions.

Multilayering of global innovation networks is the process of overlapping and interaction of various networks in the space of places and in particular cases also in the space of flows. As demonstrated by the case of the Silicon Valley, multilayering brings economies of synergy, structuring and restructuring the global innovation landscape since the emergence of the high tech industry in the Valley. Multilayering creates economies of synergy at the level of these networks because this sort of interaction increases competencies for knowledge, power, and wealth accumulation.

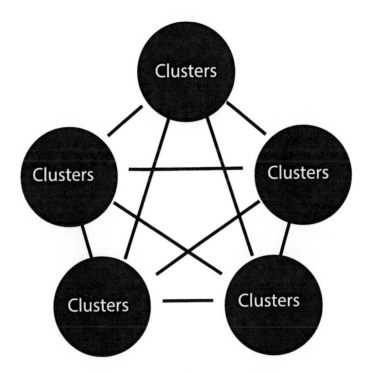

Figure 4. Tightly-Knit and Loosely-Coupled: Innovation Networks Across Clusters

Multilayering of multiple and diverse networks has a few consequences for the status of the node and for the dynamics of network diffusion. The superior capabilities of their members accelerate the dynamics of resource accumulation at the level of a particular node. Consequently, a node gains a higher status in the multilayering networks, which in return attracts more talent and investment. In a case when these multilayered networks overlap in one node, the node becomes a mega node belonging to different networks. Then participants of diverse networks interact since they are co-located at the physical distance that allows or stimulates informal socializing. Thus, they exchange information, gaining access to both the tacit knowledge and to the power networks from which they were excluded. They become connectors between networks, thus diffusing them across those networks to which they belong (Monge and Contractor 2003).

Rapid prototyping is a good example of how innovation works across local and global innovation networks. All basic devices are programmable. Most designs today are chip designs, which are programmed. If they do not perform, they are reprogrammed in a matter of days rather than a matter of months. They can be programmed because a standard exists, and they are programmed to perform only in a certain function. They are used to make a prototype, test it, integrate the results of the test into the product and change the product, and then start again. There can be a low-cost production facility in Taiwan, a semiconductor company with two or five engineers in California, and an intermediary lab.

A software company designs a chip and tests it by running it through their own software-testing program or a specialized process manufacturing activity also in the Silicon Valley, for example at Stanford or at another university. Then the chip goes to prototyping manufacturing and only ultimately is mass-produced. Another example of the simultaneous dimension of local and global multilayering of innovation networks is the formation of collaborative research partnerships.

For example, the European Union promotes transnational collaboration funding projects (e.g. the Marie Curie-Sklodowska program for mobility of researchers and young scientists), which involves a local team collaborating in partnership with other teams spread throughout at least two other EU member states, thanks to which individual researchers have their global contacts that allow them to access a wider and more diverse network in order to gain faster feedback. Venture capital networks also display the specific connection between micro and macro. While companies are managed locally, deal sourcing and raising capital are done through the global networking of, on the one hand, risk investors such as business angels, serial entrepreneurs, and local funds, and on the other hand, large financial institutions such as pension funds and insurance companies providing equity.

What kind of "multilayering" then creates most synergies relevant for innovation?

First, the critical component is the multitude of international networks of the global network of talent. It can include immigrants of different origins maintaining strong ties and supporting one another at the new location and in many cases also at the place of origin. They can also be composed of expats, the migrating talent of executives and professionals.

Second, for a node to matter in the global innovation landscape, it must have dynamic links to the global exchange of knowledge and also provide a value proposition to attract top international students and faculty. An open research environment in a node is made of networks of students and networks of researchers who came to a node for a limited period of time with their international experience and fresh ideas.

Third, the lack of an industrial network or even multiple networks for different industries could result in knowledge accumulation in the form of a flourishing node of a global research network, but not in terms of innovation buildup. Industries need first of all employees of quality to stay globally competitive, and therefore the synergy with the international networks of global talent leads to critical economies of synergy.

Fourth, a critical network for innovation is the overlapping network of the financial sector, which is especially competent in financing early stage ventures, such as a network of venture capital to take projects originating across different environments of a node to form young new firms. A network of private equity specializing in financing more mature enterprises is also indispensable for taking medium-sized companies to the next stage in establishment of a new industry in a particular innovation region.

Fifth, a network of entrepreneurs, especially seasoned, serial entrepreneurs such as business angel networks, who have the capability to integrate resources across all other networks, matters for innovation. Finally, the support networks of lawyers, accountants, IT specialists, marketing experts, and business consultants are essential not only for supporting innovation across all stages of maturation, but also for creating interconnections between different networks.

Lastly, a special sort of network is the creative network, which generates a common language of communication, giving meaning to different activities across networks in a node through communities of interest, clubs, associations, and simply friendships. In a case when these multilayered networks meet at a particular geographical location and share a node in such places, these localities become mega nodes.

Mega Nodes and Peripheries

A mega node for the global innovation landscape is a place where various innovation networks overlap. This kind of node has a special status in each of these multilayering nets, and because of its status it attracts and accumulates resources. For example, the Silicon Valley and Boston area in the US, London and Cambridge in the UK, or Beijing and Shanghai in China, are typical cases of this "multiple nodal advantage." However, while the Silicon Valley has all sorts of networks relevant to innovation, the Boston area does not reach the same level in the global innovation landscape since it lacks some of them such as, for example, financial networks. No doubt, suggests Castells, Boston is a dominant node in academic research and a significant node in technological innovation (particularly in ICT and biotechnology) (Castells 2009). However, it is only a secondary node for industry networks and subsidiary to other nodes in terms of access to global networks of finance.

In China, Beijing is a dominant node for political, financial, scientific, and technological networks and a secondary node for global trade. Shanghai, on the other hand, is a dominant node for financial networks, industrial networks, and technological networks but has a secondary status for other sorts of networks relevant for innovation. London is a global dominant hub for all sorts of networks in the innovation domain including political, financial, research and technology, talent, and wealth networks, while Cambridge is a dominant node for research and technology networks, a significant node for entrepreneurial networks,

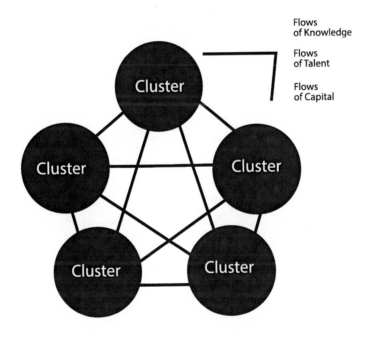

Figure 5. Flows of Knowledge, Talent, and Capital Across Innovation Networks

a secondary node for industrial networks, and a subsidiary node for political and power networks.

How then do innovation networks diffuse? What drives the emergence of mega nodes?

Mega nodes have a special status in the entire global system of innovation. This status is derived not from their node as an innovation ecosystem, industrial cluster, or venture capital hub. The Silicon Valley has all these characteristics, yet its privileged status in the global innovation network comes from its power as part of the network. It is not the critical mass, availability of risk capital, research capacity, availability of multinational talent, and entrepreneurial open culture that constitutes the phenomenon of the Silicon Valley.

While all this is important, it is underwritten by the function of the San Francisco South Bay, including the Silicon Valley and San Jose, as a switching node in the global network (Saxenian 1994). A switching functionality of a mega node lies in the possibility of creating a common space of places and a common space of flows for a number of multilayering innovation networks.

The common space of places means that high power decision makers of different networks have a possibility allowed by physical space for face-to-face interaction, which results in making investment deals, negotiating mergers and acquisitions, signing commercial agreements, making partnership and strategic alliances, and trading talent across networks. This sort of activity is critical for strategic development of large corporations in diversifying or streamlining their business activities from a global perspective. For the networks of financial investors, the switching function of a mega node provides the opportunity to exit investments, restructure the portfolio of companies, and access global deal logs.

A switching functionality of a mega node in creating a common space of flows for the multilayering networks has two dimensions.

First, virtual interaction within the node allows for more effective execution of global strategies across a network by swapping between the space of flows of these other networks.

Secondly, it involves additionally the possibility of entering into a space of places of other networks and influencing the political decisions originating in other networks, which can have impact on the wealth and power of a particular network. An example of the latter would be a case in which members of an industrial network or research network involved in implementing research and development projects have access to high-level decision makers in political networks responsible for designing assumptions for a new budget perspective, as a result of which research and innovation can obtain resources, tax advantages, and subsidies.

The multilayering of networks in a mega node may lead to breakthrough innovations giving birth to new industries. The history of Genentech, the largest biotech company is a good case to illustrate this process, where a network of cutting-edge researchers in the emerging field of biogenetics and the financial networks of Silicon Valley venture capital multilayered and triggered the emergence of a new industry (Russo 2003).

Genentech was founded in 1976 by Herbert W. Boyer, a biochemist and genetic engineer, and Robert A. Swanson, a venture capitalist. At the time when Genentech was formed, Boyer was a professor of biochemistry and biophysics at the University of California, San Francisco, as well as director of the graduate program in genetics and a faculty member in the microbiology department. Although much of the research work for Genentech was actually conducted at the UCSF in San Francisco,

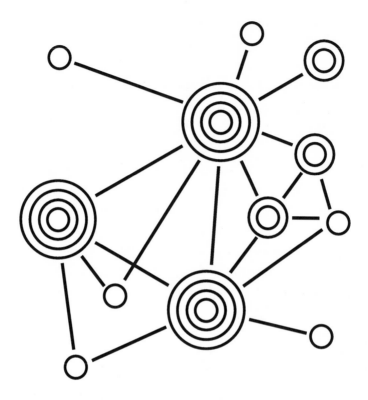

Figure 6. A Global Network of Innovation Networks

where Boyer and geneticist Stanley Cohen pioneered a new scientific field called recombinant DNA, Genentech patented its work as well. Only in 1999 did Genentech and the University of California agree to settle the patent infringement lawsuit brought by UCSF relating to the company's human growth hormone product, Protropin.

There are dozens of technical universities in the world such the University of California, so why is only Stanford renowned for its partnership with the venture capital industry?

The emergent markets, which include markets created by new technologies, are ruled by the strategic advantage of the first mover.

The entrepreneurial team that is able to outrun others in bringing the innovation to the market gets a premium. While UCSF was more important than Stanford in terms of scientific input, its culture as a public research institution prevented it from moving fast enough into partnerships with the venture capitalist industry, to protect their intellectual property and exploit the market opportunity together.

However, the logic of an innovation network allows innovation to start anywhere, both in the space of places and in the space of flows, at a major node as well as at a peripheral one. However, to mature, innovation has to be applied, tested, and reiterated, and there are usually a number of cycles before it can be commercialized and disseminated globally. This creative, value-adding process takes place more in the space of places, in the milieus of innovation.

Indeed, a minor event at the periphery of the innovation network can lead to instantaneous impact and cause major disequilibrium or a radical change. But this turning point takes meaning only if settled and framed in the context of interactions within a space of places. The dynamic social processes taking place in the Silicon Valley since 1950 led to numerous breakthrough innovations—inventions in microelectronics, biotechnology, the Internet, social networking, and green tech, which vindicate the notion of innovation networks.

How does one monitor the peripheries of an innovation network for a "black swan" event, a highly improbable event, which may occur somewhere at the peripheries of networks, yet which can potentially cause a "butterfly effect," that is a failure of a complex system such as networked innovation models (Taleb 2010)?

A "black swan" event can potentially change the business models of whole industries, even in a case when such a black swan appears in a separate network. For example, the model of the telecom industry relied mainly on subscription for services. With increasing competition, the price for telecommunication services drops every quarter to the level where the operating profits do not allow for covering the costs of the existent telecom infrastructure, not to mention investment in a new one. At the same time, the emergence of apps and in particular of social networking sites created a totally new industry with its specific business models taking advantage of the existing telecom infrastructure built before the software boom.

For example, Telefonica, a major telecom operator in Spain and in South America, searches for "black swans" by creating the "space of places" where members of various innovation networks meet, connect, and share their insights into what is happening in nodes and what is marginal to the networks of others. Telefonica Disruptive Innovation Council, which was launched in 2011, is an independent, blue-sky think tank composed of around 20 external experts in various areas. The composition of the Council seems to have a strong technology bias, yet at its core there is user-driven innovation and customer behavior in mature and entrepreneurial markets of transition economies, which are rapidly changing societies entering into mainstream consumption patterns creating, for example, vertical markets. In search of breakthrough ideas, Telefonica also supports a number of other programs, such as Campus Party/Campuseros, a massive start-up camp for thousands of entrepreneurial students developing their business ideas in the creative atmosphere of a tent community in the towns of Telefonica's South American markets. Thus, the Telefonica Disruptive Innovation Council operates to spot early new business models or opportunities and create alternative sources for growth since the existing business models do not provide sufficient returns.

Chapter 5

TOWARD NEW BUSINESS MODELS

Traditional Western business process management approaches tend to rely on highly specialized and tightly integrated activities monitored in detail from a single control point. This approach leads to decreasing returns with the increase of overheads along the complexity of process management.

Thus, the innovative process management approaches opt to rely on process networks, which are more scalable as they are based on a series of activity modules. Literature on business strategy provides a wide range of perspectives and frameworks to analyze innovation and innovating.

There is a body of research focused on structural competitive advantages, core competencies, and open collaboration as a way to build innovation-driven culture (Chesbrough, Vanhaverbeke, and West 2006; Porter 1998; Hamel and Prahalad 1994). Hagel and Brown integrate these diverse strategic perspectives and stress the "need to deploy institutional mechanisms and management practices that are designed to get better faster by working with others" (Hagel and Brown 2008). They stress that this "dynamic perception of strategy puts an emphasis on the need for movement, flow trajectories, and pace of change yet it builds upon the enterprise-centric schools of strategy, yet seeks to expand them beyond the boundaries of an individual firm by emphasizing that some of the most promising capabilities involve management practices that access, mobilize, and build complementary capabilities across firms" (Hagel and Brown 2008).

As these authors point out, such a perspective also underscores the power of participating more effectively in a variety of broader collaborative formations: process and creation networks, economic webs, local business ecosystems, and university and research partnerships. They claim that this "integrated perspective shifts the attention from ownership of stocks of knowledge or resources in favor of privileged positioning in flows of knowledge that can accelerate learning and capability building" (Hagel and Brown 2008).

In general, depending on the business culture, European and American firms remain transaction-focused. This includes practices of building captive facilities, offshoring, or acquiring innovation capabilities through mergers and acquisitions. Establishing captive facilities or offshoring is based on short-term transactions with highly specified contractual agreements. These do not induce trust, loyalty, and open exchange of knowledge.

It appears that long-term trust-based relationships give access to the tacit knowledge that is the key competitive advantage in leading-edge innovative companies and frontier research. Good practice has been used by Japanese companies, which develop partnerships within tightly coupled, trust-based relational networks—keiretsus, which are traditionally cemented through cross-ownership. However, these networks are rather inflexible and do not induce openness in innovation.

The shift from tightly to loosely coupled process management practices creates a new level of strategic advantage, which becomes progressively more valuable with the increase of the number and specialization of global innovation hotspots. Often cutting edge innovation resides in small entrepreneurial firms and the ability to tap the top talent in these remote locations in the new economies or nodes of budding innovation networks.

Hagel and Brown analyzed new management practices emerging in a networked business environment. They found that gaining a strategic advantage requires a different approach to managing processes and innovation. Their theory is depicted below in a three-dimensional figure. Axis X shows two dimensions: transactional and relational. Axis Y denotes again two dimensions: tight coupling and loose coupling. The third axis shows a shift from mobilizing existing resources to building new capacity. These three levels of management practices create a framework for strategic analysis of the emerging trends in how companies innovate.

For example, the framework allows one to trace a shift from tightly coupled, short-term, transaction-based bilateral relationships, through long-term, trust-based loosely-coupled process networks, to global creation networks opening opportunities for enhanced learning and innovating. The figure below shows their model for analyzing the strategic itinerary, in which market players move from the lower to upper quadrants, and from the upper front to the upper back quadrants, in their quest for increased innovativeness as a source of sustainable competitive advantage in an open innovation framework for a networking environment.

The loosely coupled approach to structuring innovation partnership, versus the tightly coupled approach, offers significant freedom for improvisation and experimentation at the level of activities. It shifts the focus from control of activities to assessment of capabilities and performance outputs.

The orchestration of loosely-coupled process management networks moves from "low-tech" (phone and fax) to using information technology service-oriented architectures that can automate more routine coordinating activities (e.g. Microsoft's .Net technology). Loose coupling relies on pre-established long-term and trust-based relationships linked with the capability to reconfigure collaboration partnerships in process or product design networks or supply chains upon customer or market demand. In this sense, loose coupling is by no means a short-term transaction-based relationship but a long-term strategic collaboration. Consequently, as Hagel and Brown claim, in order to exploit the potential of "creation networks" for learning and innovating , a set of new management techniques is needed.

Collaboration among people with diverse skills coming from different backgrounds by definition creates challenging situations, which can lead to creating dysfunctional teams. However, generating productive friction is characteristic of creative environments. Friction has been eliminated in the relentless quest for operational efficiency and seamless operations in multinationals.

When properly managed, friction among members of a creative team can result in unexpected novel solutions and ideas, moving performance targets far beyond the expected outcomes. These management practices involve key abilities: search and selection of network participants with adequate capabilities and skills; organization of network participants around common aggressive performance targets; acceleration of the learning process, development, and testing of prototypes in order to reach decisions over performance milestones; providing data enabling benchmarking of performance and a process for coaching network participants on closing the performance gap.

Network Enterprise: New Paradigm for Value Creation

The networking logic of the network society, and its new technological paradigm, led to the emergence of a new type of business organization—a network enterprise defined as "a specific form of enterprise whose system of means is constituted by the intersection of segments of autonomous systems of goals" (Castells 2010). The components of a network enterprise originate in different parts of large and small enterprises and can be defined using Schumpeterian terms of an enterprise as a project-oriented activity.

The network enterprise is not a firm but a project-based collaborative partnership of different divisions of multinational organizations, as well as micro, small, and medium-sized companies. The firm as a legal entity continues to exist, yet it has lost its dominance as a basic operational unit of a business practice. Unlike a firm in the industrial age, a network enterprise is not a separate, legal entity, although it does enter into business partnerships, strategic alliances, and social contracts for the duration of a specific project.

The emergence of a network enterprise as an actual operational unit in the global economic system has created a new logic organizing resources between and across interlinked networks of clusters (also referred to as innovation pikes, ecosystems, regions, cities). A project, or rather projects as such, have become vehicles driving economic growth, wealth creation, and the redefinition of relationships in the network society both at the level of competition and labor. While a firm continues to exist as a legal entity, it disintegrates into divisions, departments, or other functional units, gaining independence and entering unilaterally into specific contractual agreements and strategic partnerships.

Indeed, in the process of globalization and deployment of digital communication technologies, many MNCs have become decentralized. They moved away from their specific organizational form based on a vertically integrated bureaucracy with institutionalized functions and power relations described as "Taylorism." This organizational design was deployed both in capitalistic enterprises, such as in Henry Ford's automobile plants in Detroit, Michigan, as well as under the communist regime, where work organization and output was planned in a five-year time horizon following scientific methods.

While innovation depends on resources available and multinational corporations dispose of significantly larger assets than small companies, the latter have gained a special status. Smaller companies have become more powerful by operating as subcontractors or collaborators in networks with MNCs and other SMEs. They continue to remain part of their networks despite their much smaller size, limited resources, and power. The reason for this is their value, which resides in the accumulated knowledge, especially in its tacit dimension, which they have acquired in the process of execution. More and more often, a new type of a network enterprise emerges linking the counterintuitive qualities of being at the same time local and global.

The micro-multinational is a particular manifestation of a new emerging genre of a network enterprise. It functions as a one-person operation or as a small, often virtual team, and by orchestrating globally available resources rather than owning or controlling them, accomplishes the goals of a project (Metler and Williams 2011). With the organizational evolution, which followed the diversification of markets, and the increasing unpredictability of demand and consumer "wishes and wants," the mass production model was replaced by flexible models (Cohen and Zysman 1987).

The new flexible model was manifested by different approaches. For example, mass-customization allowed customers to design their products and services by choosing modules or components "a la carte," as they began to be deployed in the automobile, furniture, or housing industries in the 1980s. Flexible specialization followed the traditional craftsmanship model, where local producers possessed particular skills and adequate resources to follow short batch production, thus adapting to volatility and unpredictability of fashion or design industries and applying this model even to financial services such as personal banking and asset management. Finally, dynamic flexibility linked the economies of scale (high-volume production) with economies of scope (customized production systems), enabled by technologies capable of easily reprogramming product design as well as production processes.

Decentralization of large multinationals and the rise of status of small companies as critical agents of innovation led to new practices, such as co-opetition. The process of co-opetition takes place when competitors, or rather particular units of globally competing organizations, become partners in strategic alliances united by the specification and purpose of a project in which they have decided to engage. Small companies continue to remain part of these networks because they not only are subcontractors or service providers but also hold project-specific knowledge. This tangible and tacit knowledge constitutes their value in the business network and protects their interests.

Thus, it is no longer a firm as such but a project that becomes a competitive unit in a project-specific network of divisions, departments, and subsidiaries of multinationals and their local or regional firms linked by a number of multi-party contractual agreements limited to achieving a particular objective over a specified period of time with particular rights and duties of parties involved. For example, in the energy sector, Vattenfall, a Swedish state-owned company, competes in a number of European markets with Electricite de France, the second largest electric utility company headquartered in France. Their different units at the same time collaborate on particular goal-oriented and time-bounded projects such as developing new technology in the process of pre-commercial development. In the ICT sector, chip production often becomes a project in itself, and this project becomes an operational unit in the global economy.

The transition from industrial to informational economy brought a new business landscape marked by the emergence of inter-firm networks of intra-firm networks.

There are different types of these business networks, always based on the networking logic and leading to the development of radically new business models as a source of new sustainable competitive advantage. The Internet and Intranet allow companies to manage their major functions through different types of business networks:

- Suppliers networks: manufacturing is organized around a network or networks of subcontractors, often small and medium-sized companies as in the case of South East China and the Romagna district of Northern Italy. Outsourcing of manufacturing through ODM (original design manufacturing) or OEM (original equipment manufacturing) allows the contractor, usually a large multinational, to minimize in-house production and logistics costs and thus radically increase profitability;

- Producers networks: co-production cooperatives allow the pooling of resources (production capacity, human resources, finances) in order to integrate across value chains and offer solutions rather than products or components, which leads to higher value added as it forms a basis of competitive offering;

- Customers networks: client relationship and management, including marketing and sales, partnerships with distributors and value-added resellers, as well as post-purchase customer service, takes place through combined real or virtual channels where clients' relationship and service costs are lowered, thus increasing profitability;

- Users networks: online social networking sites provide interactive space for community building, user-driven innovation, and learning, thus diminishing the cost of marketing research, offering insights into the upcoming trends, and increasing the speed and quality of innovation, thus providing value added and competitive advantage of a market leader and creator;

- Employees networks: flexible, part-time, labor-sharing management practices are based to a large extent on the Intranet, which provides instant communication, training, and knowledge management of an integrated organization, while at the same time optimizing labor cost;

- Strategic alliances: a network of companies engages in temporary, contractual collaboration agreements in various areas of concrete business projects, which allows them to share informational sources, gain access to privileged information or markets, and develop jointly new knowledge and technologies, especially at the pre-commercial stage. Strategic alliances offer companies optimized value chains and access to market segments;

- Standard coalitions: networks of companies engage in standard-setting for an industry, such as for example telecom, which allows the network to lock in particular technological or design solutions, thus enabling sharing of generic knowledge, research, and development costs.

Until the late 1980s, many multinationals conducted processes, such as pricing, by sending faxes around the globe. To get a pricing approval, a manager from the US had to send a fax, and within five days or so the pricing department would respond with bidding availability. This led to a decentralization of the procurement management process and pricing in the regions was based upon guidelines and procedures. The process would be divided and the company would see fast rather than monolithic action. All business administration that had been provided by people who would complete and process paper documents has now been automated and is done by logarithm software and is handled through a network. Automation of services is designed in multiple dimensions.

For example, companies alienate particular, concrete tasks that are part of a value chain and have them done at cheaper locations in Poland, India, or China. The basic aim of applied research and innovation is to exploit the potential of basic techniques. This happens through integration of existing and new technologies in the final solution. In the ICT sector, this may imply creating new applications, software modules, architectures, protocols, control mechanisms, and service concepts. This concerns all big companies in the service industry, such as telecoms, banks, insurance companies, and new economy firms such as Google, eBay, and Facebook; they all compete in the area of automation of services. Still, for many manufacturing companies originating from the developed markets, innovation is strongly linked with scientific discovery and is technology-driven.

A well-known example of a company completely redesigning its business model and basing all its processes on the logic of networking was Cisco, producer of Internet and networking equipment, based in San Jose, California. In 1999 Cisco acquired Cerent, a start-up, with only USD 10 million in sales for USD 6.9 billion. It caught public attention as the most costly acquisition of a privately held technology company, but was just one milestone in Cisco's growth strategy based on its ability to develop as a network.[11]

The "Cisco Model" became known as the ultimate example of a competitive, network-based type of organizational structure. More recently, a new sort of hybrid organization bringing a network enterprise back into the realm of face-to-face interaction is Apple Inc., based in Cupertino, California. Apple designed its breakthrough product lines—iPod, iPhone, and iPad—with all manufacturing, distribution, and logistics organized around the Web and located outside the company.

In 2010, a new strategy for client sales and service was deployed to compliment the online store and Apple opened 284 brick-and-mortar stores, offering its clients a unique experience of face-to-face interaction with passionate Apple employees, for learning and entertainment encounters with its carefully designed products. The strategy proved to be successful and in 2012 the Apple brand was ranked by Forbes magazine as the most valuable and exceeded Microsoft and Coca-Cola. The same year, Apple Inc.'s market value reached USD 623 billion and exceeded the record set by Microsoft Corp. in 1999 during the Internet bubble.

Power of Social Networks

The analysis of global accumulation of resources shows dynamic flows of people, knowledge, and capital leading to restructuring of the global landscape of innovation. There is a cyclical mode of birth and death of industries. There are success stories of the emergence of global mega nodes beyond Silicon Valley, which remains an ultimate point of reference inspiring efforts to replicate it. Communication is the key underlying process through which an innovation network is held together.

---

(11) The deal was widely discussed in the media, e.g. WSJ, Aug. 26th, 1999; NYT, Aug, 26th, 1991; SFGate, Nov. 1st, 1999.

In activities related to innovation, the Internet, the World Wide Web, and wireless telecommunication have become the dominant modes of communication. They interweave the fabric of the "space of flows." These multimodal forms of communication gradually enter also into the "space of places," in some cases even replacing to a certain degree face-to-face communication. Communicating via e-mail and text messaging has become so ubiquitous that people start to use these person-to-person forms of communication even if they sit at adjacent desks in the same office. There is a new pattern of horizontal communication characteristic of innovation networks. This is a more general pattern specific to the network society. It has been defined as mass self-communication.

Social Networking Sites (SNS) provide users with social networking experience on the Internet. Distinctive features of SNS include making one's personal social networks visible to selected others through technological platforms that users can easily adopt to leverage their social ties, particularly with pre-existing connections (Boyd and Ellison 2007).

SNSs have their own characteristics relating to their digital product and digital process. The digital product is "anything that one can send and receive over the Internet (i.e. paper-based products or multimedia products)" while the digital process refers to any process involving multiple human interactions and communications. The digital product is tangible and includes information and entertainment. The information is not interactive (e.g. books, journals, newspapers, magazines, databases, and software), while entertainment involves interaction with the user or between users (e.g. video and audio signals, multimedia products, such as movies, television programs, and sound recordings).

The digital process is intangible too. It exists as a knowledge base with continual access or real-time coordination with multiple users or processes, including communication (e.g. electronic messaging, video conferencing, access to news clipping services), trading services (e.g. e-commerce, electronic auctions, shares and option trading), and all sorts of support services (e.g. banking, government services, shipping, and flight traction).

The value of social networking sites powered by digital communication infrastructure is captured by Metcalfe's law defining the self-expanding characteristics of telecommunication networks. SNSs grow exponentially with every new member joining the network and tend to expand to infinity. Their expansion fuels the qualitative dimension of the quantitative increase of the value of a network.

The exponential growth and qualitative increase are enabled by mass-self communication, which allows each member of the network to transmit a message to all other network members (Himanen 2001; Castells 2011). It is "mass" since it enables creating and disseminating "many-to-many" messages, and it has a "self" dimension since a person is able to create a message and share it with other members of the network through multimodal channels of communication. This mass-self communication is a key characteristic and the source of power in the global innovation network and in the global network society in general.

Mass-self communication is a game changer of the power paradigm and the new source of power in a network. It scales up and across the globe the ability of an individual actor to inform, influence, negotiate, build relationships, and create networks or interconnect them. Power resulting from the ability to mass self-communicate across an innovation network takes different forms. Castells distinguishes four distinct types of power in a network society, and since an innovation network is a manifestation of a network constituting this kind of social structure, this typology finds application in the analysis of mechanisms driving the diffusion of innovation networks and accumulation of resources in chosen network nodes (Castells 2009).

First, there is Networking Power. It is based on the principle of access to an innovation network, privileging some members and excluding others from the backbone of the global innovation network. Second, there is Network Power. It resides in the ability to control the membership and traffic in a network. For example, a network administrator authorizes entry and exit, defines hierarchies of access, designs protocols, controls intensity of traffic, and monitors social interaction in a network. Third, there is Networked Power. It is related to a specific social status of certain members over others within an innovation network. A brand name of an active blogger, anonymous or not, gathers traffic and this gives her leverage in the process of mass-self communicating. Fourth, a distinct form of power is Network-making Power. This is the power of dominant members to program the content of a network, connect it with other networks, or switch it thanks to their presence in the "space of places."

Designing SNSs involves understanding the features that affect how they can be used. Among various attributes of SNSs, two are considered critical: usability and sociability (Shackel 1991; Preece 2001). Usability refers to the capability of a system to be used easily and effectively, which can be measured in terms of efficiency, effectiveness, and users' satisfaction with the design (Brooke 1996). Sociability online is the quality or state of being sociable— enjoying a high quality of social interaction in a networked environment.

Sociability can be defined in terms of social psychology, as a mix of empathy, trust, identity, and reputation; or in terms of social dynamic, which includes the concepts of networks, reciprocity, and social capital;

or in terms of meeting the objectives of the users' access to information, support, and contacts, contributing to content, and coordinating processes; and finally from the perspective of policies expressed as cultural norms and rules (Preece 2001).

Sociability can also be defined from the perspective of the user's experience as a computer-supported collaborative learning (CSCL) environment (Kreijns et al. 2007). The concept can be extended by linking groupware (task-oriented group applications) with social ware and redefined sociability as the degree to which the communication environment mediated by social software is perceived to facilitate social interaction and to enhance social connectivity.

Innovation in the digital content service can be determined by changes made to platform, product, and process, separately or in conjunction. Dong refers to a typology of innovation relating to these three attributes (Dong 2012). According to this typology, innovation can relate to changes in the system performance by increasing the reliability of the system, including the speed at which information for social activities can be transferred; to decreasing system disturbances in that a user can distinguish between wanted and unwanted content and block the latter; to increasing privacy so that users can control private information in the system; to providing more information bandwidth, the maximum amount of data that can be simultaneously transferred within the system.

A number of innovations can result in altering the social climate of the SNS, which can become more direct, open, respectful, and polite, yet affectionate (Dong 2012). Dong claims that the innovation can also involve benefits by changing the meaning to reality, that is the extent to which social activities in this system contribute to events and people in the real world, and reciprocity, that is the ratio of effort invested in the system and payback. Tangible as well as socio-emotional rewards are real life or virtual life payback—in return for their effort and time invested in the system.

Innovation can also concert the control of content quality by changing the level of censorship of information transferred during social networking. SNS innovation can include changes in the number of contacts in the system, changes of the quality of existing social contacts in the system, and the overall number of system users. Innovation can also relate to the modifications of the richness of interaction, customizability of the content and format of exchanged information, and integrationability, the ability of the system to adapt and integrate content from other systems.

Finally, she concludes in her analysis that the adjustment in SNSs may result in alteration of users' virtual self-image building and increased reputation through support of formal interaction of group activity by increasing the perceived authenticity of content exchanged in the system and proposing a variety of operation modes, such as drag-and-drop, mouse clicks, and shortcuts (Dong 2012).

From the users' perspective, usability and sociability are two salient features applicable to knowledge seeking, sharing, and exchanging, and result in "stickiness" of social networking sites. Depending on the purpose of social networking, different measurements are relevant. When users seek knowledge, ease of use and system reliability are considered important for usability.

On the other hand, it is the perception of the moderator's integrity that is more relevant than sociability, if network participants search for or want to share knowledge. While tracking fulfillment is more important for usability, social interactivity is more valued for sociability. When members look for social entertainment, symbolic physicality, inherent sociability, multi-play asynchronicity, and inter-application interactivity are major measurements (Phang, Kankanhalli, and Sabherwal 2009; Wu et al. 2010). There is no instant process to make a member of an innovation network a prominent agent.

The innovation networks are held together by communication processes that result in developing, strengthening, or loosening relations between network members. The only way to get into the global innovation network is to associate with its participants, for example with Stanford or MIT. There is no instant success when entering the network. Reaching certain power and influence is related to a brand as perceived by other network members, and building trust takes time. A brand that gives Networked Power and Network-making Power means in practice a history of interaction in the space of places and the space of flows. For example, Apple, which became the most valued brand in 2011, was launched in 1978. It took time to take off. The critical turning points in the history of Apple were not only the availability of technology and products but also the recognition by other members of its innovation network. The market success followed the recognition of industry mavens paid to the key people at Apple, its technology, and its products.

Openness of Innovation

Global competition is a major driving force for increased openness in innovation, although the operating model of leading research centers is still based on IP protection. Open innovation is seen as a way to speed up the innovation process when product life cycles become ever shorter and mass-customization or batch production becomes more widely spread. The discussion of openness in innovation concerns primarily the free flow of information within and between participants of the process of production and consumption. The term "open innovation" describes the process of collaboration where information and knowledge are shared without limitations of proprietary rights as they relate to the content of the collaboration among service providers, users, and customers (Chesbrough 2003). Chesbrough views a firm as a nexus of transactions.

With the underlying assumption that most knowledge and capabilities are available in the market, he sees the function of the firm in minimizing transaction costs and coordinating transaction flow (Chesbrough 2003, 2005). Open innovation refers to the acquisition of knowledge or solutions on the market and extends beyond contract-based R&D (Granstrand et al. 1992; Fey and Birkinshaw 2005). Innovation sourcing includes acquisition of technology firms for the purpose of its own technological renewal, licensing technology, purchases of patents, machinery, and components (Herstad, Bloch, Ebersberger, and van de Velde 2008; Lazonick 2007; Chesbrough 2003).

Open innovation does not mean free innovation. Openness may concern the process or the product, or both. Collaboration established with external partners, i.e. customers, consumers, universities, researchers, students, open source software (OSS) projects and other creative communities implies direct and indirect costs in terms of license fees or some other financial arrangements, like sponsoring or in-kind investments in time or attention of employees, or other resources to external public or private projects.

Open source software projects such as the Linux operating system are public and share development costs among a globally distributed community of developers, who consider themselves "hackers." In certain cases, it is the product that is free as well as the process. Open content allows the whole global society to benefit from a project such as Wikipedia, or open courseware at MIT and Harvard. Creative Commons is a product-related model of openness. It enables content sharing on the web, for free, yet with a requirement for users to inform others about the authorship. Through promoting attribution, Creative

Commons builds the reputation of authors and also a shared identity of users—a common culture of open innovation.

Open innovation forces and at the same time enables companies to renew their business model (EIT 2009).[12] The unconstrained exchange of information and/or open solution challenges the existing world's biggest companies in the ICT sector. Good examples include the Linux operating system, Firefox browser, Skype, MySQL, Google Mail and Maps, and Wikipedia. The term "open" signals a fundamental shift in business thinking. A company may decide to leave a specific market and open its patents as OSS for the commons. It must involve a business model innovation since the profits do not come from exploiting the intellectual property in the software or solution itself, as users are often different from paying customers. For instance, Google, a web-based browser and search engine, is free for users and makes its profits from advertising income. During the "First Browser War," Netscape decided to open up its Navigator, which led to the formation of the Mozilla Foundation and the successful OSS browser Firefox, diluting the market (Berghel 1998).

Open innovation may allow the deployment of lower margin business models by using OSS components, rapidly developing new value proposition and thus shortening product life cycles, or serving lower market segments. Examples of these are cases like MySQL vs. Oracle and ventures localizing OpenOffice vs. Microsoft Office; companies that interact with OSS projects by investing in participation, sponsoring, hiring, and access to the most recent trends in market evolution. Companies may search for new technologies and set up partnerships in order to reach new niches or adjacent markets. While pursuing new territories, not all of the required knowledge is available in-house,

---

(12) The discussion on openness of innovation and the examples below are based on insights the author of this book gained from the working group on Research and Innovation led by Prof. Yrjö Neuvo at the Governing Board of the European Institute of Innovation and Technology and its *Report of Governing Board Working Group on Research* (2009).

forcing them to gather external expertise necessary to create value and to achieve a competitive advantage.

Some large multinationals rely on open innovation and have included it in their core business models. IBM contributes to its development by respecting the rules of openness as non-proprietary contribution to the source code, reserving patents only for applications. Nokia and Apple source application development through open online communities, producing innovation along with or in substitute for the in-house R&D. The sourcing firm is concerned with the output of the contract, and not with the learning, which happens during the development process. Open sourcing offers companies greater flexibility and responsiveness, without necessarily incurring huge costs of innovating. It enables new start-ups to explore technologies and possible markets with low cost, and more swiftly than before.

Open innovation is the opposite of closed innovation models designed to minimize "false positive errors" (Chesbrough 2003). Ignoring the right to make "false negative errors" is well documented in the cases of Xerox Corporation and PARC, who are known for losing technology to others. Chesbrough tracked thirty-five projects initiated at PARC, when the internal funding of the lab stopped. The collective market value of ten of these projects exceeds the value of Xerox.

PARC (Palo Alto Research Center Incorporated), formerly Xerox PARC, is a research and development center that was established by Xerox Corporation in 1970 as its West Coast facility.[13] It is renowned for its blue-sky inventions and innovations such as laser printing, Ethernet (a local-area computer network increasing its computational power and secure communication), the personal computer, graphical user interface featuring windows and icons operated with a mouse,

---

(13) The author's interview with John Seely Brown, former Chief Scientist of Xerox Corporation and the director of its Palo Alto Research Center, gave direction and insight for this section of the book, Palo Alto, 2010.

and ubiquitous computing. Xerox PARC is often cited as an example of a business's failure to commercialize and exploit inventions by the commercial arm of a corporation. Its innovation unit (PARC) was not able to properly convince the East Coast engineers to deploy a number of breakthrough inventions. GUI, graphical user interface, is quoted as one of the examples.. A group of researchers from PARC led by Charles Irby and David Liddle, a Stanford professor of computer science, founded Metaphor Computer Systems, further developed the concept of GUI, and later sold it to IBM. The first wide-scale application and commercial success of deploying GUI was Apple Macintosh. Xerox allowed Apple engineers to use GUI in exchange for pre-IPO Apple shares.

The first desktop Apple computer deployed a user-friendly interface by enhancing the Xerox prototype using menu bars, pull-down menus, overlapping windows, the trash icon, and the mouse (invented originally by Douglas Engelbart in 1963), which allowed for direct operation of widgets by a few functions such as drag-and-drop or scrolling.

Fostering open innovation models is being accepted with varying degrees in different industry sectors since open innovation models are to a large extent sector-specific. It is widely spread in the ICT sector where product lifecycles are too short and success is dependent on speed-to-market rather than IP protection. Many companies from non-ICT areas do not appreciate the benefits of innovating in an open environment. More importantly, they do not know how to effectively participate in this exchange without risking the confidentiality of proprietary information. Yet more and more firms in retail, climate, or energy search for ways to experiment with different ways of opening their innovation models to formal or informal external networks. Some use joint ventures, corporate venturing programs, corporate venture capital funds, and other softer forms of collaboration agreements, like joining or sponsoring OSS projects.

Opening to external networks creates an open culture and at the same time a sense of urgency since internal groups are in a way competing with external groups. The openness of open innovation resides in the ability to mobilize resources not directly under control but as a benefit of being part of a network. The network members are rewarded for the openness since the more they share the more they receive access to. The strategic choice between "use it or lose it" in relation to internally available technologies makes strategy more focused and clear.

Creating open innovative corporate culture requires proper human resource management practices and incentive structures recognizing and even rewarding failure and learning as part of the innovation process. Promoting innovative business leaders as role models, public recognition for scientific achievements or contributions to OSS, and mentoring schemes may be as important as monetary rewards. These talent management practices enable and encourage creative individuals to dare to think beyond existing technology frameworks and current markets.

Process Networks and Creation Networks

The model of the economy has significantly changed since the early 1980s from a model of vertically integrated, co-located industries, with a stable product cycle and a mastering of novel products (Akamatsu 1962; Krugman 1979; Vernon 1966), into a world of fragmented production; specialization not only in specific industries but also in specific stages of production. Truly novel products are produced or sourced globally without being produced in the countries where they were designed and developed.

There are multiple strategic perspectives and modes, which confer competitive advantages relating to some stages of production but not others. Former Asian NIEs adopted a model of the "follower" countries based on the assumption that they first should imitate others by utilizing economies of scale and scope, and using the latest technologies developed elsewhere (Gerschenkron 1962).

The "run of the Red Queen" model differentiates China in that it has chosen the "fast-follower" model, which differs from the one declared by the communist government (Breznitz and Murphree 2011). It happened as a bottom-up development of an entrepreneurial economy, partly as a result of local experimentation and partly as a result of the specificity of the network society. China has surpassed its initial stigma of low-cost production grounded with a number of original and unexpected networked innovation models.

Process networks coming from China are new and competitive business practices for the global value chain management paradigms. The model of the process network is based on managing a network of suppliers rather than a chain of subcontractors or in-house units. Computational microelectronic networks allow real-time feedback loops in what is usually a network of small entrepreneurial ventures, specialized in a particular production or service. Companies operating in a given area, such as Chongquing city in central China, compete among one another to enter into and remain a valuable link in the network. The competition drives them to innovate in order to enhance their own capabilities. Being part of the process network, they at the same time collaborate with each other directly to satisfy given specifications of a product design or rough design blueprints for a client (e.g. a Western multinational).

Such a network is self-navigating, self-controlling, organized along a common goal, and working along a predefined time schedule and deadlines. One company, a network orchestrator, has direct access to the customer and loosely controls the flows in the network to ensure timely delivery. This master of networking makes sure that, for example, a network does not depend on one supplier, since losing it and its specialist knowledge could hurt network members. It also maintains the compatibility of a network, for example by aligning short-term and long-term goals of its members in terms of profit maximization.

The key success factors for network orchestrators include a combination of management practices. They manage by setting clear performance targets openly articulated and disseminated in the process or creation networks. They foster an unconstrained environment for finding creative solutions, sharing prototypes across organizational boundaries using co-opetition and thus changing from collaborators to competitors and vice versa depending on a particular module of a product or service. They develop processes with the new generations of information technology to ensure dissemination and synchronization of information across the network.

A learning opportunity in a network is also provided by "dynamic specialization." The scalability of networks allows and rewards specialization, which rapidly evolves. The dynamic of collaboration of loosely coupled networks shifts the incentive from short-term cost advantage to long-term opportunity for learning and innovating. Since innovating increases the resource base and opportunities for all network participants, it fosters more collaborative behavior and limits destructive zero-sum behaviors such as cheating, moral hazard, and withholding information. The process networks become creation networks since they mobilize, organize, and monitor existing resources, but also encourage the creation of new capabilities, thus creating value for all network participants.

Process networks develop new products through a new architecture based on modularization of assembly parts (components and subsystems). As a result of dynamic collaboration and negotiations at the level of suppliers—often competing and at the same time collaborating with each other—the process of production is optimized through a bottom-up approach rather than as a result of value chain optimization based on large data processing.

Hagel and Brown describe a number of practices emerging in Asian entrepreneurial economies (Hagel and Brown 2008). The combination of product innovation (modularized production) and process innovation driven by collective responsibility in a loosely-coupled network of assemblers competing and collaborating in local business ecosystems challenged established Japanese producers such as Honda Motor, Suzuki Motor, and Yamaha. Innovation in China went beyond simple imitation. It redefined product architecture and business processes by allowing local suppliers to find creative solutions at the component and subsystem level.

As Hagel and Brown demonstrate through numerous examples, modularity enables innovation in the process networks (Hagel and Brown 2008). It can be driven by suppliers as in the case of Chinese motorcycle manufacturers. It can also be driven by customers as in the case of fast moving consumer goods, which are packaged into small units and thus become affordable for low-income customers, e.g. Coca–Cola introducing 200-mililiter bottles in India in 2003, and Cummins offering low-horsepower engines (under 100-kilowatt) to Indian retailers, farmers, and hospitals who were not able to afford high-horse power sources. Cummins redesigned its distribution channels from direct distribution to the use of third-party distributors able to provide the minimal technical support to simplified, modularized power engines called generator sets ("gen sets"). Modularizing the engines meant smaller manufacturing runs, which by definition increase price per unit. The company had to look for extra cost savings in other parts (even peripherals) of its products and encouraged standardization of design, e.g. of noise-abatement hoods. The accumulation of these minor innovations led to batch production at an affordable price, another possible solution to those already developed by Western companies for their short-run or mass-customization production.

They continue the analysis, pointing at western companies that also deploy network-based processes of production such as Cisco Systems, PortalPlayer, Apple, and Nike, and showcase yet another model of networks developed by innovative Chinese firms (Hagel and Brown 2008).

Hagel and Brown give concrete examples of novel network-based processes. For instance, Cisco Systems is a successful network orchestrator. The company invested in distributed learning platforms building to share learning, culture (meaning), and trust. The competitive advantage of network orchestrators is the result of their ability to learn how to navigate more quickly in the network in order to gain access to specialized resources. PortalPlayer, a micromultinational from California, which played a key role in the introduction of Apple's iPod product line, provides a useful example of leveraging its global "creation network." iPod was a new breakthrough product and a business concept linking a new MP3 product with an online music store product. Apple focused on external design and user interface design. PortalPlayer used its ability to design and manage networks across multiple geographic innovation hotspots in the US, the UK, Japan, and China to coordinate design and deliver prototypes of the final product. The innovation process took only nine months from approving the initial business concept to delivering the product to the customer. Nike, a sport fashion company, is another example. The company constantly searches for new designers, suppliers, and manufacturers. It encourages its partners to integrate others into the existing networks. This diverse, dynamic collaboration enables the enhancement of its athletic high-tech shoes through a sophisticated tutelage system of learning.

Entrepreneurial Chinese companies developed a unique model, taking process networks one step further into "creation networks"— distributed, loosely coupled, long-term collaborative partnerships. Hagel and Brown describe this phenomenon and claim that thanks to these "creation networks, entrepreneurial Chinese companies appear to be especially well-positioned to succeed in the most competitive global markets" thanks to the strategic choice of how they structure interactions with other companies. Such a model of process network works for motorcycle assemblers near Chongquing, for example Dachangijiang, Longxin, and Cixi Zongshen Motorcycle.

Another example is LiFung, a Hong-Kong based apparel business, which deploys a network of 7,500 specialized business partners. The company structures the relationship with its suppliers using a "30/30 rule." The rule commits the company to subcontract a minimum of 30% of the production capacity of its new business partner, and at the same time specifies that it will never exceed 70%.

Tracing how networking logic is deployed in networks leads Hagel and Brown to interesting conclusions (Hagel and Brown 2008). As a consequence, they claim, the customer base of a supplier remains always diversified. This leads to more trust, resulting from less dependence and exposure to competitors, which allows the company to stay close to the most recent market novelties. This management practice helps find appropriate partners, helps them stay competitive, and increases the effectiveness of participation in relevant innovation networks. LiFung, as the network organizer, created a platform for developing networks of long-term, trust-based relationships via a number of initiatives organized by deploying "institutional mechanisms and governance processes to ensure effective collaboration". It is an orchestrator and a gatekeeper. It defines protocols for participation and in this way coordinates over ten thousand business partners in its apparel business. This network enables them to customize a supply chain for each apparel line. The same model of "creation network" is used in other industry sectors, for example consumer electronics and other high-tech products by original design manufacturers (ODMs) in Taipei.

Moreover, creation networks intervene in the inertia of organizational practices, generating friction and acting as a catalyst for driving change in the systems of innovation of an individual enterprise as well as entire industries. They incite systemic innovation by allowing the compounding of a number of incremental innovations through rapid prototyping and iterations of small enhancements at the level of products and processes. This accelerated process of experimentation creates tacit knowledge. Enhanced access to the tacit knowledge as a source of competitive advantage becomes a strategic priority for innovators, who in a systematic way increase their participation in the creation networks, making them more long-term oriented and sustainable as open learning labs.

Summarizing, what counts in the process networks and in creation networks is the speed and quality of the innovation capabilities of network participants. The multiple learning loops enabled by process networks provide feedback that reinforces learning-by-doing, dynamic specialization, and supplier driven innovation. Small changes at the periphery of the process networks can result in unexpected consequences and disrupt established processes in distant parts of the network. Once the network coordinator masters orchestration across participants from various geographic locations, the ultimate challenge is to amplify innovation and learning opportunities to enhance capabilities of network participants.

Chapter 6

MEANING AND POWER IN THE GLOBAL INNOVATION NETWORK

The emergence of the global knowledge economy under new technological advances enabled by advanced computing in the financial markets and real-time management of global enterprises questioned both established business models as well as conventional economic models. The radical shifts in power, wealth, and knowledge at the micro and macro levels on the local and global scale calls urgently for a deeper understanding of drivers, mechanisms, and impact of new networked structures stimulating accumulation of assets and talent. Under new technological conditions, traditional innovation policies display low effectiveness in adjusting national innovation systems in a timely manner to operate effectively under changed mechanisms of wealth creation and accumulation in the networked structure of the global network economy. This fiasco opens opportunities to redesign these policies, experiment with radically new, networked innovation models, and redesign strategy to compete at the level of a firm, as well as the level of whole economies.

The most fundamental contradiction emerging in the network society is dissociation between meaning and power. In the globalized, urbanized, networked world, nodes are populated to a large degree by migrant professionals and by immigrants. These individuals carry certain, more or less common characteristics, such as for example propensity for risk-taking. However, they feel stronger links to their culture of origin, ethnicity, or nationality than to the culture of the place in which they temporarily live and work. This dissociation between their identity and the transient place of their living creates a gap between the space of flows and the space of places. The value of the space of flows resides in its functional dimension. The value of the space of places comes from the locality of a personal network. The former gives the power of execution. The latter gives meaning, bonding, and social status.

The decision to locate resources in a certain physical space is based on the existence of micro networks of high-level decision-making, linked to macro networks of decision implementation. Direct, face-to-face interaction is particularly important for innovation based on collective creative processes rather than individual processes, or those specific to the IT sector, which are by nature abstract and virtual. Face-to-face interaction cannot be replaced by virtual communication in cases when confidentiality of information is an issue, access to information gives a competitive advantage, and strategic choices require collective brainstorming. This is why decisions of where to place R&D facilities of business organizations are based also on intangible factors such as access to micro networks of partners, collaborators, and competitors converging in certain selective physical innovation "milieus" (Castells 1989). They can be technological, like in Silicon Valley (Saxenian 1994) or other centers of technological innovation (Castells and Hall 1994). They can be related to media like in Los Angeles and New York (Abrahamson 2004). Since key innovation processes occur during face-to-face contact, they still require a shared physical space. This also explains the process of metropolitanization by concentrating the production of services, finance, technology, markets, and people in innovation regions. The clustering creates economies of scale but also, what are more relevant, economies of synergy.

The interaction between multilayering networks is facilitated by their spatial convergence at a mega node (Castells 2009). In other words, continues Castells, they are co-located in what evolves as a global innovation region. Each mega node attracts resources such as capital, labor, and innovation and accumulates opportunities to increase wealth and power. At the same time, because it rarely has institutional capacity or political capacity to design and execute plans in order to meet the needs of the locals, notes Castells, it can hardly implement "redistributive policies," that is, allocate income from taxes, and thus a mega node imposes the logic of the global over the local. As a result, the dissociation between meaning and power takes the form of dramatic growth of breach between investment in innovation and social returns from this investment. In other words, mega nodes become an expression of extreme wealth and extreme misery. This is troubling in itself, and leads to questioning the sense of continuous push for more consumption, more innovation, and more wealth accumulation.

This poses a serious challenge for policy makers responsible for public investment in innovation. Rarely having political power over mega nodes, people, knowledge, and funding flow freely across the innovation networks attracted to the new emerging opportunities in the ever-changing global innovation landscape. What are the most effective policies and policy instruments to prevent the dissociation between investment in innovation and reaping returns from this investment elsewhere?

These mega nodes are not global cities but they are global innovation hotspots. They are spatial urban areas composed of multilayered global networks residing in interconnected neighborhoods, which hardly ever have common municipal or regional institutions or local governments able to make autonomous decisions and manage them as an integrated metropolitan region. This kind of power could stimulate the development of inclusive and meaningful urban planning. The consistent regional investment policy in innovation could then energize the node by building infrastructure connectivity for innovation. Such an arrangement would have pragmatic implications for alleviating daily commuting routines of knowledge workers. At the level of the local community it would also erase the punchy contradiction of metropolitan regions where areas of wealth and power are located side by side with zones of poverty and social exclusion, putting in question the very sense of innovating. What is the meaning of investment in innovation, accumulation of wealth, and power in mega nodes if it brings benefits and profits to a few global elites cruising across the global network rather than a better future for many locals, permanent residents, and less privileged migrants of these mega nodes?

The mechanisms for knowledge and wealth accumulation dominant in the network society induced a new geography of social, economic, and technological inequality and exclusion. The dissociation between the structure of the network society and geopolitical barriers has created a challenge for traditional municipal, regional, and nation-state institutions, which were tailored to the contours of an industrial society. While they kept their institutional authority, they lost the executive power to monitor, control, and regulate the flow of information, knowledge, talent, and capital.

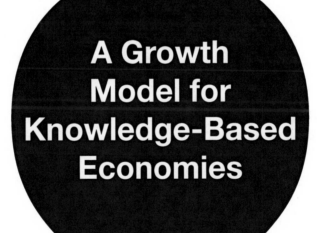

A Growth
Model for
Knowledge-Based
Economies

Research evidence points to a set of typical success factors for an innovation cluster to succeed (OECD 2011; WEF 2011; EC 2010). These factors include: intensive co-creation along the entire innovation chain; a critical mass of activity concentrated and focused over extended periods of time; entrepreneurial culture of risk-taking and venture capital funding; and an attractive environment for top talent with a high rate of exchange between different sectors. However, when observing how innovation processes take place in the networked knowledge-driven economy, it becomes more and more clear that it is the access to the global innovation network, rather than being part of a cluster, that is critical. Interconnections with diverse networks are as important as exposure to opportunities offered by socializing in an innovation hub.

The structure of this open innovation system consists of nodes, or spikes, which cumulate talent, knowledge, and capital, as well as connections between spikes in different geographical locations. Members of the innovation networks maintain tightly coupled local connections and are at the same time loosely coupled with other members of their own and different innovation networks. A local innovation ecosystem of different networks can be looked upon as a network of multiple stakeholders ranging from businesses to universities and research organizations, government agencies, and not-for-profits. Innovation can start anywhere in this innovation networked space in any of the organizational settings. The multilayering of local innovation networks with other networks is a new aspect that corporate and public innovation policy makers have to focus on when creating framework conditions to stimulate innovation.

The idea of an innovation network was conceptualized in the context of national innovation systems by Freeman and Lundvall, and later developed by Soete and others (Lundvall 1985; Freeman 1988). Freeman defined a national innovation system as "the network of institutions in the public and private sectors whose activities and interactions initiate, import, modify and diffuse new technologies" (Freeman 1987). Lundvall put emphasis on "the elements and relationships which interact in the production, diffusion and use of new, and economically useful, knowledge ... and are either located within or rooted inside the borders of a nation state" (Lundvall 1992). The concept was further developed into the direction of regional studies and policy making as the top-down approach to stimulate local or regional innovation of enterprises through applied new technologies as the core element of competitiveness.

In this context, Metcalfe specified that the national innovation system is "a set of distinct institutions, which jointly and individually contribute to the development and diffusion of new technologies, and which provides the framework within which governments form and implement policies to influence the innovation process. As such it is a system of interconnected institutions to create, store and transfer the knowledge, skills and artefacts, which define new technologies" (Metcalfe 1995). Patel and Pavitt further elaborated the definition as "national institutions, their incentive structures and their competencies, that determine the rate and direction of technological learning (or the volume and composition of change generating activities) in a country" (Patel and Pavitt 1994). Every country has its own networked structure of innovation nodes connected internally and also externally to the strategic global innovation networks. Within the geography of a nation-state, the nodes, because of their connectivity outside the national dimension, trigger the expansion of urban areas into metropolitan regions. These regions determine the level and dynamics of connectivity between the local and the global and thus design a spatial structure of each country. The areas left outside the metropolitan regions are deprived of this multilayered local/global connectivity. As a consequence, they become excluded from value creation mechanisms and deprived of access to talent and capital, and deteriorate into areas of structural poverty.

The spatial articulation of innovation networks has implications for national innovation systems. With the growth of the networked model, the entities in the national innovation system become increasingly interconnected with other local, regional, and global innovation networks. The multilayering of networks over time attracts more quality resources, and by accumulating them, changes the status of a node, which may develop a switching capacity. This means that people in networks relevant for innovation, such as venture capital industry networks, SME networks, science parks, and university networks, will build relations and develop a capacity to interconnect them.

This capability to interlink various networks will enable or accelerate processes transforming the node. During these evolutionary processes, a peripheral node—if characterized from the perspective of a global innovation network—can gain importance and become a significant node and maybe even a mega node. A different scenario is also possible. A relevant node in Europe will slowly lose its status because it will not build this "switching capacity." Whatever the dynamics of network dissemination, connecting ecosystems matters. Placing a node of a pan-European innovation network in a particular geographical location generates in itself an opportunity for growth at the local, regional, and national scale.

Global networked innovation models introduce indeterminacy into the national and global innovation systems. They blur the borders between different kinds of networks, as well as systems. However, it is by no means chaos. Just the opposite, there is a structured order with specific mechanisms fueling the dynamics of interaction and apparatus for power and wealth accumulation. This order is not stable though, since volatility and failure are embedded in the system. The Babel tower of the space of places and the space of flows creates a communication error, a misunderstanding or a slip of the tongue that can trigger an idea, potentially turning into a "black swan."

What kind of innovation network or networks should policy makers sponsor and stimulate in order to increase the competitiveness of an innovation system? What policy tools should be used? Is it at all possible to influence the global innovation system and, if so, what policy brings the emergence of mega nodes into the origin of the investment of public funding and not elsewhere?

The answers to these questions are anchored in the understanding of new emerging business models—how value is created in the global networked environment.

Chapter 7

KNOWLEDGE TRIANGLE: A NEW CONCEPT OF INNOVATION NETWORKS

A lot of ideas and a lot of initial impetus to innovate came and still comes from global mega clusters such as Silicon Valley (Saxenian 1990, 1994; Brown and Duguid 2000; Zhang 2005). Technical universities in the Valley provide a lot of forward thinking that is mitigated through the marketplace and taken up by entrepreneurial companies. Firms with the highest growth potential attract venture capital investors, who have the competence to either grow them fast or fail fast. If successful, these companies become vital for creating new industries or they revitalize bigger companies and ultimately reinvent them. There are examples of ongoing attempts to replicate Silicon Valley elsewhere, such as the Skolkovo Institute in Russia (Liuhto 2010). There are also numerous cases of failures to copycat the Valley (Castells and Hall 1994; Saxenian and Hsu 2001). It is a long-term process during which a complex innovation ecosystem is created and emerges as an industrial cluster (Porter 1998).

These failures originate in a misunderstanding of the nature of innovation mega nodes such as Silicon Valley. Indeed, it is a dense innovation milieu constructed in widely spread metropolitan areas and marked by a myriad of overlapping innovation networks. However, the Valley gains its meaning and status only as part of a global innovation network, not as a stand-alone innovation ecosystem. It is this simultaneous global and local networking aspect from which mega nodes derive their relative value in the age of ubiquitous digital communication and physical and virtual mobility of talent and capital.

The question then arises—if Silicon Valley, as the ultimate symbol of a successful innovation ecosystem, cannot be simply imitated elsewhere, what would be an alternative approach to stimulate innovation at the peripheries of innovation networks? How can one conceptualize and ultimately redesign on a systemic level a model for innovation processes so that it could be applied as a growth model beyond existing mega nodes in other metropolitan areas, regions, countries, or free trade zones?

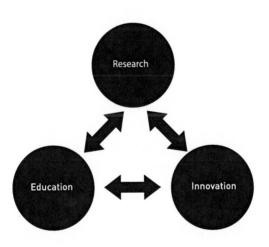

Figure 7. Knowledge Triangle Model

The Knowledge Triangle is a new approach to designing a growth model based on a specific type of an innovation network. The term appeared in the context of the mid-term review of the Lisbon Strategy (EC, 2005; Potocnik, 2006). Innovation is an engine of economic growth and job creation, an enabler helping to solve societal challenges, a critical learning process, and a driver of cultural transformation. Therefore, understanding, designing, and calibrating a new, networked paradigm of innovation is essential for the society-at-large as well as for individual firms.

The Knowledge Triangle is proposed as a concept where three sides of the triangle are referred to as research, education, and innovation. It is manifested through a set of innovation-related activities taking place during a process of interaction between organizations representing these three areas: universities, research labs, and industry.

The Knowledge Triangle as an innovation network is discussed as formalized collaboration of research institutions, universities, and industry partners located in geographical proximity of an existing innovation ecosystem and linked to similar networks operating in comparable environments, in which the majority of innovation value chains or value webs already exist. Therefore, the understanding of the model is based on the important inter-institutional aspect of innovation. It represents a perspective relevant for policy makers but also for leaders coming from each of the "sides," who are responsible for setting out and implementing a long-term innovation strategy for an individual academic or business organization.

The Knowledge Triangle gives a lean descriptive image, a handy model that can be easily used when designing or explaining an innovation strategy or policy. However, it is too simplistic to capture the complexity of what is innovation; how innovation processes actually have been redesigned in the networks of innovation; how innovation networks interlink, collaborate, and compete; and how these dynamics and mechanisms impact the globalized context of knowledge flows, talent mobility, and capital accumulation. The notion of each "side" of the Knowledge Triangle has become quite complicated and often blurred. At first glance, the Knowledge Triangle may indeed seem to be an inter-institutional network of academic and business organizations involved in research, education, and innovation.

However, in a networked world in constant flux with ever changing rules of the game, the self-interested rational choices of an organization or an institution, understood as an agent, may collide and at the same time coincide with what the principal—an institution in this case—desires. The formal aspect of bilateral or multilateral relationships and the asymmetry of information resulting from legally binding contracts is no longer such a discriminating factor.

Creativity and innovation appear to have no boundaries. The tacit knowledge, which cannot be cast in protocols and procedures, turns the cultural aspect of innovation into a tool to handle the abundance of information, share, or give open access to information and the freedom to use or misuse it. Freelancers, self-employed professionals, and micro-multinationals have gained the ability to turn their creativity into projects, earlier reserved for large organizations owning or controlling assets and resources. They independently search, select, and frame pieces of information flowing through networks, turn them into knowledge generating value, and ultimately—in some cases— also equity exceeding market capitalizations of old, reputable, large companies.

This is the case, for example, of Facebook, Skype, and Instagram, all of which come from the ICT industry, though this phenomenon is also true in manufacturing, logistics, and financial services. Entrepreneurial teams and individuals organized around a project with or without formal contractual agreements with large institutions or organizations, which structure and thus limit institutional relations, undermining the seemingly "cast in stone" image of the Knowledge Triangle. Innovation is a mosaic of diverse activities performed in a wide range of innovation settings by agents and principals with stable but also often transient properties and identities changing their roles, displaying different interests, and changing the rules of the game. This is the world in constant flux.

Activities related to science, technology, and innovation are carried out in a number of diverse settings. In some settings, fundamental or deep technological research is protected by tight intellectual property rights (IPRs) policies and procedures. In other environments, protection of intellectual property rights is not that important or neglected in principle, as success depends on the speed of business or industrial application of an idea, often using a wide range of users who copy, exploit, and improve the initial product.

For certain market segments, such as those at the "bottom-of-the-pyramid," or for the societies in the emerging economies, non-technological innovation often delivers significant impact with little, if any, technological input. Even in the most advanced industry sectors, the competitive advantage comes more from the competence of leveraging technological and non-technological innovation rather than from scientific or technological excellence in itself. For example, the inability of major European firms to combine the two elements is considered as one of the reasons for the competitiveness gap between the European Union and the US, especially in the service sector, where it is both much more R&D intensive and client or user interface focused (Uppenberg 2009).

In the context of the Knowledge Triangle, parties enter into dynamic, reciprocal relationships and depend on each other. Their relationships are underlined by a series of discontinuous flows that include core drivers of innovation: knowledge, talent, and capital. Research and technology activities in interrelation with business activities generate new knowledge, which is the source of innovation, and business activities interplaying with knowledge production are a source of new pathways for research and technology development. Higher education institutions along with peer-to-peer learning, and individual contextual learning journeys through life and WWW, add value by producing new research and enhanced or novel technology and thus develop more relevant skills for conducting research, which improves the quality of education.

Through the knowledge of new markets, customers, and business world practices, understanding the translation process of knowledge into products and processes makes education especially relevant to the labor market if education provides people with a relevant set of skills for innovation in business. How is value created within and between them? What kinds of flows take place in the value creation process manifested by integration of cutting edge innovation, entrepreneurial talent, and risk capital? What accelerates knowledge, talent, and capital flow; what slows down the velocity; what brings qualitative change?

To shed some light on these questions, it is necessary to understand in more depth the processes of knowledge production, dissemination, and commercialization in the context of interlined, distributed learning environments.

The analysis of innovation in the Knowledge Triangle goes against an underlying assumption that knowledge is generated in research labs, disseminated by universities, and turned into innovation, implemented and commercialized by industry. The innovation processes can originate in any of the settings, distributed in real and virtual space around innovation projects, which may involve parties temporarily anchored in a geographic location or a few locations, as well as detached from any by virtue of constant commuting.

The apparent interpretation of the Knowledge Triangle implies that there are three core settings where knowledge is produced, knowledge is disseminated, and innovation takes place. However, knowledge is produced in a number of diverse settings beyond academia and business. Business helps develop new knowledge also in terms of financing the development of the society. Research and universities expect to receive funding from business, e.g. via taxation of profits, research grants, sponsoring, internships, scholarships, and professorships. Business expects to have access to research that is relevant for commercial aims, and to skillful graduates apt to tackle challenges posed by the global competitive business environment. The exchange is based on different types of flows and involves different mechanisms, dynamics, and reasons for discontinuities.

New knowledge is often developed in the grey space between domains rather than strictly within them. Connection between innovation and the private and public sectors is fundamental in health, public security, climate change, and other sectors. The government itself is an innovation setting where a number of innovation activities are applied, for instance, in order to improve government efficiency, as was the case with the e-government in Estonia. The government is yet another element of the model. If so, it transforms the Triangle into a quadrilateral. Including the non-profit sector, yet another important innovation setting, creates a pentagon.

Since more and more innovation happens also at the end of the value chain and is also driven by individual or collective users, the Triangle becomes a complex, multidimensional network of multiple innovation settings integrated into a network by common goals, yet driven by different and sometimes divergent interests.

For example, climate innovation requires collaboration and private-public partnerships at the municipal, regional, or national levels, since solutions include large infrastructures and capital-intensive, long-term projects with political implications. For example, more and more regions highlight local needs and want to become test beds for pilot implementation of climate-related projects stimulating innovation by creating user-driven demand especially by pre-commercial procurement.

Conceptualizing the Knowledge Triangle is an ambitious attempt to develop a new model of economic and societal growth and development based on inter-institutional relations, but it does not explain or take into account a number of issues important for stimulating or engaging in innovation activities. The architecture of the network, the dynamics of interactions and mechanisms for the diffusion of networks and differentiation between different types of network nodes, as well as identification of the integrators, drivers, and stimulus to change the velocity and quality and different kinds of flows taking place within and across networks, are not explained by this conceptual framework.

In fact, the model implies that all networks are stable and that the interaction between the actors is seamless and quite mechanical. In reality, innovation networks are diverse, dynamic, and morphing like a living organism rather than structured like rational architecture. There is a high level of conflict in the interactions as a result of team diversity and fundamentally different organizational cultures. This creates a creative tension, a space for "false positive errors," and a level of indeterminacy, which is quite often uncomfortable for individuals and destructive for organizations.

The model also suggests that the networks are similar to each other in terms of architecture, quality, and specificity once they include organizations or individuals from the three domains—research, education, and innovation. In order to improve the understanding of the Knowledge Triangle as a concept, it is important to critically analyze bimodal and multimodal relationships, interdependencies, and dynamics of flows between what have been named the three "sides" of the Knowledge Triangle: research, education, and innovation.

The Knowledge Triangle as a conceptual model is important in that it brings forward a framework underlying an innovation-driven alternative growth model where knowledge production, dissemination, and commercialization are conducted in the context of globally interconnected innovation networks. The linkage of innovation and entrepreneurship has been broadly discussed in the context of growth, mainly in its economic dimension.

While expressing growth solely as a percentage of gross domestic product has become inadequate and much too simplistic for the complexity of the global network society, innovation and entrepreneurship in the innovation networks remain powerful tools for reinventing a number of stagnating, underdeveloped, or underprivileged, yet aspiring, innovation nodes located at the peripheries of networks. As a concept for an alternative growth model, the Knowledge Triangle is based on the underlying assumption that growth depends on qualitative rearrangement of innovation processes rather than the quantitative increase of available resources, their distribution, and their exploitation.

Collaboration Between Industry and Academia

The prevalent model of thinking about research and innovation, such as for example the Triple Helix concept, was originally developed around manufacturing in contrast with the practice of innovation developed in industries such as software or bioengineering (Etzkowitz and Leydesdorff 2000). At the level of a single manufacturing company, as well as in the aggregated industry, competitiveness was based largely on the degree of production line automation. During that time, many industries in Europe, in the US, and in Japan developed, flourished, and vanished as the automation of manufacturing became the norm and shifted to Asia. In the period following the Second World War, it happened so for historical reasons.

On the one hand, there was a need to use the defense industry for non-military purposes. On the other hand, recovery funds invested into Germany and Japan were used to fund automation of far-reaching, large factories, which led to the development of the automotive industries in both countries. The same innovation model later became true also with the semiconductor and microchips industries, where governments invested both in research and development, as well as in fully automated, mass manufacturing facilities.

The embedding and cross-fertilization between particular stages of innovation processes come from advances in the application of ICT in innovating. For example, virtual representation and modeling techniques enable ex-ante evaluation of the potential effects of an innovative action on engineering and production. In consequence, an innovative action can be used until the preliminary phases of the production process. Exploiting ICT techniques in innovating substantially improves the competitiveness of manufacturing sectors in terms of investment and speed in innovating, as well as the strategic fit with market expectations and demand. Thinking of business as a service even if it is product-based helped to keep the user/customer interface.

The shift from manufacturing to the service industry and convergence of technological and non-technological innovation in the manufacturing sector created a lot of uncertainty and intensified competitive tension in the innovation-driven global business environment. The innovation in service economy has its specific features (De Jong and Den Hertog 2007). They include intangibility, high level of interaction, and increasing importance of organizational innovation in global value chains. The scrutiny of these specific factors underlies innovation models in the service industry (Gadrey, Gallouj, and Weinstein 1995; Sundbo 1997; Salter and Tether 2006; Gallouj 2002).

The main differentiating factor between the product and service industries is separability between the place of production and consumption (Erramilli and Rao 1993) and intangibility (Jacson, Neidell, and Lunsford 1995). Since competitiveness of traditional manufacturing industries relies more and more on extending the value chain by integrating service components into product packages and offerings, digital artifacts such as software and content integrated into the value offering have become a separate line of study (Giarini 1994; Gronroos 1990; Jack et al. 2008).

The traditional and sequential phases of basic and applied research-innovation-engineering are much more interrelated and often embedded in each other. The traditional linear model of innovation put science at the beginning of the innovation process. Thus, it interpreted the new role of science due to the context in which technological change originated. In the 1980s, a chain-linked model of innovation was proposed. It encompassed and surpassed the linear model by emphasizing that science is an element of the innovation process but not necessarily the context in which innovation originates. As the economy became more and more industrialized, the service industry grew as well.

Moving toward the service industry, a manufacturing company had to provide different kinds of resources, as well as on-going service and customer support. To remain competitive in the service industry, companies needed to automate. Service—contrary to product—is consumed locally and thus needs to be delivered locally.

Technology-driven innovation is no longer a sustainable competitive advantage and becomes a legacy of established industry players.

It is neither science nor technology that constitutes a value in itself. Innovation, which serves people and societies, fulfills the needs of markets and is able to create a "tipping point." For different stakeholders of the innovation process, this "tipping point" will be by definition different. It may lead to higher contributions to R&D by the private sector, an increased concentration of high-tech manufacturing and a smaller size of manufacturers, more start-ups or spin-offs in fast-emerging sectors, less dispersion of scientific knowledge, and more interaction between science and technology, or higher R&D intensity in small and medium-sized companies, which usually display a higher propensity to grow and expand internationally.

In either case, strength in scientific and technological research and protection of intellectual property do not compensate for the inability to exploit applied research and innovation.

The recurring problem of academia and industry collaboration—besides IP issues—is the step from the prototype stage to mass manufacturing. Scientists carry out experimentation successfully but they have not been able to overcome barriers between small scale and industrial production. Technological advances—especially in the ICT sector—have changed innovation paradigms in a way that still needs to be understood and fully exploited.

The core competencies in the traditional manufacturing industries came from patents, hardware technologies, and technical knowhow. Applied research and innovation still define new configurations for products, systems, processes, or services. Adopting outcomes of the scientific and technological research and building new solutions on top of the existing technology is a natural maturing process of an industrial sector.

However, as industry matures, its technology often becomes a commodity and the differentiating competencies come increasingly from its service components, switching the innovation paradigms from product innovation to service innovation. The question arises whether the collaboration process between academia and industry should always be open. Usually, beforehand, partners agree on IP policy and enter into contractual agreements regulating the rights to the outcome of the collaboration (e.g. a piece of technology, a product).

The agreement between UC Berkeley and BP concerning energy research is often considered an interesting model of partnership, although strongly opposed by some of the Berkeley faculty and not always functioning well. It protects academic independence and at the same time specifies in the pre-established procedures of agreement how the proceedings from the patents are to be shared between the firms and academics. For academics, the incentive to collaborate with industry is the most relevant when it leads to publication or patents. For businesses, the incentive for the collaboration with academic partners is the product and the protection of the rights to exploit it commercially.

Successful open collaboration between academia and industry is preconditioned on understanding and respecting separate interests and incentives, while recognizing the synergies and logic of reciprocal interests (Chesbrough 2003, 2005, 2011). He explains the open innovation model, bringing in a number of examples from different industries including Nanosys, PayCheck, and car2go.com.

A model of an academic-industry network disseminating knowledge has been developed and tested by Nanosys, a nanotechnology company founded in 2001 in Palo Alto, California. The venture capital industry, vital for technology dissemination and driving the growth of innovative firms, is usually not interested in funding research. However, it is eager to engage in technology development and plays a vital role in the diffusion of technology, and it is an important economic force that has emerged over the last thirty years. Nanosys managed to establish a collaboration with the VC industry.

Nanosys was established as a consortium of research advisors/partners from Berkeley, Stanford, Harvard, Technical University in Israel, and Cambridge, UK. They worked on a number of different research projects mainly in nanotechnology. The partners were aligned by an incentive system stimulating collaboration and knowledge sharing. All researchers were given stock options on top of a fee for their advice and an additional fee for lab support. The portfolio of Nanosys consists of over 750 patents. The venture capital funds invested USD 80 million to carry various lab projects to the next stage and finance commercialization. It took a while to develop a line of products with medical and fuel cell applications, and a wide range of creative inventions still need to find their application. This innovation network was fundamentally interwoven by a group of diverse scientists conducting basic research based at various geographically dispersed research universities.

Another example of successful open innovation model scrutinized by Henry Chesbrough is when increased specialization reduces transaction costs. He argues that, thanks to open innovation, the market expands, leading to lower cost and more specialization, as in the case of Paycheck, a payroll processing service, which did not exist 30 years ago. Specialization may also be the result of utilization differential. Yet another case is www.car2go.com, a Daimler car-sharing program launched in Ulm in 2008 and in Austin in 2010. Amazon, started as an online bookstore, offers a number of open services, which create economies of scope through a consistent shopping experience for users. A large market attracts merchants, and a large selection of goods and services attracts a big market. Amazon shifted from its online bookstore model to become a one-stop shop for consumers (Chesbrough 2011).

Designing a business strategy in a relatively stable competitive landscape, within known boundary conditions and accepted rules of the game, was quite straightforward. Michel Porter proposed an analytical model of sustainable competitive advantage built around structural barriers to entry. Gary Hamel and C.K. Prahalad developed a concept of core competencies as a strategic tool to refocus a strategy on mobilizing internal resources in the context of absent structural advantages (Hamel, Prahalad 1994). Porter's value chain model (Porter 1985), relevant to product economies, is of limited use in explaining the competitive advantage of the service economy. Innovation in the latter is a service value web, and not a chain, where customers and their experience are at the center of value creation.

However, the paradigm shift required a new strategic understanding of how complex adaptive systems work and how individual companies can discontinue their operations and rapidly build new competencies through various forms of collaboration. Concepts such as co-opetition (Brandernburget and Nalebuff 1996), value nets, and business ecosystems discounted the increasingly uncertain business environment by putting emphasis on mobilizing external resources through leveraging broader networks of collaborators and competitors. Hagel and Brown proposed an integrated strategic perspective (Hagel and Brown 2008). It stimulates a new approach to innovation beyond the paradigm of manufacturing—service industry and places innovation in the knowledge of knowledge-driven economy.

Scientific Excellence, Education, and Innovation

Education is not necessarily only about knowledge production. It is also about socialization, legitimization of dominant values of a society, organization of social stratum, and meritocracy. The real issue is how to extract from the university system the real value: students. How can students remain immune to a system that stiffens creativity and curiosity? Students need knowledge and skills to deal with complex problems, while in an authoritarian environment only highly structured problems can be dealt with. When it comes to complexity, a hierarchical model of a university with a professor as the only and ultimate source of knowledge is no longer acceptable.[14]

While the requirements of the job market change dramatically, universities do not always seem to follow these changes at the same pace. Although creation of a balanced social system is underpinned by a balanced education system, it seems that many universities still accept rather traditional approaches to higher education.

Not only students but also academics themselves critique universities as "medieval" institutions allowing ex cathedra teaching methods with one-way communication rather than class interaction, action-based learning, and teamwork. Flat organizational structures and inclusive open culture create more favorable conditions for learning how to solve problems, deal with ambiguous situations, mobilize resources, and manage projects. Students need both deep understanding of research as knowledge production but also transversal skills and a broad emphatic understanding of the world. Questions of ethics, accountability, and sustainability, although universal and important, are not often part of the curricula.

Industry quite frequently raises the point that the system of scientific excellence is often detached from the system of higher education and innovation. It is a complete social elite system, which reproduces itself doubled with a pseudo-democratic system. In principle, even if university education is free, the university system is not competitive, and in reality, it is elitist. The reform of the higher education system

(14) The following paragraphs give an account of numerous discussions and interviews held by the author of the book with university leaders, students, and employers over the period of 2009-2012. This account may give a rather grim outlook and it should be interpreted as an endorsement of a more radical shift of higher education in Europe required to face the unexpected difficulty of overcoming the economic crisis.

in the United Kingdom has budgets for teaching and increased tuition fees. This will surely impact the quality of research as well, although this part of the budget has remained largely unchanged. There are still few examples of change in some university systems.

However, in many cases the system perpetuates itself, replicating a model based on the academy of science in the Soviet Union and many Eastern European countries or a model in France where most of the quality research is done outside of the universities, with approximately 70% conducted at CERN, or in Germany where a big part of research activities take place in institutes such as Max Plank Institute, Fraunhofer Institutes, or Julich. In Europe, most universities appear to be bureaucracies rather than modern, globally competitive knowledge organizations.

While they declare an ambition to be research-driven and excellence-focused, in reality, they do not apply market-driven criteria for excellence like American universities. In France, and until recently also in Finland, professors are appointed public servants, and given a guarantee of life-long employment. Endogamy rather than meritocracy prevails and feudal relations between professors, assistants, and students happen to exist. The rigid system of promotion and lack of a competitive, equitable incentive system preserves the status quo. Promotion often results from seniority rather than scientific achievements, with some notable exception of medical and engineering schools, which often provide market-related entrepreneurial possibilities. With the interests of professors dominating the interests of students, the latter are far from being perceived as clients.

Linking knowledge production in a university setting with markets and society is a "people's issue" related to strategic human resources management, culture, leadership, and teamwork dynamics stimulated by remuneration and incentive systems. Bringing the human resources perspective into the process of strategic change in academia gives new tools for establishing collaboration between culturally separated worlds.

In fact, in many cases, neither industry nor academia has managed to build sufficient cross-cultural literacy or abilities to network, build relations, and work in multidisciplinary teams. Solving complex problems requires more often a shift from multidisciplinarity to transdisciplinarity. In the former case, a competence is required to manage teams with various backgrounds. In the latter, the challenge is to integrate these perspectives. Blurring of institutional boundaries, switching across roles and organizations, and taking on multiple tasks simultaneously requires new competencies exceeding the transfer of knowledge, especially in its codified dimension.

One of the aims of reforming the higher education system in Finland was to create environments where these kinds of competences could be developed. For example, a merger between three universities in Helsinki into a transdisciplinary Aalto University enabled a new academic milieu linking technology, business, art, and design. Aalto University has six schools and three platforms to bring students and faculty across the traditional silos of departments and disciplines: Design Factory (Aalto Design Factory 2011), Service Factory, and Creative Learning Environments. For example, Aalto Design Factory is an experimental co-creation platform for all members of the Aalto community. Established and managed by Kalevi "Eetu" Ekman, it is extended on an annual basis. Every year, Design Factory reinvents itself, avoiding the stiffness of permanent projects, which are difficult to terminate in the university setting. Aalto Design Factory has no long-term institutional arrangement securing its sustainability, but it is anchored in the living organism of the Aalto community as a seasonal service provider also in the international scope since its facilities in China and Australia serve the whole Aalto community as an entry point to these countries.

The system is not competitive if universities do not compete for the best students. In some countries in Europe, for example in Italy and Spain, most recruitment at universities is driven by the place of residence.

Many universities do not have a marketing policy or alumni relations department. A university degree from France, Spain, or Italy, a degree from Rome, Milan, or Naples gives nothing more than access to the job market. There is little differentiation in terms of the value of a university degree in Europe. Except for a few cases of some elite and some private institutions in management education like INSEAD, London Business School, or Bocconi University, European university degrees seem to have a comparable market value.

Role of Universities

"Free flow" of knowledge has always been a distinctive feature of the academic culture and the academic community. On the contrary, companies have relatively recently started to learn how to benefit from open innovation. But industry does not want to corrupt university research. On the contrary, it needs good researchers to commit in return for a fair reward. Universities try to stand up to these expectations, developing different kinds of cooperation with industry. There is evidence that some universities change their strategy to become increasingly more capable of engaging in collaborative partnerships with industry (Etzkowitz and Leydesdorff 2000; Etzkowitz 2008). Open innovation allows more diverse forms of cooperation between the academic world and the business world. The key issue is how business firms engage in and finance the process, how they may still obtain competitive advantage from the collaboration and ultimately a return on their investment, and how these goals are compatible with the incentive structure in the university system.

Universities have multiple functions in the society and economy. These functions include creating and legitimizing the dominant values of the society, creating and consolidating the elites of the society, conducting exploratory research and producing new knowledge, producing mass market labor force, and stimulating science and technology application and diffusion as in the case of the entrepreneurial university. We realize that the vast majority of European universities declare to perform most or all of these functions at the same time.

As a result, knowledge production is but one function of the universities in Europe predominantly focused on mass-production of university degrees and graduates with general qualifications suited to perform a middle class function in the economy and the society. Universities are not stand-alone institutions—they are part of a system. In Europe there is a wide range of university systems, which are country specific and quite distinct from each other. The paradox is that while the systems are different, particular institutions offer degrees of similar quality and— with few exceptions—there is little differentiation in terms of branding and identity.

Universities play a critical role in educating next generations for meeting the requirements of the innovation driven economy. Production of new knowledge and applying science for the benefit of a society as a core function of the university was articulated in a model of a "research university" developed in early Renaissance and spread across Europe during the Enlightenment.

A new generation of research university was conceptualized in Germany in the early 1800s by Wilhelm Humboldt, a reformer of the Prussian educational system. He based the model, later called a "Humboldtian university" after his name, on liberal ideas of Friedrich Schleiermacher and envisioned the University of Berlin founded in 1810 as an academic institution with student-centered activity of research. This new model engaging students in exploratory research and in knowledge production was spread across Europe and also the United States. This modern notion of a research university achieved great success in particular in some originally theological schools like Oxford, Cambridge, and Harvard. It happened so because the elites were already established and the function of producing and applying science, that is the appropriation of the knowledge, became fundamental for their prosperity and self-procreation in a modern society.

A new function of a university emerged as a response to the demands of the industrial revolution. At this point in socioeconomic development it became important to create a university performing a function of a "mass university," which was producing labor force for the labor market. It emerged in the mid-nineteenth century and catered to the needs of the labor market in the industrializing economies by providing educated labor force to fuel the economic development of agricultural regions and urban areas. This was the case of the so-called "land-grant" universities, which were founded in the United States in the 1860s with federal grants of land estates to individual states to establish educational institutions with a mission to teach practical skills and applicable knowledge in the area of agriculture, science, and engineering. Another example is the model of European polytechnics or technical universities such as ParisTech in Paris, Technische Universitat in Berlin, KTH in Stockholm, ETH in Zurich, and Imperial College in London, which also conducts research and educates medical doctors. Some medical universities, such as Karolinska Institute, focus on combining the education of engineers, scientists, and medical doctors.

The creation of the "working-class university" came as a consequence of market pressure and the increasing need for a better-qualified labor force, especially after the Second World War. It was also a consequence of pressure from the society, since the working class wanted to educate their children to secure a better life. While it was and still is possible to get a mass degree anywhere in Europe, it is unlikely that a child of working class parents will be accepted to one of the elitist schools like the French Grandes Écoles. In the vast majority of cases, mass universities educate medium level labor force without any specific skills to a required level of understanding and literacy to match the needs of the job market. Graduates have general qualifications when entering the job market, which allow them to accept medium level positions, and they are usually trained on-the-job to match the industry's needs or the needs of public administration.

However, the most interesting model, the model of an "entrepreneurial university," emerged in the 1940s and 50s. It declared and deliberately fostered connection and collaboration with the industry, the government, and the society for stimulating applications of research, trading patents, or simply diffusing technological and scientific capacity initially in the productive sector or later in the service sector and the creative arts.

The first entrepreneurial university was Massachusetts Institute of Technology located in the Boston area in the United States, which was originally founded as one of the land-grant universities. The most famous one, which has become a point of reference, is Stanford University in California. While there were many interlinked and converging factors that resulted in the development of Silicon Valley, the establishment of Stanford University, and in particular Stanford Industrial Park in 1951, was one of the absolutely critical factors in the development of this largest entrepreneurial ecosystem in the world.

Knowledge production in the university setting poses particular challenges because of the cognitive and experiential barriers between academia and markets. This gap can be bridged in a number of ways. For example, design thinking methodology applied originally in the Stanford University d.school (the Hasso Plattner Institute of Design) in California has also been deployed elsewhere, for example in research projects of Aalto University Multidisciplinary Institute of Digitalization and Energy.

Design thinking is a toolbox for innovating and learning how to redesign customer experience. Design thinking includes a wide spectrum of research tools for gathering data, such as service touchpoints, mapping and visualizing customer experience, and co-creation workshops. The user-driven innovation, in this case by crewmembers and ship customers, allowed improvement of service quality through the enhancement of work environment. Student-led research teams use various methods of collaborative research, such as probes, empathy mapping, and affinity mapping, as well as ethnographic methods including shadowing, observation, and participatory design. The testimonies and joint workshops with service providers working at the customer and user interface are a learning environment for user-driven innovation.

One of the novel approaches to creative learning environments is "Bit Bang," launched in 2008 as a one-year post-graduate course for doctoral students anchored in the Multidisciplinary Institute of Digitalization and Energy. It attracts international and multidisciplinary graduate students with the objective to help them acquire such skills as teamwork, multidisciplinary collaboration, scenario building in the broad view of global perspective, and business foresight. Each year, students undertake and manage a project for their learning journey. They document and publish it as a collection of papers, photos, and insights. "Aalto on Waves" is a collection of essays and memoirs of a student-driven innovation project, which took 110 members of the Aalto community from Finland by ship to Brazil (Guseynova 2011).

"Aalto on Waves" included a number of student-designed and led research projects, the trip itself, and fundraising. The research was based on participating and observing the teamwork of the ship crew. For example, "Crew Environment" was to examine public spaces on board and identify design opportunities for helping crewmembers better cope with the challenges of living and working during long-distance trips. The project was divided into three phases: a set of lectures before the trip on design process, methodology, and ethnography practices; immersion in practices as a crewmember; and surveys, interviews, and feedback sessions where ship workers co-created solutions.

In the process of knowledge production and dissemination, intentional or unintentional sharing may lead to development—at hazard—of unexpected side effects or projects. The serendipity results from accidental meeting, coincidence, and exchange of opinions between researchers and innovators. A spectacular example of serendipity is the use of the missile guidance technology developed within the Star Wars program in the US for Navigator, a GPS-based service enabling positioning, localization, and routing of objects in space.

Quite surprisingly, serendipity can be an outcome of a clash of libertarian academic culture and bureaucracy. In the case of Paul Baran's research on distributed communication infrastructure funded by the Pentagon, an unintended consequence was the development of the Internet, first deployed as a virtual cross-culture communication tool among academics, then by business, and only ultimately by the military and the governments. A particular aspect of industry-academia in the funding model in Europe and a well-deployed model in the 1970s was pre-commercial procurement, wherein governments funded research for developing particular solutions. It was later replaced by a system of grants for industry, which was in essence a system of subsidies for developing projects in more than one European country.

On the contrary, the system in the US is an extreme, where research is flooded with funding to open new horizons and see what will come from universities and research labs, as was the case of microchips. In the 1950s, after the government had funded the research, both the military market and public demand expanded. Another extreme of the funding model for stimulating knowledge dissemination in the context of industry–academia collaboration has been developed in the Soviet Union and inherited by Russian researchers. It is a centralized system of deployed funding based on a long-term plan for outcomes of research, which is conducted in an environment of bureaucratic control and supervision.

Chapter 8

EXPERIMENTING WITH THE KNOWLEDGE TRIANGLE: KNOWLEDGE AND INNOVATION COMMUNITIES

The concept of the Knowledge Triangle as an innovation network can be manifested in a number of different ways. One model for which the Knowledge Triangle was used as a conceptual framework was the Knowledge and Innovation Community (KIC). KICs are manifestations of the Knowledge Triangle as Europe-specific innovation networks. Initiated by a policy action, they were expected to respond in a more effective way to an increasingly aggressive and dynamic global innovation landscape and make Europe more competitive.

The first three Communities of Knowledge and Innovation were established in 2010. The basis for their launch was the framework of the European Union legislation [EIT Regulation (EC) No 294/2008] and their governing body was a new European agency, the European Institute of Innovation and Technology.

In 2010, the European Institute of Innovation and Technology announced the "Call for KICs," a public tender process for selecting three consortia, each in one of the following areas: climate mitigation and adaptation, sustainable energy, and future information and communication society. The call defined KICs as innovation networks in the following way:

KICs will be characterised by geographically distributed people who are brought together for significant periods to work in centres where individuals from different types of organisations and cultures (nationalities, industry, academia, research etc.) are co-located in significant parts of the innovation chain (co-location centres). This co-location of people will allow stakeholders to work together face-to-face and move forward effectively towards KIC goals. The co-location centres are expected to be the lead nodes amongst a much larger number of partners in the network. It is anticipated that KICs will typically involve four to six co-location centres or lead nodes. Where an exceptional case for this is made, applications involving more than six may be considered. Notwithstanding geographical co-location, all necessary means should be used to ensure a continuous linkage between all the partners in the KIC (Call for proposals EIT/2009/KICs).

The three KICs interpreted the general outlines specified in the call in three different ways depending on the strategy of their partnership. While each of these networks is distinct, they share a number of characteristics.

A KIC is an excellence-driven, autonomous partnership of higher education institutions, research organizations, companies, and other stakeholders [EIT Regulation (EC) No 294/2008]. A higher education institution was defined as an organization that, in accordance with national legislation or practice, could offer master's and doctoral degrees and diplomas. A research organization was to include any type of private or public lab, whose main task was to undertake research or technological development. Companies were to be represented by large global and European corporations, as well as small and medium-sized companies, and the category of other stakeholders implied institutions and public bodies relevant for designing and implementing innovation projects, such as municipalities, local or regional governments, and non-profit organizations.

A KIC was to be a legal entity. Its legal structure was not precisely defined in terms of for-profit or not-for-profit. Whatever the legal entity of a KIC, its strength and governance model was to constitute a base for setting up sustainable and long-term self-supporting strategic networks in the innovation process. The collaboration of stakeholders in a KIC as a partnership was to be legally binding in a long-term time horizon, specified as a minimum of seven years, and in general between seven to fifteen years. For this period, core stakeholders were expected to keep their commitment to a KIC. In this context, the European Institute of Innovation and Technology was the EU body committing itself through a Seven-Year Framework Agreement to support a KIC financially for a period of seven years. Subject to the outcomes of periodic evaluations and to the specificity of a particular field of a KIC, the EIT financing could be prolonged beyond the seven years if the extension of a KIC's operation could help meet the objectives of the EIT, that is to catalyze the innovation process leveraging the European single market.

According to the Call's text, a KIC was to involve at least three independent partner organizations, including at least one higher education partner and one private company, which are established in at least three different EU Member States. The call did not specify what kind of legal entity would fit best. Taking into account the diversity of legal systems in Europe, it was left open to the leading partners preparing the call proposal to choose whether a for-profit or not-for-profit type of legal structure would best fit the objectives of the KIC and under which legislation such an entity should be incorporated. KICs were to propose how they planned to maximize the share of financial contribution from the private partners engaged on the basis of a formal and long-term contractual agreement, or project-based with a KIC.

The formal role of the EIT toward KICs, based on the Seven-Year Framework Agreement, is to provide financing and in return implement a transparent governing process, through which these excellence-driven innovation networks are monitored and evaluated. The regulation foresaw that in case of inadequate results, the EIT could take appropriate measures penalizing a KIC by reducing its contribution, by modification or even withdrawal of its financial support, and in extreme cases by terminating prematurely the framework agreement with a KIC. However, in 2010, KICs were often referred to as "five-legged animals," which reflected the complex concept of a new type of innovation network.

Therefore, there were and still are a number of pending questions concerning the evaluation of the three existing KICs, as well as the KIC model as such. Since KICs have been operating as consortia for slightly over two years since signing the formal agreements with the EIT, there is an emerging picture rather than an established model of a KIC and its network dynamics.

KICs are legal entities with the financial commitment of their partners for a period of between seven and fifteen years. This duration exceeds standard projects funded within the Framework Programs for Research and Technological Development, which are grant schemes to encourage and support research in the European Research Area. It allows the undertaking of projects requiring long-term research, which makes it a competitive framework to usually shorter, industry-led research projects. These types of research projects tend to dominate in an increasing way in the United States, so the KIC gives a specific competitive advantage to its partners. The longitude of the partnership brings stability and allows long-term planning, which is crucial when solving complex problems, integrating business models across value chains, and building trust for open innovation.

Some KICs reported that "certain industrial partners, who were in competition across the CLCs came together as partners in the KIC Steering Committee—a move which may have a positive impact on common standards in the European market" (Technopolis 2011). There are diverse forms of partnerships in the consortium. The partnership includes core partners and a KIC-specific structure of affiliated partners, associated partners, and project partners. The core partners commit financially and have formal power over the KIC. Other partners have a varying degree of involvement, some kind of commitment and power as a member of a formal structure (e.g. governing board, IP board). The legal partnership allows for exit and entry of the parties, which makes the structure flexible, making a KIC network a morphing organism rather than a fixed and bureaucratic structure.

Each KIC is headed by a management team with a Chief Executive Officer. The CEO has executive decision power over all the resources of the KIC including tangible and intangible assets, as well as the financial and in-kind contribution of all partners. It is one of the key elements that the CEO's scope of responsibilities includes all KIC resources and not only the EIT financial contribution. A management structure mimicking the best practices of private sector organizations induces accountability and results-oriented performance assessment. The CEO is appointed by the board of the KIC. The board has supervisory duties and monitors the management performance and the KIC deliverables. It also governs the KIC in terms of providing strategic guidance, representing the KIC to the outside world, and strengthening its position in the process of brand building.

As a result of the call, two Seven-Year Framework Agreements were signed at the end of 2010, and one was signed at the beginning of 2011. Climate-KIC was the winning consortium in the thematic area of climate mitigation and adaptation; KIC InnoEnergy won in the thematic area of sustainable energy; and EIT ICT Labs won in the area of future information and communication society. The Call's text emphasized the networked character of a new innovation model a KIC was to become in the context of and in line with the logic of the global innovation network of networks.

The concept of "geographically distributed people who are brought together for significant periods to work in centers where individuals from different types of organizations and cultures (nationalities, industry, academia, research etc.) are co-located in significant parts of the innovation chain (co-location centers)," pointed not so much to the importance of the legal framework for inter-institutional collaboration of a KIC's partners, but to their particular division, departments, or other organizational units, which dedicated their employees to work together face-to-face for a limited period of time on a project in the so-called co-location centers (CLCs).

This project-based collaboration as the dominant operational structure defines the KICs as a new manifestation of a network enterprise. While a KIC as a network enterprise is defined as a portfolio of projects, each KIC is also a legal entity with a defined financial structure and a governance model. This legal arrangement gives the long-term stability critical for developing complex research and technology solutions. At the same time, keeping the flexibility of a network enterprise suited the stimulation of open innovation, keeping the process agile, lean, and adaptive to the changing competitive landscape.

Spatial Articulation

The spatial articulation of the KICs is quite specific. Their architecture is one of the differentiating factors from other innovation networks in Europe. KICs with their CLCs differ also between each other and within each KIC in terms of their geographical spread, specialization, and functionality. There are certain KIC-specific features characteristic of all CLCs within a KIC.

However, there are a number of questions that will still need to be addressed with the maturing of the KICs. What drives these particularities and differentiating features? Are functional differences a result of the specialization, or maybe of the managerial skills necessary to manage distributed networks? To what extent does the political decision to strongly embed a CLC in a national innovation system change its status? Do they take a leading role in activities related to education and/or innovation and/or business creation because of partners' strengths? How is the CLC related to other networks and their nodes, in particular in the case of Climate-KIC, with its CLCs network of Regional Implementation Centers? To what extent does the status of a CLC differ as a result of its interconnectedness with the global innovation network? What are the KIC's policies shaping the dynamics of interaction between the CLCs and their transformation in the KIC and to the outside world? Are CLCs needed at all, or could a network exist without physical (office) space? What is the optimal number of nodes for a KIC? Do they depend on the industry sector? Should some nodes be located elsewhere, for example in mega nodes of global innovation networks like Silicon Valley? How can innovation be leveraged at the peripheries? Is there a difference for regional specialization if nodes are located in neighboring countries? Is clustering still so relevant? What are other networks that could accelerate innovation in the KICs? Is the RIC network the only structure, and what function does it play in increasing a KIC's output and impact?

Another set of questions related to the concept of the network architecture: What is a co-location center? What is its function and role in the network? What are the differences between different models? In what ways do a particular set up and a specific function of a co-location impact the network dynamics and the effectiveness of the network in producing quality outputs? What processes take place if nodes of different KICs overlap? How then would these diverse functions allow a CLC to become "a leading node?" What does it mean and what does it mean in a given context? Does a co-location center influence local, regional, or national innovation systems and, if so, how does it change the innovation strategy of Member States and Europe's innovation capacity as a whole?

The architecture of KICs as innovation networks is defined through "co-location centers," otherwise called "lead nodes." Each KIC has five or six of them spread across Europe. The concept was described in the call for KICs and raised a wide range of questions as to their set up and function. A diversity of the manifestations of these "lead nodes" across and between the KICs points to significant differences in how the concept has been understood and consequently applied. KICs have interpreted it in diverse ways adapting to specific conditions of partnerships, thematic focus, industry, and strategy.

The specificity of the spatial articulation of the KICs relies on the fact that a KIC as an innovation network is at the same time tightly-knit locally and loosely-coupled globally. It is tightly-knit locally at the level of its co-location centers or the nodes. It is loosely-coupled globally with other nodes across the KIC and with nodes of the pan-European KIC network, and beyond this intra-KIC network with other innovation networks in the global world through multiple connections of the KICs' partners.

The characteristic spatial arrangement of a KIC is expressed through a network consisting of a limited number of co-location nodes. A CLC is a physical location that is a part of the pre-established innovation hub, a place where a major part of the innovation value chain is already located. The CLCs are linked with each other in a number of ways. As reflected in the organizational charts, there is some kind of matrix showing vertical and horizontal interdependencies, direct and indirect reporting lines.

A KIC as an innovation network is composed of lead nodes, which display some apparent features and functions in the network. The articulation of CLCs varies. The CLCs themselves search for their meaning in the KIC structure. They change locations of offices. They move from a partner's premises to an independent setting. Sometimes they are given a prestigious localization in a representational spot of one of the leading partners. Spatial and organizational articulation of a KIC was an important criterion in the selection process.

The quality of the co-location plan comprised up to 10% of the total score (maximum 20 points out of 200). The call for KICs specified that a KIC was to consist of a small number of co-location nodes, ranging between four and six. A special justification was needed to include more nodes into the network. The co-location plan was in fact a kind of feasibility assessment of an operational aspect of the KIC as an innovation network. The degree of its completeness and of the complementarities of the nodes was assessed in terms of a strategy for managing geographically distributed people in innovation networks so that they could work in their original node and also work on assignments of significant duration (from a few weeks up to a few months) in other nodes.

The early assessment of impact of the spatial articulation of the KICs' networks, and in particular its co-location nodes, concluded that the network concept is widely understood and accepted and that the physical presence of the CLCs as places for implementation does not seem so important and should not be emphasized in future calls for KICs (ECORYS 2012). Indeed, implementation seems to take place in the "space of flows," which redefines the initial role of the CLCs as research labs and education and incubation facilities.

The vertical reporting lines between "pillar" or "thematic line" directors shows the hierarchical interdependence between a CLC and the KIC as an umbrella organization. It is a result of legal arrangement and the governance structure. A CLC director reports to the KIC CEO. The horizontal direction is a sign of operational activities related to the intersecting agendas of the KICs, namely education, innovation, and new business creation. The directors responsible for each of these agendas collaborate across CLCs. They report to the KIC CEO and at the same time are indirectly bound with the CLCs' directors.

There are also a number of ad hoc working groups, which bring experts from a given area (e.g. simplification of procedures, communication and branding) and which operate in an octagonal way across a KIC or between the KICs. These organizational activities show distinct features of networked articulation of the KICs. The nodes are the places for strategic discussions and decision-making. The flow between the CLCs is a myriad of activities related to the implementation of these decisions in the virtual space of the World Wide Web, through the Internet and by communicating via fixed or, more often, mobile phones. In this sense, the CLCs are the "space of places" and the links between them are the "space of flows."

The networks established within Framework Programs usually include a large number of partners spread across Europe in an effort to include institutions and organizations coming from countries described as "Followers" and as "Lagging Behind" (OECD). The networks are project-based collaborations established for a short period of time. The networks are not legal entities and consequently they are coordinated rather than managed since there is no source of executive power in the hands of a network coordinator.

The joint projects in the networks funded within the Framework Programs are considered transactional, and they are usually based on previously established connections. But it is also common that a partner is invited to join because of his or her country of origin and convergence of research interest and not necessarily because of excellence as such. The Framework Programs have induced massive mobility across Europe, building innovation capacity and stimulating creativity through diversity and cross-cultural literacy. The participants of the collaborative projects under the Framework Programs often express disappointment with lack of follow up practices. When the collaboration project is terminated, its outputs are not exploited.[15]

Geographical distribution of partners in the KICs is different and reflects on the one hand the fragmentation of the innovation capacity in Europe, and on the other hand, thematic convergence between different locations. In some cases the CLC office is located at the premises of one of the leading partners. In other cases, it is placed in an independent office in an innovation hotspot, a science park, or a business accelerator. The distribution of partners in a CLC should allow daily commuting to the CLC office, if necessary. Each of the three KICs has five or six co-location centers. The Climate-KIC has an additional network of Regional Implementation Centers and the EIT ICT Labs has a supplementary network of Associated Partners. These are both based on a different concept than the CLCs. The map below shows the distribution of eighteen CLCs, six RICs and two EIT ICT Labs Associated Partners across Europe. The CLCs are located in nine countries, eight of them Member States. RIC and Affiliate Partners are present in six Member States. Overall, some sort of an organized unit of the three KIC networks cover eleven states; ten of them are EU Member States, of which one CLC in Poland, and one RIC and one Affiliate Partner, both in Hungary, are located in the states which joined the European Union in 2004. Two other KICs also have offices in Brussels, the exception being KIC InnoEnergy.

(15) The frustration regarding the set up of collaborative partnerships under the Framework Programs is not specific to any particular group and is often voiced by academics as well as by industry representatives.

KIC network participants can also have strategic discussions via teleconferencing or videoconferencing. This is possible, however, only after establishing a trust-based relation through face-to-face international meetings in the CLCs. It will become more and more often the case that people engage in workflow in different geographically distributed CLCs while working on development or implementation of short to mid-term projects, which require mobility of students, faculty, innovators, entrepreneurs, or KIC management and support staff.

The work design makes the participants commute through real and virtual space between the co-locations, staying there or becoming engaged for a significant period of time. This is part of the implementation process, and despite the physical proximity, the pure implementation could probably be done via the Internet. Working and collaborating with people from different CLCs or in a CLC by representing diverse organizational and national cultures creates the space for mutual understanding, bonding, and forming a team. Each KIC will develop its own patterns of intra and inter co-location center organization. The mechanisms to integrate these geographically distributed "innovation factories" will be based on the specificity of the network: the "space of places" and the "space of flows."

The analysis of the applications of the CLC concept has conceptualized it as "fundamental architecture of the KICs" (Technopolis 2011); "backbones of the KICs and a sort of operational units that bring together groups of people, regional and local clusters and nodes of excellence" (ECORYS 2012); "the primary delivery mechanism for KICs, and as such are essential mechanisms for implementing a range of activities underpinned by the aim of integrating the three dimensions of the knowledge triangle (education, research and innovation)" (EIT 2012). ECORYS notes that CLCs are not entities in their own right and that their existence results from being part of a KIC network (ECORYS 2012).

These descriptions are quite broad and there is an impression that on the one hand, a CLC is a large extended area (e.g. a cluster), and on the other hand, it denotes a specific office or lab of a KIC, which is part of this geographically focused ecosystem. They also do not explain the difference between what kind of work is done at the CLCs and what kind is done in the continuous linkages between them. This distinction can be better understood in the framework of KICs as the combination of "space of places" and "space of flows."

Early analysis of the articulation of the CLCs provides evidence that the CLCs are in fact a manifestation of the former, while these linkages between them are manifestations of the latter. The CLCs are the space for face-to-face interaction during which collaborative creativity leads to generating new ideas and political capacity brings strategic decisions. The linkages—calls, e-mails, teleconferences, and videoconferences— are the process of implementation. In this sense, the CLCs are conceptualized as nodes of an innovation network.

Tightly-Knit, Loosely-Coupled: Emerging Business Models

The concept of the business model of a Knowledge and Innovation Community may have seemed quite unexpected, taking into consideration the tradition of research and innovation networks sponsored and supported by public bodies at the European or national levels. The call for KICs requested that the proposals of the consortia applying for the EIT funding and new innovation brand in Europe also present a document in which they define their value proposition, business case, and a business model as a roadmap to reaching financial self-sustainability within a maximum of seven years' time. The business model of the KIC can be analyzed on macro and micro levels. The micro level indeed focuses on the "KIC as a business" concept. The macro level responds to the phenomena of accumulation of resources and knowledge flows, which are catalyzed by the KICs in the European economy.

The business plans of the KICs at the moment when they were incorporated were not clear concepts and were translated in a number of ways by the winning consortia. The KICs' funding structure was quite complex and largely based on the assumption of bridging the public-private gap in funding R&D.

The sources of the KICs' funding were to include a number of revenue streams. First, the contributions from companies or private organizations were expected to become a substantial portion of a KIC's budget. The general budget of the European Union was to be another major source of funding, yet KICs were not to be privileged with any sort of special treatment and would fall under the same rules and procedures as all other EU funded programs and entities financed from the Seventh Framework Program, Competitiveness and Innovation Program, Life-long Learning Facility, or Structural Funds. Some portion of the KIC budget was to be financed from contributions from Member States, third countries, and public authorities within them, as well as from bequests, donations, and contributions from individuals, institutions, and foundations, from national and international bodies and institutions. All contributions could be in-cash or in-kind.

The European Investment Bank was mentioned as a possible source of funding, including but not limited to funding a KIC from the Risk Sharing Finance Facility if a KIC was eligible and met the selection procedure criteria. However, a KIC was also expected to generate revenue of its own. It could come from its own activities, as well as from royalties from intellectual property rights.

The EIT contribution to a KIC's budget was to cover its establishment, administration, and coordination costs. At the moment of launch,

Climate-KIC's partners had a vision that the value added would be a result of integrating the value chain of climate change-related solutions. Rather than offering a technology, partners would be able to offer a solution with the incorporated service component, thus increasing the profitability of commercial activity of universities and industry partners in the KIC. In case of the EIT ICTLabs, future revenue streams seemed to be less evident, however. The value added resided in creating an open innovation environment, invigorating flows of knowledge, talent, and capital in the network and creating platforms for development of industry standards, vital for the entire industry as in the case of GSM technologies. KIC InnoEnergy had a model based on taking equity stakes in companies that they could provide added value for by connecting to the first customer and offering robust educational programs and executive education.

The concept of co-location located in an ecosystem where significant elements of the innovation chains are located was aimed at changing the qualitative arrangement of innovation processes in Europe. It was to move away from the campus-based model to an innovation network model. KICs were brick-and-mortar operations. Individuals linked to KIC projects were at the same time involved in different projects with local and non-local partnerships or organizations.

The CLCs were distributed across Europe and they infused mobility into the innovation system in Europe with people commuting and working on a project based at these centers from different geographical locations with their individual connections and projects in other innovation networks. The more a co-location center was open—in the sense of having a more open culture—and welcomed interactions beyond traditional academic silos, institutional boundaries, and the gap between academia and business, the more diverse people were attracted. This contributed to the creation of a more fertile ground for collective creativity and innovation and a learning process. The CLCs are not simply office spaces for administrative purposes of coordinating the network. They were conceived as creative zones, meeting points, and political spaces for strategic decision-making.

The analysis of two years of operations of CLCs within and among the KICs at the national scale points to some phenomena specific for the "space of places" and "space of flows," as well as mechanisms of the global innovation network such as multilayering, developing a switching capability, and eventually changing the status of a node. For example, three KICs located their CLCs in France. They have become the space strategizing, lobbying, and negotiating with the government.

For example, the CLC Climate-KIC France is located at Paris-Saclay campus, 20 km south of Paris[16]. It is the largest research and technology campus in France, with two billion Euros invested by the French government, 10,000 researchers and teachers, 1,500 PhD students, and 22,000 students within 9 km2. The total output of the campus is 180 patents per year, 160 people for knowledge transfer, and 30 start-ups annually on all topics. Additionally, some specific research and innovation activities are also managed in the Paris-Est campus, at a distance of 20 km, where Advancity, a "competitiveness cluster" with universities and incubators, is located. The organization of the French node reflects a centralized research model with a cluster in the metropolitan area including long-established, prestigious partners, such as CEA and École Polytechnique. The CLC receives funds from both regional and national sources. Mainly it is sponsored by the French national government as part of the overall strategy to develop Saclay as a future global innovation hub. This CLC is part of a larger innovation web of the Paris-Saclay campus.

(16) Data available at www.climate-kic.org

However, the Climate-KIC CLC is connected at the French level with two CLCs in France: CLC Alps Valleys of InnoEnergy and the Paris Node of the EIT ICT Labs. Regular monthly meetings at the management level have been set up between the CLCs' directors to discuss, strategize, and decide on their negotiating position versus the French national government, in particular the French Ministry of Higher Education and Research. The three French CLCs do not consider each other competitors but allies in building and leveraging the EIT brand across the KICs, although they apply for funding at the national level separately. The CLC Climate-KIC France is also in constant contact at the operational level with other CLCs in its network (EIT 2011).

The business models at the micro level of a CLC, at the KIC level, and at the macro level—that is, the inter-KIC level or pan-European context—introduced a new organizational scheme linking two network dimensions: closely-knit and loosely-coupled. In this sense, the co-location plan was a new operational pattern for innovation networks in Europe—the network architecture.

It seems too early to investigate what the emerging map of innovation networks in Europe is and how certain nodes change their status in the global context. When networks diffuse, some nodes will develop the capacity to switch and this capability will drive growth and development beyond mere investment. Their connectedness at the international level will increase and this will attract talent, hopefully creating competitive conditions attracting Europeans back from Silicon Valley and other innovation hubs. Mobility, the flow of people, and project-orientation, the flow of knowledge and capital, are vital carriers of value creation in the emerging business models of the KICs at macro and micro levels.

Learning-by-Doing: Integrated Entrepreneurial Education

Model

An intersecting dimension of the three Knowledge and Innovation Communities is entrepreneurialism and entrepreneurial education. The KICs develop different models of non-degree and for-degree programs at master's, PhD, and executive levels. The curricula focus on teaching a set of entrepreneurial skills, creativity, leadership, and teamwork. Integrating entrepreneurship into standard curricula of engineering or science education is important.

This integration is a serious challenge for Europe with respect to its talent development and brain drain, especially in the context of people who are not risk-averse and who take their chance to emigrate. Graduates of excellent European universities choose to build their careers elsewhere, in an environment conducive to attracting and growing entrepreneurial people. Top talent is discouraged by Europe's bureaucracies, rigid hierarchies fostered by fragmentation of the scientific potential. Some obstacles that prevent drawing on the talent from Central and Eastern European countries include poor English skills, inadequate educational qualifications, and cultural issues such as lack of experience on teams and reluctance to take initiative or assume leadership roles.

Entrepreneurship is both a skill and an attitude for integrating resources and deploying creativity to organize capital, labor, and knowledge in order to exploit an opportunity. Entrepreneurship as a set of skills can obviously be taught. The teaching includes creativity, interdisciplinarity, skill enhancement (for example, business plan writing), fundraising, and management of fast growing businesses.

Socialization in an entrepreneurial culture is conducive to growing entrepreneurs. The entrepreneurial culture of Silicon Valley rewards the next big idea, which carries a sense of edginess. A common thread among entrepreneurial behavior is a basic, preemptive fight of boredom.

Entrepreneurs feel an imperative to create some chaos once things get too neat. In sharp contrast to the United States, the potential reward for taking risk in Europe is limited, while potential downsides or costs are relatively high both in financial and societal terms. There is in fact no need to take risks in Europe if one is a fresh graduate, since pay-off for not taking risks is high, as the labor market level of analysis shows.

Some academic institutions seem to be better at developing entrepreneurial culture than others. The student population can be divided into three groups: students who, no matter what is done, will never become entrepreneurs; students who, no matter what is done, will become entrepreneurs anyway; and the vast majority of students who simply do not consider an entrepreneurial venture as their career choice.

Therefore it is important to create a framework for collaboration between faculty, industry, entrepreneurs, business angels, and venture capitalists. A university becomes a meeting point and it happens so that the university as an institution is usually not a driving force.

Stanford University is widely perceived as a university that trains entrepreneurial people. This brand is based on such success stories as HP and Google. However, Stanford only relatively recently began teaching entrepreneurship courses in a more systematic manner. The secret of Stanford is that the university did not teach entrepreneurship but attracted entrepreneurial people. Actually, looking up to the Stanford University as a model for teaching entrepreneurship is a misconception. The Stanford University brand is based on attracting top students interested in starting a business and faculty with entrepreneurial interests, rather than having a systematic model developed over the decades as the new industries were created around Stanford. At Stanford, students develop the tools that will increase the likelihood of their success in the business world, but they are not taught to be entrepreneurial. There is a natural pre-selection process as people who get accepted to Stanford already dream of becoming entrepreneurs, and part of this entrepreneurial myth is that success is determined by an ability to create market value, which leads to personal wealth.

However, activities fostering entrepreneurship and centered around schooling may not be necessarily part of the curriculum. For example, in American high schools there are initiatives like Junior Assembly, which inspires and supports students to start their own businesses, prepare a business plan, and participate in business plan competitions. But otherwise, in the formal sense, the system of education has little to do with the training of entrepreneurial people.

The level of entrepreneurial activity is high in certain parts of Europe. In Italy or Greece there is a high level of self-employment and family business tradition. There is also an impressive track record of entrepreneurial behaviors in the post-communist societies of Central and Eastern Europe. Under communism, where the supply side was a key issue due to supply shortages and breaks, businesses used to keep high inventories, which meant high operating costs and the need to switch rapidly to increase the efficiency of operations as the cost of capital was driven by market prices and a high level of short-term assets. Ignoring the rules of the demand driven free market economy led in many instances to liquidity and solvency issues. Their entrepreneurialism can be expressed in the responsiveness of these enterprises to develop under communism or right after its collapse in their adaptability to free market economy, by acquiring entrepreneurial skills in marketing, sales, finance, and human resources management.

In the United States, a key factor contributing to the creation of entrepreneurial students is competitive sports, which are part of early education. Soccer players are formed in kindergarten, not upon graduating from high school. Five-year-olds who have a desire to play are selected and trained. There is a culture that produces these people and at the university level they are taught the rules of the game, which makes it more probable that they will succeed once they start a business. The teaching is more about how to write a business plan, what language to use in order to raise money from a venture capitalist or get a bank loan, and how to present the business for the purpose of selling it.

In a similar manner as in a film or design school, students are taught how to write a good script, make a good project, and write and draw in style. The desire to become a film director or a famous designer must already be intrinsic in these students. They are the people who have a desire to be taught the techniques to reach success. Therefore, teaching entrepreneurship means teaching techniques and not teaching how to be entrepreneurial. The pre-selection is critical. People who will be put into the system and taught certain skills must come with a dream and an ambition. If this is the case, the challenge then is how to identify and attract these people into the system.

Teaching entrepreneurship skills can be effective, yet possessing these skills does not guarantee that one will be successful in business to the same extent an MBA degree does not automatically bring success. However, there is a fundamental difference and responsibility. Teaching entrepreneurship skills and building on the desire of people who do not necessarily want to work for other people requires demystifying a risky career choice. Among a handful of success stories are thousands of people who are not successful, and there are many stories of personal failure, family break-ups, and spoiled lives.

The chances of success in business are not high, although many entrepreneurs share a false belief that success is within their reach. The myth of the gold rush and money making resonates in humans' nature as hunters and hustlers. In the 1980s a book, "The Pursuit of Excellence" by Tom Peters, made it to the New York Times best seller list. The truth is that its success did not derive from the merits of the book as such but from the fact that McKinsey Consultancy, which co-authored it, bought the first 50,000 copies and distributed the book for free to their customers. With such a marketing campaign, the volume of books "sold" jumped immediately to the level of "best seller," triggering the real sales that followed. The success then was the result of being a member of a powerful network rather than the merit of the product. A degree, therefore, is not a guarantee of success in business. There are a number of famous examples of drop-outs, such as Steve Jobs, Bill Gates, or Mark Zuckerberg, who created multibillion dollar companies from scratch while not completing their education.

An interesting model for entrepreneurial training is "T-shaped" (Pendelton-Jullian 2009). The "T-shaped model" means that there is deep, vertical knowledge in science, math, and design, as well as a horizontal, broad set of skills such as creativity, teamwork, interdisciplinarity, integrity, communication, and interpersonal skills. In the "T-shaped model," hard skills are complemented with soft skills. Quite often, the best universities, including Stanford, were choosing the best students based on the skills and competences included in the horizontal element of the "T-shape" without necessarily acknowledging it. Students would be chosen for being, for example, a top debater, a top sportsman, or a community leader. Relatively recently the effort has been made to capitalize on the brand of Stanford and formally capture entrepreneurial thinking. The teaching on becoming more entrepreneurial is about learning-by-doing, not by discussing and writing a report but by delivering a prototype, or fundraising rather than writing a business plan. The expectations for students' work are set clearly to solve problems under given circumstances and under time constraints. This is how creativity somehow happens in a collective process of co-creation.

Fostering entrepreneurialism through the educational programs of the KICs is urgently needed to shake conservative curricula and teaching methods. It is a question of two different models and approaches. One is a crash course integrated into science, art, or technology-driven curriculum. Another is a degree approach modeled as an MBA in entrepreneurship.

Whichever the model deployed, it should be, however, noted that a particular demographic challenge comes from Generation Y—the Internet generation of people born after 1980—whose outlook has been shaped by connectivity, constant access to the World Wide Web, information overload, and a new generational value set marked by rejection of participation in the "rat race," unsustainable growth, and irresponsible consumption. The values of this generation are manifested by movements such as "Occupy Wall Street."

Over the last decade, the war for talent has intensified and Europe suffers from a painful brain drain of the top talent and emerging academic and business leaders. Increased global competition and strategy by investment in research, innovation, and entrepreneurship, mobility of knowledge workers, and demographic changes will only intensify the brain drain.

Effective talent strategies cannot focus solely on short-term goals but must create a context for top performers to deliver in the long-term and for average performers to maximize their potential. Good talent management requires the attention of senior leaders, who usually do not spend enough high-quality time shaping the strategy of talent development and developing talent themselves. Organizations need to encourage a culture of collaboration, teamwork, and knowledge sharing. The incentive system should promote top performers in the long-term perspective (stock options and revenue sharing mechanisms) and not erode the contributions of capable and steadily delivering average performers. Inclusiveness in the broadest sense and responsible local and global citizenship becomes more and more important to top talent.

After two years of operations, there is some early evidence of how the model of the Knowledge Triangle has been translated in three different ways in the three existing Communities. It is too early to assess impact and evaluate the outcome of each KIC, in particular since they are evolving networks of partners, who experiment and search for the most adequate legal, market, operational, and financial solutions for the industry sector in which they operate, the level of Europe's competitiveness in the given sector, and global competition for talent and other resources as well as the structure and maturing of a sector.

There are some common denominators of the model. For example, their excellence-driven ambition refers to the quality of research projects undertaken by the KICs. However, the degree to which these projects will turn out to be cutting-edge and breakthrough will be known most probably in the mid to long-term future. While it is not possible to assess the impact of the innovation projects undertaken by a KIC, a proxy conditioning this impact is the ability to attract talent and growth-oriented people by creating a learning environment in the open innovation mode.

Mobility programs for students and young researchers across the KICs and beyond the KICs are one of the instruments to form such a creative and stimulating distributed ecosystem. The assumption is that the activities of a KIC in linking research with education and with innovation will help overcome fragmentation in Europe and attain a critical mass by creating synergies between dispersed geographically and culturally distinctive innovation hubs in Europe.

Understanding and assessment of the KIC model value is not only about how it creates synergies, but to what extent and how quickly the

KIC and its partners are able to exploit the results of their innovation projects and how leveraging available resources can create value in the economic sense and in the social and societal dimensions.

Chapter 9

RE-CONCEPTUALIZING THE KNOWLEDGE TRIANGLE

The Knowledge Triangle becomes a new, Europe-specific concept of a network of innovation networks. It is particular in that unlike other models, it epitomizes a network of partners within and between established and emerging innovation ecosystems. What hold the network together are flows of knowledge, talent, and capital between and across them. The analysis of the nature of innovation and entrepreneurship in the information age has introduced the idea of a physical and digital learning environment. Networking within and between these creative spaces where innovation is delivered and ventures learn to succeed or fail fast occurs in the process of migrating across the "space of places" as a milieu where collective creativity meets demand.

In empirical terms, the Knowledge Triangle can be conceptualized rather as a learning environment detached from a physical location such as a cluster, where institutional partners engage in innovation activities. The Knowledge Triangle becomes a model of multimodal, multidimensional networks of distributed learning environments held together by flows within and between real and virtual worlds rather than a geographical location. The learning environment can be designed as an interactive space where organizations, teams, and individuals become in turn agents and principals and interdependent in a temporary situation, with their incentives aligned to perform the best along the logic of a project, which is a precondition for either retaining or expelling them.

A creative learning environment is a space where innovation as a learning process takes place with all its specific conditions characteristic of the world-in-constant-flux, with a World Wide Web constantly available for "hanging out," "messing around," and "geeking out," and an open innovation paradigm endlessly accelerating feedback loops and thus bridging more quickly and efficiently the world of ideas with markets and societies.

There are many specific learning environments and the Knowledge Triangle exists as a network of these rather than a stand alone, alienated place. The pictograms of the Knowledge Triangle spell out three sides: research, education, and innovation. It is perceived as a set of innovation-related activities taking place during a process of interactions between these institutions. Interpreting the concept as a network of research institutions, universities, and industrial organizations provides a descriptive image but is too simplistic to capture the complexity of networked innovation. The notion of a "side" in a Knowledge Triangle is quite complex. At a first glance, the Knowledge Triangle may indeed seem to be an inter-institutional network of academic and business organizations involved in research, education, and innovation.

However, in a networked world in constant flux with ever-changing rules of the game, the self-interested rational choices of a "party," understood as an agent, may collide and at the same time coincide with what the principal—an institution in this case—desires. The asymmetry of information is no longer such a discriminating factor as the abundance of information, open access to information, and freedom to use or misuse information. The ability to search, select, and frame a piece of information, turning it into knowledge, blurs the divisions.

Entrepreneurial teams and individuals organized around a project with or without formal contractual agreements with institutions or rather certain parts of institutions, which limit yet always obligate institutional relations, make the Knowledge Triangle into a mosaic of diverse innovation settings, agents, and principals with transient properties and identities. The learning environment is then an interactive space where organizations, teams, and individuals become in turn agents and principals and interdependent in a temporary situation, with their incentives aligned along the logic of a project, which is a precondition for inclusion.

In a learning networked environment depicted by the Knowledge Triangle, parties enter into dynamic, reciprocal relationships and depend on each other. Their relationships are underlined by a series of discontinuous flows, which include core drivers of innovation: knowledge, talent, and capital. Research and technology activities in interrelation with business activities generate new knowledge, which is the source of innovation, and business activities interplaying with knowledge production are a source of new pathways for research and technology development. Higher education institutions along with peer-to-peer learning, and individual contextual learning journeys through life and the WWW, add value by producing new research and enhanced or novel technology and thus develop more relevant skills for conducting research, which improves the quality of education.

Through the knowledge of new markets, understanding of customers, and familiarity with business practices, commercialization of innovation becomes a steep learning curve. The demands of implementing new product and processes and designing new experiences makes education more relevant not only to the labor market but to the competitiveness of the individual, self-employed entrepreneurs as well as companies born to grow fast.

Adequate education provides people with a relevant skill set for innovation in business. How is value created within and between them? What kinds of flows take place in the value creation process manifested by integration of cutting edge innovation, entrepreneurial talent, and risk capital? What accelerates knowledge, talent, and capital flow, what slows down the velocity, and what brings qualitative change? To shed some light on these questions, it is necessary to understand in more depth the processes of knowledge production, dissemination, and commercialization in the context of the interlined, distributed learning environments recently established across Europe as the Knowledge and Innovation Communities.

Launching The First Knowledge and Innovation Communities

Innovation is a driver of growth and development. While this statement is backed by available evidence, there are a number of vital questions regarding what it actually means in the context of increasing competitiveness as a result of multifaceted dimensions of innovation, its inherent link with entrepreneurship, its new meaning in the network society, and new dynamics and logic in the global network of innovation networks, with emerging new business models for value creation, and new globalization dynamics accelerated by the financial crisis started in 2008. To what extent and in what way could Knowledge and Innovation Communities contribute to the elaboration of a new model for growth in Europe? What are the key characteristics of this model, and the drivers of processes within the Knowledge Triangle as well as the limitations and obstacles to their potential impact?

European clusters lack a critical mass of vibrancy and energy of emerging clusters, especially in the markets in transition, to change the dynamics of process in the global innovation network and become major nodes, although current size, excellence, and industry specialization is definitely a big asset to many innovation hubs in Europe. Connectivity has such a significant value because it is an enabler, which can change the status of a node or industry cluster. Because of the nature of innovation networks, regional clusters will become strengthened in the process of diffusion of innovation networks across Europe. This will become a driver for synergies across innovation capacity at the European scale and integrate, across and beyond borders, national innovation systems. The impact of co-location centers is achieved through their capacity to "bring people together conceptually through shared goals and operationally through shared infrastructure, capacity and activities" (ProInno 2010).

It can be assumed however that the Knowledge Triangle as a concept and its embodiment in the Knowledge and Innovation Communities will change the dynamics of innovation processes and resource accumulation in Europe. After two years of operations it may be too early to assess the model and draw conclusions, as the first analysis of practices emerging from the implementation of the Knowledge Triangle through three Knowledge and Innovation Communities was undertaken (Technopolis 2011). It would be interesting to take a snapshot of KICs moving from "naissance to toddler" stage and try to understand the dynamics of this evolution, the challenges encountered, and the solutions tested.

Under the logic of the global network of innovation networks, some nodes will become mega nodes, others will become significant, and others will remain peripheral. This stratification will result from their interconnectedness with other, global nodes of innovation networks relevant to the specificity of a KIC. The mega node will attract enough quality traffic to develop a "switching capability" through the critical mass of multilayering, multidimensional innovation networks. They will accumulate not only traffic but also quality resources: talent,

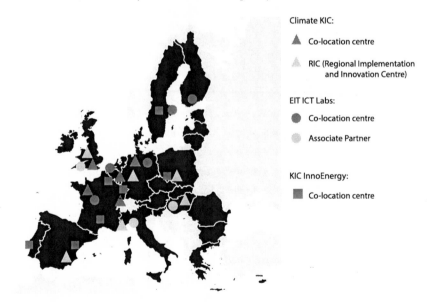

Figure 8. Map of KICs' Co-location Centers (2013).
Source: EIT

knowledge, and capital. Accumulation of resources will not be an automated process.

The case studies of the first three KICs will provide material for reflection on the possibilities and shortcomings of new innovation models. These cases are limited to the initial launch of the KICs between 2010 and 2013. In this chapter, the essence of the findings of the case studies will be presented, referring the reader to the appendix of the study for more details and a snapshot of partner institutions, themes, specializations and programming as of 2013.

Chapter 10

Climate-KIC

Climate-KIC was selected in the competitive Call for KICs organized in 2010 by the European Institute of Innovation and Technology for the thematic area of "Climate Mitigation and Adaptation." Climate-KIC addresses the global challenge related to climate change, which requires a major transformation of institutions, innovation models, and consumption patterns. Its mission is defined as a catalyst for these transformation processes in Europe by qualitative rearrangement of available and future resources and funding for innovation. Europe has taken a global leadership role on climate change with its 20% reduction target for 2020, its rapidly developing adaptation policy, and complementary national policies (Green Paper 2007). Europe 2020 shapes the EU's thinking about smart and sustainable growth, taking the "comprehensive path for the transition towards a low-emission economy" (European Economic Recovery Plan 2008).

The objectives of the KIC embrace and take to the operational level the European environmental strategy based on the research projections that global warming beyond 2°C above pre-industrial levels constitutes a dangerous interference with the global climate system. Since global economy needs to reduce CO_2 emissions by at least 50-85% against 2000 levels by 2050, while it is expected to grow by a factor of four, 10-fold growth in European carbon productivity is required by 2050 (IPCC-WGIII 2007). In the perspective of the European policy framework for coupling mitigation and adaptation of climate change with innovation, knowledge creation, and economic growth, Climate-KIC becomes an operational arm of the policy.

In the medium-term, Climate-KIC wants to become the place that businesses and governments come to for help in generating technical and policy solutions to their climate change challenges, and where top students go to become climate change innovators and entrepreneurs. Climate-KIC focuses on eight platforms defined by climate change mitigation and adaptation as shown here.

Network Governance

Climate-KIC, or "Association Climate-KIC," is a non-profit entity duly incorporated under the Laws of the Netherlands, and registered in Utrecht. Climate-KIC core partners include major companies, academic institutions, and regional agencies that collectively assign several billion Euros a year to climate activities. In 2010, the KIC's partners committed over 250 million EUR in projected annual KIC-led activities and asked for EIT contribution at the level of 120 million EUR over four years.

Climate-KIC brings together research institutes, universities, businesses, governmental bodies, and non-governmental organizations that are leading players in climate change innovation. Many of the governmental bodies are part of Climate-KIC's network of regional public agencies and municipalities from Eastern, Southern, and Western Europe. Its business partners include a high proportion (circa 50%) of SMEs and early stage innovation companies. These Climate-KIC partners are engaged via one of the co-location centers or regional implementation centers. They represent different sized institutions and organizations with global and local geographical reach.

Depending on their share in the liabilities of the Asssociation Climate-KIC, Climate-KIC offers two different types of partnerships:

- Core partners are members of the global Climate-KIC community, who share equally in any potential liabilities incurred by the Association Climate-KIC. They have a vote in the Assembly of the Association and can be elected to the governing board. They have the power to strategically shape the research focus, education program, management, and organizational structure of Climate-KIC.

- Affiliate partners are members without shared liability for the Association. They work through a co-location center or region on Climate-KIC through activities.

Climate-KIC was initially constituted as a foundation under the Dutch law. The governance model of the foundation did not turn out to be the optimal model, and Climate-KIC transformed it into an association established under the Dutch law. The restructuring of the governance model resulted in a growth in partner numbers, with a loss of some (three) former core partners, who were unwilling to take on shared liability for the Association, but with a net increase in new core partners who were keen to take on new powers and responsibilities.

According to the KIC management, issues related to governance allowed for clarifying the vision and business model of the KIC and ultimately positioned it for a rapid and multidimensional growth. The evolution of Climate-KIC may lead yet to another transformation, and the KIC leadership has declared the possibility of restructuring its legal set-up and governance structure in the foreseeable future into a company, which could better fit the emerging business model of the Climate-KIC[17].

Climate-KIC's supreme decision-making body is the General Assembly, a representation of each of the core partners and of two elected affiliate partner representatives. The General Assembly meets twice per year. This governing organ supervises and gives strategic guidance to the Governing Board comprising representatives of CLCs and RICs in the case of the Climate-KIC. The General Assembly handles major decisions regarding the partnership, while supervision and strategic guidance is provided to the KIC by its eleven-person Governing Board, chaired by Professor John Schellnhuber. The Governing Board includes nine representatives from the five co-location centers and one representative from the six regions of the Regional Innovation and Implementation Center. The representative does have a vote, providing it comes from a core partner. The board members are a mix of business, government, and university partners. Over its monthly meetings, the Governing Board oversees the mission and strategic vision for the KIC and appoints, appraises, or dismisses the CEO. The European Institute of Innovation and Technology, the supplier of up to 25% of the KIC's annual budget, is not represented either in the General Assembly or in the Governing Board.

Operationally, Climate-KIC is driven by a Chief Executive Officer, Professor Mary Ritter, and her executive team, which reflects its matrix organizational structure. The CEO has an executive function over all resources of the KIC and leads the KIC operations with a lean executive team, which slightly differs per KIC. In Climate-KIC, it is made up of the directors of the three core pillars (education, innovation, and entrepreneurship), its Director of Operations and the directors of its

(17) According to Mary Ritter, the CEO of Climate-KIC, it was unclear as of early 2013 whether Climate-KIC should become a limited liability company that is for or not-for-profit.

CLCs and the RIC. The management team is responsible for operations of the KIC and strategy implementation across the network.

Multilayering and Switching Capacity

Climate-KIC has developed a broad implementation and innovation network for knowledge sharing and dissemination, in which knowledge, talent, and funding flows take place at an accelerated pace. The organization of Climate-KIC tests a new Europe-specific innovation network, creating a new pattern of interlinked ecosystems built around co-location centers.

The Climate-KIC is designed around five nodes geographically distributed and located in established clusters. Being part of an ecosystem provides local support to innovation and in return feeds new dynamics into local innovation hubs by connecting with other ecosystems and attracting new resources in the KIC's co-location centers. Climate-KIC operates in five co-location centers located in London, Paris, Eindhoven, Berlin, and Zurich. Each co-location is responsible for interlinking with the local and regional existing structures and thus invigorating local innovation ecosystems. Following a model of a network enterprise, it involves partners at the level of their institutional units, which drive entrepreneurship and venture creation. A parallel network to CLCs is a network of six Regional Implementation Centers or RICs, which are interconnected with CLCs through implementation projects.

In co-location centers students find a new type of educational program with a strong focus on entrepreneurship. They are offered support when turning their entrepreneurial ideas into prototypes, and succeed or fail fast, which—in either case—builds hands-on experience in business. It is a fertile ground for start-ups to be incubated and for industry to locate their R&D centers. In some cases, CLCs are located in hubs where venture capital investors are concentrated as in the case of London. In the case of the Climate-KIC model based on a small number of CLCs, it is designed to overcome critical gaps in the growth phase of start-ups and SMEs, where classical venture capital models are not suitable either due to the length of investment into research and innovation or because at the earliest stage of emergence of climate mitigation and adaptation as an industry, the industry business model is based on or requires political support, funding, or subsidies.

Climate-KIC's CLCs are still "in-the-making," with each of them trying to find an optimal way to leverage its local resources and connections and the KIC's transnational network. For example, Climate-KIC's CLC in London is located within Imperial College's South Kensington Campus in the city center. Its office has a prestigious seat in the main location of the campus next to Imperial College's Incubation Centre and Imperial Innovations. Imperial College, as an academic institution, has an excellent track record in structured collaboration and networking with key stakeholders of the climate change knowledge cluster in the London metropolitan area and to some extent in the UK. Its established network includes academics, as well as policy makers and science and industry leaders.

In keeping with the original EIT vision for co-location, a major innovation campus is being built by Imperial and will become Climate-KIC's UK home in 2015. Climate-KIC Germany has already established itself within Berlin's climate change innovation hub at EUREF. This has enabled them to create a vibrant community outside of their parent institutions (TU Berlin and PIK). The site has been host to numerous pan-European idea marketplaces and student summer schools, and now hosts a significant number of start-ups in its Green Garage.

Many alumni of the Climate-KIC's summer school (the Contextual Learning Journey) have started companies or become intrapreneurs within multinational companies and governmental bodies. From the first year, five student companies were created and have continued to grow. One of the students, Moritz Meenen, started Electric Feel in Zurich. The company provides solutions for urban mobility, targeting corporate clients who want to enhance the benefit programs for their employees by offering one-way rentals of electric equipment.

The Technology Transfer Office (TTO) of the ETH Zurich has a remarkable track record of technology out-licensing to existing companies and spin-offs from the university, which is well integrated into the world-class level of the national innovation ecosystem. VentureKick, as a fund of Fondation des Fondateurs, is an umbrella foundation, monitored by the Swiss Federal Supervisory Board of Foundations, which has a mission to support spin-offs from Swiss academic institutions and increase their survival rate and fundraising capacity. CLCs provide future start-ups the ability to connect with this early stage seed fund to bridge their liquidity gap.

CLCs and RICs actively search for opportunities in the open innovation framework where they are fertile for spillover of knowledge and serendipity. During this learning process, unexpected opportunities may arise as in the case where Sainsbury's, a supermarket chain and CLC partner, considered becoming a customer in the process of developing and implementing environmentally responsible strategy and turning their stores "green" to fit with their customers' expectations and values. In other cases, joint research activities are developed, as in the case of PhD funding with the Grantham Institute and Master's scholarships from Santander.

Another example includes YESDelft!, student entrepreneur facilities developed with local TTO partners. The CLCs evolve into cross-CLCs projects, managed in an octagonal way across the KIC network. For example, the CLC in London and the CLC in Zurich leverage their resources through "The Smart Urban Adapt" project, which is the first applied research program between Imperial College London and ETH, launched within the framework of their partnership in the Climate-KIC.

Regional Implementation Centers form a network of implementation sites or regions in Poland, Hungary, United Kingdom, Germany, Spain, and Italy. Experimental solutions for innovative businesses and public institutions along with technology solutions for metropolitan areas or neighborhoods developed in CLCs are tested, reiterated, and calibrated. The six regions coordinating and delivering the Pioneers into Practice Program and the RIC Venture Support Program are pilot schemes taking the KIC Incubation Model one step further into the innovation process in reaching markets and society.

The RICs offer a model for integrating and leveraging the innovation capacity and potential of countries in Europe where CLCs are not located due to the lack of sufficient excellence-driven competence in climate change research innovation, or which for some reason did not partner with the Climate-KIC consortium. RICs as a model supplementing the CLCs network create an advantage for Climate-KIC by giving access to a broader range of knowledge, talent, and funding. They create a direct link between those who develop climate-related innovations and an open community of customers and end users of these innovations. The governance model of the network of Regional Innovation and Implementation Communities' is modeled after the European Regions Research and Innovation Network (ERRIN) of over 90 regions in Europe.

The collaboration model between the CLCs and RICs and between RICs is still in development. There is some early evidence of good practices. For example, RIC Lower Silesia region located in the south of Poland is strongly supported by the municipality of Wroclaw. EIT+ is a joint venture between the city and the five largest multidisciplinary universities in its metropolitan area. The company, launched as a potential partner for the Climate-KIC, has emerged as a competence center in Poland in climate related technologies and is looking into options for how to integrate and leverage the innovation potential of the Czech Republic in this area. The RIC took the initiative to host a two-day seminar, "Low Carbon Crucible," during which specialists from Great Britain, Hungary, and Holland prepared a compendium of best practices following the learning of the KIC's Pioneers into Practice program, which can help reach the targets of the EU 20/20/20 strategy in the Lower Silesia region, that is, lowering CO_2 emissions by 20% compared to 1990 levels, using 20% of renewable energy sources, and increasing energy efficiency by 20%.

The portfolio of projects and programs in innovation, commercialization, and education in the CLCs and RICs is monitored on a daily basis within the KIC's operational structure. Organized as a matrix structure, coordination activities between and across CLCs and thematic pillars ensure maximum interaction, synergy, networking, and effective allocation of resources at the pan-European level. Regular staff exchanges, management, and activities are organized throughout the network and by different partners to facilitate and encourage the flow of knowledge, talent, and funding both locally and internationally.

There is a similar pattern within the KIC in coordinating the activities of the CLCs. Two weekly formal conversations take place between the KIC CEO and the CLC directors on an operational level. Video conferences take place every few weeks, and one physical meeting is organized every month. The members of the working groups at the CLC level, which are similar to the KIC level, also conduct regular meetings and then report back to the KIC-level working groups. There is a dedicated effort to have members of the CLCs tour different CLCs so as to create opportunities to get to know each other and to not leave any node out.

Sheltered Innovation and Entrepreneurship

Climate innovation in Europe is driven by regions and cities. Climate-KIC drives innovation in climate change through new multimodal types of partnerships between business, academia, and public entities offering activities in three areas: education, entrepreneurship, and research and innovation. Climate-KIC enters a new, largely still non-consolidated market where private-public partnerships are often the only way to develop and implement integrated solutions to mitigate and adapt to climate change. The sector is very entrepreneurial and fragmented with small and early-stage companies rather than leading industry enterprises. Climate-KIC searches for a business model, which would offer a value proposition to its existing and new partners and in time develop revenue streams or equity stakes that would allow the Community to continue its activities and make impact when the grants within the Seven-Year Framework Agreement with the European Institute of Innovation and Technology end in 2018.

Strategies to address and help develop an integrated value chain in this emerging and fragmented market is a market opportunity for the Climate-KIC and its partners. The business model of Climate-KIC is based on a need for academies, industries, and governments to co-create innovative business and technology solutions to meet the climate challenge in the areas of four thematic specializations. Climate-KIC includes structural elements of the networked innovation processes and multidimensional value webs embracing education, commercialization, and new business creation.

It is still to be proven to what extent KIC partners will find this offering competitive enough to allocate quality resources and to what extent potential customers, for example KIC partners, municipalities, and regions, will find the KIC's solutions credible and feasible and scale them up so that they can generate revenue for the KIC. An option the leadership explores lies in an equity agreement with the KIC's start-ups, where the KIC would receive an equity stake in return for support and connection to the KIC network. As of 2012, these options were at the early stage of exploration and validation of emerging elements of the KIC's business model.

Climate-KIC receives funding from its core and affiliate partners, as well as a grant from the European Institute of Innovation and Technology within the Seven-Year Framework Agreement. The EIT grant constitutes up to 25% of the KIC's annual budget, which, when the KIC is fully operational and integrated, will reach the level between 50 and 100 million EUR per annum.

The KIC funding is used to fund its management costs and value-added activities in each of the three pillars—education, innovation, and entrepreneurship—in a way that integrates the Knowledge Triangle, that is, the institutions involved in the partnership. The flow of knowledge between education, research, and innovation is facilitated through three mechanisms: innovative projects sourced in open calls and developed in the sheltered innovation model within the entrepreneurial interconnected ecosystems; PhD and post-doctoral scholarships and fellowships for program-specific research and innovation projects; and mobility schemes for researchers, scientists, and entrepreneurs to work and socialize between and across co-location centers.

Contextual Learning Journeys

Innovation activities of Climate-KIC are driven as pan-European programs organized and integrated under the eight platforms. Some of these activities were started less than a year before and so it is too early to assess their impact. Each of the innovation projects within the platforms is led by a researcher or innovator responsible and accountable for the delivery of the project to its commercializable endpoint. The CLCs and RIC provides business and education support to accelerate and facilitate projects. The Platform team (a maximum of five experts) helps the CEO to shape and focus the portfolio of innovation and integrate across platforms. Operational decisions about project activities within platforms are conducted by the Innovation Team on behalf of the CEO. The objective of this approach is to enable the Climate-KIC to focus on market creation and exploitation for climate change innovation. The Innovation Team and Platform work together to run a project stage-gate process to enable the CEO to manage innovation failure and success dynamically.

Climate-KIC programs were planned to be operational for at least five years. The roll out of activities started with education and innovation. Entrepreneurship activities took a more robust shape in the second year of operations. The programs' topics were a result of discussions among partners, as well as an open challenge call for proposals to enable the KIC to take on-the-radar, emerging new opportunities with funding outside the existing programs.

Climate-KIC innovation activities are designed in line with the eight Platform objectives, and assessed by the probability of having a high impact on climate change mitigation and/or adaptation. Most projects involve several corporate, academic, and regional partners. High potential for market and economic value creation, which also leads to new jobs, is leveraged by the strengths of core partners. Each platform is facilitated by a CLC or the RIC. They provide administrative support to the platform team and to the workshops (idea marketplaces) that they run.

Climate-KIC education and training programs are designed to inspire climate change entrepreneurship. Climate-KIC provides added-value education programs that are taught entirely in English to hundreds of students and leading professionals. The courses, studies, and academic degree programs combine climate change science and entrepreneurship with an emphasis on learning-by-doing through hands-on participation in innovation and entrepreneurship activities.

Climate-KIC education is integrated into the platforms and their innovation projects. Students are exposed to action learning by working on real industry projects, case studies, and lectures, which are distributed across different settings in all co-locations, including Regional Innovation Implementation Communities and industry partners. Student projects and PhD theses are directly linked to Climate-KIC research and innovation projects characterized by their focus on commercial development and implementation programs rather than blue-sky research. Students are encouraged to use their skills, creative thinking, and risk-taking to develop new ventures and novel ideas.

Climate-KIC entrepreneurship activities involve a wide range of climate change entrepreneurship communities including students, young entrepreneurs, research and development centers, and venture capital investors. Their goal is to revisit European incubation models so that the existing business incubators and accelerators generate more born-global, high quality climate-related business start-ups. The duration of support is normally three to six months for each of the stages, depending on the development path of a startup.

The Climate-KIC model for new business incubation and acceleration is integrated, community-wide, and open to the general public, and it exploits the Climate-KIC partners' existing facilities, thus linking them into international networks, creating critical mass and synergies. It is composed of a number of short and long-term duration structured programs along a yearly cycle of building the entrepreneurial community.

Chapter 11

EIT ICT Labs

EIT ICT Labs focuses on the theme of the Future Information and Communication Society. The KIC leverages existing regional, national, and EU funding instruments with its partners' contribution and EIT grants to speed up innovation in Europe. The vision of the KIC is formulated in action terms as the ambition to "drive European leadership in ICT Innovation for economic growth and quality of life" by establishing a new type of partnership between leading companies, research centers, and universities in Europe with ICT as "an enabler to enhance the quality of life for everyone." The Knowledge Triangle conceptual model is a direct and straightforward model for the KIC to design its actions in a way to facilitate knowledge flows between its three sides. It catalyzes flows of knowledge integrating the three elements of the Knowledge Triangle—education, research, and innovation.

Industry-led Collaborative Partnership

EIT ICT Labs is a non-profit association established under the Belgian law. The overarching body of the association is the General Assembly. It consists of representatives of founding members of the KIC Association and includes initial partners of the first application for the EIT Call for KICs, who signed the first Seven-Year Framework Partnership Agreement with the EIT. The KIC's partners represent global corporations, universities, research institutes, and small entrepreneurial companies in the ICT sector. The Executive Steering Board is the governing body reporting to the General Assembly and carries the duty to oversee performance of the KIC's executive team.

The Executive Steering Board reflects the combined industry and academic leadership of the EIT ICT Labs. The board decides on the strategic direction the association takes, monitors and controls the KIC's activities, and appoints and appraises the KIC's CEO. All members of the association's Executive Steering Board have equal voting rights. Each member carries responsibility for management and operations of one of the co-location nodes. The Chair is Henning Kagermann from Acatech. The body has balanced representation of industry and academia. Each node is led by representatives of core partners.

There are three different categories of the KIC's partners: core, affiliate, and associate, each of them defined by a different contribution to the KIC budget and governance rights. Core partners are members of the KIC Association. Affiliate partners are typically universities, SMEs, or venture capital funds and other companies. They have a contractual agreement with the EIT ICT Labs KIC Association and a mandate to supply competence and human resources to one of the CLCs. They have access to general information on all activities, but no governance rights of the KIC. Associate partners are involved on a project basis with the KIC. They also have a contract with EIT ICT Labs KIC Association to obtain general information and have access to all EIT ICT Labs activities but no governing rights. The bulk of the EIT ICT Labs partners represent in a balanced way institutions and organizations from the initial policy concept of the Knowledge Triangle.

Spatial Articulation: Extending the Network

The KIC is an integrated network with six co-location centers or nodes in Germany, the Netherlands, France, Finland, Sweden, and Italy. It has been formed by leading European companies in the ICT industry and serves as an open innovation platform through networking, mobility, and international and interdisciplinary programs and projects.

EIT ICT Labs has six co-location centers or nodes located in the metropolitan areas of Berlin, Eindhoven, Helsinki, Paris, Stockholm, and Trento. An operational differentiation is visible in the structure between them, which, rather than being based on core competencies in terms of industry subsectors, undertakes a cross-disciplinary approach through each of the nodes, leading a "thematic line." The concept of "thematic lines" is an element of the KIC's strategy in organizing its activities in such a way as to integrate approaches to deliver solutions rather than services to satisfy particular needs. EIT ICT Labs speaks of itself as "an Innovation Factory for ICT Innovation in Europe and the innovation action lines are our production lines." The thematic lines "are a way to address key societal issues in a number of selected areas for which ICT can bring forward significant improvements."

The CLCs display interesting differences in an emerging node's identity and positioning within the KIC. Some nodes are described through their core competencies (e.g. cloud computing); others market themselves through focus on education (Berlin, Stockholm), business (Berlin), research (Berlin, Helsinki, Paris); while others emphasize their leading role in particular action lines (e.g. Smart Energy Systems, Intelligent Mobility and Transportation Systems). The functional specialization in education is visible in the case of the Stockholm Node, which leads the Master schools, and the Berlin node, which is also responsible for education catalysts and the software campus. Quite a distinctive case is the Eindhoven node. It offers its space as the physical and virtual meeting point for KIC-level workshops and SMEs expanding their operations in other EU countries. The table below presents the specific characteristics of the EIT ICT Labs' CLCs.

There is a built-in resilience at the KIC and CLC levels against the differentiating of nodes in terms of their status in the network. Action line matrix is one of the mechanisms to keep nodes valuable in the network. Each node has a field specialization as a "pillar" or leader of an action line. However, the process of program stratification and thematic differentiation will gradually take place. For example, the KIC management sees added value in strengthening the Berlin node, which is in itself a hotspot for technology but also for avant-garde art design, culture enabling the integration of digital media and services in a multidisciplinary and multidimensional way characteristic of the network society.

The dynamics of collaboration with industry partners depends on the structure of the national system. At the CLC level, the interaction is quite different in Finland or Sweden where there is one dominant industry player, Nokia and Ericsson. A different type of project is developed in Germany, where the Berlin node consists of six core partners (Deutsche Telekom AG, Siemens AG, SAP AG, Fraunhofer Gesellschaft e.V., DFKI GmbH, and TU Berlin) and six affiliate partners (Max Planck Institute for Informatics; Saarland University; TU Darmstadt, The Center for Advanced Security Research Darmstadt (CASED); TU München; Karlsruhe Institute of Technology (KIT); and EICT GmbH). Linking the Berlin node internally within the KIC and within Germany with partners in the Munich region (Siemens ICT corporate research, Technische Universität München, with its associated institutes CDTM, Unternehmer TUM, and fortiss) builds tightly-knit and at the same time loosely-coupled connections within the German innovation system.

The dissemination of the EIT ICT Labs' network is dependent on personal connections of individuals and good connections point-to-point at the institutional level. A contractual "umbrella" between the partners and the EIT is built over a personal connection through a formal collaboration agreement drafting the framework conditions of cooperation and securing financial support. Existing industry contacts are a good link with international ecosystems. For example, Phillips is well connected to China and the Unites States, especially with MIT and Stanford. The Stockholm node also has a good connection with Asia, especially in the field of education. Trento has connections with Israel. The KIC's network will extend to Brazil through new collaboration with a Spanish entity as an associated partner group. Berkeley Institute is well linked with German, Finnish, and Italian nodes. Often the existing exchanges, while exciting and valuable, do not bring expected value in terms of helping the nodes become better connected due to the dominance of one-way communication and outflow of human resources rather than exchanges. This is because this connectedness is not balanced in terms of two-way quality flow.

As a result of collaboration, nodes are at risk of losing resources—in this case, human capital. While a stay of two or three months abroad or at a different CLC seems too short to develop meaningful relationships, the probability of return after two years' work elsewhere decreases significantly. Being too connected puts at risk the existing ties with a node.

Catalyst-Carrier Model

The catalyst-carrier model developed by the EIT ICT Labs is based on a concept that the EIT funding should act as a catalyst for leveraging and rearranging existing ICT capabilities and resources in Europe, especially those represented by the KIC's partners. The KIC's business model is underwritten by the accessible innovation resources of partners such as on-going innovation projects, patents, and licenses. According to the KIC management, the catalyst-carrier model leads to strategic evolution of ecosystems at the EU level and at the level of co-location centers.

Based on the catalyst-carrier concept, EIT ICT Labs proposed a business model. It is driven by digital communication in the network society and is focused around screening innovation-driven ICT market opportunities, applying ICT to other business domains, identifying new research areas, and adapting to social changes arising from open innovation.

According to the EIT ICT Labs, its business model entails: implementing a lean and agile governance structure, which is reaching out on a European scale to ensure free flow of ideas, innovations, business, and venture capital across geographical, organizational, and cultural borders; creating an innovation flow between different stakeholders in the innovation web and integrating education and research into innovation activities at the earliest stage of ideation; and facilitating access to critical and relevant knowledge and expertise, through the network of co-location centers interconnected with national innovation systems and global innovation chains.

The EIT ICT Labs catalyst-carrier model is applied to processes and knowledge flows in the Knowledge Triangle, among and between education, research, and innovation—interpreted as business or for-profit activity. Creating interfaces between education, research, and innovation, the KIC's activities are "catalytic" to innovations in the sense that they address a barrier to the free flow of knowledge within the Knowledge Triangle. A portfolio of carrier activities includes EIT ICT Labs' projects, to which innovation catalysts are applied, such as co-funded research projects, and co-funded educational and business programs. Projects eligible as a carrier activity are financed with the co-funding from EIT grants.

The catalyst-carrier model is underwritten by connectedness among the KIC's partners at the personal and institutional levels. Connectedness is defined through public acknowledgement of a mutually recognized and respected relationship. Connectedness also means having a relationship at the right level of the network. For example, the Chair of the ICT Labs Governing Board is an advisor to Angela Merkel, which means that he is politically connected within the national context. Connectedness at the level of partners is vital to keep the KIC high on their agenda. The KIC's CEO has direct contact with university presidents and industry partners at the level of the CEO or CTO with the possibility for personal interaction and direct contact. KIC's Education Director interacts at the level of Vice-rectors for Education. Action lines/pillar directors and project managers have connections at their respective levels in partnering organizations.

The portfolio of EIT ICT Labs activities combines research, education, and innovation projects. They are executed in academic settings, in established industry partners, and in newly founded companies in the entrepreneurial ecosystem of the CLCs. They are focused around action lines addressing selected grand societal challenges and driven by community needs and available opportunities phased out in a three-step process moving from ideation and creation, through bridging the gap between the world of ideas and labs with the market, to the last phase, during which projects are accelerated to rapidly build value or fail fast. The KIC has chosen strategic action lines, including: Smart Spaces, Smart Energy Systems, Health Wellbeing, Digital Cities of the Future, Future Media and Content Delivery, and Intelligent Mobility and Transportation Systems.

The KIC interprets the Knowledge Triangle model as a starting point for the development of a number of initiatives to facilitate the collaboration between academia and business with user-driven innovation and technology-driven venturing. It implements this strategy through a catalyst-carrier model.

The educational programs, both the Master and the Doctoral schools, have a focus on entrepreneurship education. They aim to inspire and empower students by integrating them vertically and horizontally in innovation ecosystems interlinked by the structure of CLCs. This starts with redesigning the curricula, teaching methods, and student and faculty mobility programs across countries and between academia and business. Programs offered fulfill quality criteria for EIT labeled education and are supported by the EIT grants. Education activities include three-level graduate and postgraduate degree programs: Master school, Doctoral school, and the Post-doctoral program. Non-degree training is in the portfolio as an outreach toward the stakeholders outside the KIC. Programs share infrastructure for teaching and mobility. Some of them, in particular Innovation Entrepreneurship Education for Doctoral Programs and Innovation Entrepreneurship Education for Master Programs, are co-designed and delivered in partnership with European business schools.

Business-related "catalyst" activities foster innovation linked with entrepreneurial activities in the industrial setting. The KIC supports entrepreneurs with a business idea that falls within EIT ICT Labs' focus areas. The KIC has an ambition to revisit incubation models in established companies and help start-ups go to international markets. The KIC provides help in facilitating access to finance, business networking, working with Technology Transfer Offices at its partners' premises, and soft-landing services allowing local entrepreneurs to explore possibilities of entering markets where other CLCs are located. The Innovation Radar of EIT ICT Labs is an example of a project targeted for industry partners. It offers a continuous platform of collaboration between companies that are often competitors in the market—Siemens, Ericsson, Nokia. This open framework for co-opetition helps them come together in a neutral environment and identify emerging trends in the ICT market or work on industry standards.

Emphasis on entrepreneurship is a common denominator for all programming. An early phenomenon, which is a result of this focus on an emergence of a new type of researcher, is quite absent or marginal in a number of universities which partner in the KIC. It is an "entrepreneurial researcher," who can be defined as a scholar who is well respected in the academic community and at the same time engaged in entrepreneurial activities characterized by generating one or more start-ups along with the master's or PhD students. The researcher can be involved directly as an investor, which is usually linked with membership on a Supervisory Board, or even an executive position as CEO or CTO of the start-up.

The contribution to creating spin-offs or start-ups can also be indirect. A researcher is a consultant, coach, or mentor, who helps, on the basis of research experience, translate research into a venture; if he has hands-on entrepreneurial experience, he leads the management team and helps the business grow and expand. This phenomenon of the emergence of a new legitimate type of researcher is quite unusual for example in France, which is known for its rather conservative research culture. Since the KIC has a network-making power, it can connect networks of SMEs based in the Paris metropolitan region and international networks of its partners and CLCs, which leads to the emergence of a new type of academic professor with a new code of acceptable behavior of what can be done and what cannot be done at universities and research organizations.

Chapter 12

KIC
InnoEnergy

KIC InnoEnergy is the Knowledge and Innovation Community selected in 2009 by the European Institute of Innovation and Technology as an outcome of the EIT Call for KICs in the area of sustainable energy. The KIC activities are based on integrating the Knowledge Triangle—the domains of education, research, and innovation—by fostering the culture of innovation and entrepreneurship. KIC InnoEnergy wants to become the "leading engine for innovation and entrepreneurship in the field of sustainable energy." The question of sustainability is objectified through cost reduction in the energy value chain (supply, transport, storage, distribution, and retail), increase of security (both as independence from external suppliers and as operational security), and reduction of CO_2 and other greenhouse gas emissions. These three goals are addressed by six thematic areas: Clean Coal Technologies; European Smart Electric Grids (Electric Storage); Intelligent, Energy-efficient Buildings and Cities; Energy from Chemical Fuels; Renewables; Sustainable Nuclear Renewable Energy Convergence.

The strategy of the KIC is based on the collective strength of its founding shareholders, which include 28 top industrial organizations, higher education institutions, and special energy industry small and medium-sized enterprises that complement the value chain. Given its clear business focus, the KIC mobilizes underexploited resources, leverages the network, and builds commercial value through a number of processes ranging from education, business creation, and innovation to technology development. They catalyze the speed and quality of technology translation and dissemination, and deliver a new breed of entrepreneurial graduates with understanding of the energy sector in different markets; new products, services, and standards; and novel business models and start-ups.

KIC InnoEnergy is a commercial company, incorporated as Societas Europea (SA) and headquartered in the Netherlands. SA has 29 shareholders, who represent key industries, research centers, and universities in the energy field in Europe. While KIC InnoEnergy is profit-oriented, it claims to have a "not for dividend" financial strategy and a commitment to reinvesting the company's profits back into the KIC's activities. The shareholders committed 700 million EUR over seven years for the period 2010-2014. Other partners contributing to KIC activities have different statuses as formal partners, associated partners, or network partners. Each type of partner has rights and obligations, but only the so-called formal partners or the shareholders have governance rights.

Tightly-Knit, Loosely-Coupled

KIC InnoEnergy is a six-node network. Its co-location centers are located in France, Germany, Holland, Poland, Iberia, and Sweden. Co-location centers are embedded into local innovation ecosystems. For example, the office of the CLC Iberia of KIC InnoEnergy is located within the UPC campus in the same building as various different SMEs and the creativity departments of large companies, e.g. Intel and Gallina Blanca. The KIC's incubator is hosted by "Creapolis," the ESADE Business School innovation center in San Cugat, a small town in the Barcelona metropolitan area.

Geographically, the KIC's partners are spread from Barcelona, to Madrid, Northern Spain, and Lisbon in Portugal. KIC InnoEnergy CLC in Alps Valleys is located in the Giant Innovation Campus of Grenoble, in a central location of the city, in the same building as the CEA. In the same area there are also many excellent research centers and universities ranked among the best in France, and several examples of fruitful synergies between research, higher education, industry, and local government. Large investments for research and innovation as well as Capenergies and Tenerrdis, two industrial clusters, are dedicated to energy technological innovation at the national level. Other vital stakeholders for innovation include technology transfer subsidiaries, incubators, venture capitalists, and an Economic Development Agency.

The CLCs include also Cadarache in Provence, because of its competencies and unique facilities in the nuclear field, gathering fission and fusion. The CLC is in charge of the scientific coordination of activities in its core competencies. The CLCs of this KIC specialize in projects related to the convergence of nuclear and renewable energy. The Rhône Alps is a region with a highly developed innovation ecosystem and a sound industrial background both in terms of presence of major corporations and dynamic SMEs.

This type of collaboration between research and industry partners co-located in this area existed before the CLC was created. CEA, INPG, GEM, and Schneider have been located in very close vicinity along with different regional structures for stimulating growth of high-tech companies such as Gravit, Grain, and Pétale. They have successfully contributed to developing innovation chains from the proof of concept to the creation of start-up in biotechnologies and microelectronics. The idea is that because of the CLC's activities, this ecosystem will produce many new start-ups in nuclear and renewable energy technologies principally or in any of the other thematic fields of KIC InnoEnergy.

While each CLC of KIC InnoEnergy has its own area of expertise, all CLCs are also involved and carry out joint cross-CLC activities.

Placing a CLC in an ecosystem changes its status and meaning in the local community and as a node of international innovation networks. The results and benefits can spread from more investment to various non-monetary outcomes, sometimes a result of serendipity. For example, KU Leuven has a comprehensive entrepreneurial ecosystem, which includes business accelerator and venture funds. In 2011, the university managed to attract an additional 22 million EUR because of its affiliation with the KIC, which enhanced its educational offers and standards. On the other hand, language barrier was a major obstacle to interconnect KU Leuven University students and faculty with other universities and with industry. Traditionally, classes in the region of Flanders were held in Dutch. Following a letter from Karen Maex, EIT Governing Board Member, to the Belgium Ministry of Education, KU Leuven succeeded in getting the permission to teach all EIT-label programs in English, triggering a batch of new English-language master's programs.

The establishment of the CLC at the campus in Leuven introduced a new culture-shaping element. The common model of silos approach began to be replaced with a more collaborative mode of sharing research results rather than competing for resources. The shift toward a more market-oriented and solution-based attitude among researchers is in fact a shift of mindsets from the prevailing purely research oriented approach dominant in the Framework Programs. An emerging phenomenon is cross-KIC synergies with direct collaboration developed not only at the KIC level but also by CLCs with other CLCs in different KICs. As of 2012, collaboration is envisaged between partners of the EIT ICT Labs and Climate-KIC, led by their partners, TU Berlin and Imperial College.

InnoEnergy Highway as an Emerging Business Model

The KIC InnoEnergy Highway is a novel accelerator model developed by the KIC in order to "nurture" entrepreneurial ventures coming out of its distributed and interconnected ecosystems of the co-location nodes and beyond. The KIC revisited the traditional incubation concept and proposed a new kind of pan-European incubator with six entry points physically located at the premises of its co-location centers and virtually in the Web.

The model has a few distinctive features. First, it is a hybrid between a traditional incubator and a virtual crowd-sourcing model. Second, it facilitates deal flow across Europe, leveraging the advantage of the free flow of capital, people, and knowledge in the European Single Market. Third, because of its focus on sustainable energy, it has a clear specialization in six energy fields ranging from nuclear and clean coal to renewables. It has an advantage of developing ventures at the borderline of energy subsectors and offering unique crossbreed technology solutions such as nuclear and renewables. Fourth, one of the unique selling propositions of KIC InnoEnergy Highway is the commitment to get the first customer to its clients—born-global start-ups. It seems quite feasible, taking into consideration the extended participation of energy companies as its shareholders and partners. Finally, it is a "one stop shop" and supports a start-up through an integrated process from the earliest stages of incubation to post-revenue.

The value proposition offered by the KIC InnoEnergy Highway has been successfully implemented process-wise and has brought first results demonstrated by first formal shareholders agreements, where the KIC is a minority shareholder, as well as by the growing deal log pipeline and signed term sheets. During the first year of operation, eight green field start-ups have been created, which have signed the first commercial contract with a real customer. It links transnational incubation processes with specialization in the sustainable energy sector and has direct access to potential strategic investors and customers, which are leading European companies in the energy sector.

The approach of the KIC toward business incubation is to develop a pan-European test-bed with six entries and to enhance the capabilities of its CLCs, whose partners may not have proper incubation infrastructures with competence in the thematic field. This is compensated by access to developed generic facilities, incubation networks, and venture business offices. This particular incubator, unlike existing models, is not only a physical office space by a pan-European innovation network interconnected with the global network. The KIC's model may in time become a European brand for innovation in this sector and enhance the innovativeness of its industry partners.

Through this networked model of innovation, new ventures are exposed to global opportunities. They receive advice on reiterating technology if needed, access to labs, protecting IP, organizing marketing and sales, structuring finance, and shareholding, and access to talent, especially KIC InnoEnergy students. For start-ups, which enter into the InnoEnergy Highway, acquisition of their first customer is a turning point. Bridging the gap between labs and market in the energy sector is difficult not only because of competition but also because of the specific safety and security requirements, confidential and highly protected deployed technological solutions.

When tested in real-life circumstances, technology can be both demonstrated and validated, which allows further experimentation, enhancement, and calibration of solutions. For a young venture, being part of the Innovation Highway provides an opportunity to attract talent and develop its operational structure. Ventures that already have the first customer and are at a certain operational stage of growth have a significantly higher probability of finding an investor. The valuation of the company at the pre-revenue stage is dramatically increased after the first paying customers prove the solution credible. The incentive structure for the KIC InnoEnergy is aligned with offering service for KIC InnoEnergy Highway customers. The KIC signs a partnership agreement and in return gets for its service an equity stake up to 10% or a share in future revenue streams and licensing fees depending on a company's business model.

Measuring Impact

As a for-profit company, KIC InnoEnergy's strategy is output driven. The Community defines its business goals, milestones, and key performance indicators quantified in terms of output, e.g. number of students, patents filled, and new business ventures. It aims to deliver outputs defined as entrepreneurial people, innovative products and processes, and new companies. To get to those results, the KIC offers a set of novel educational programs (Master's, Executive, and PhD levels), runs technological innovation projects in selected topics of the six described thematic fields, and offers a portfolio of added services or business incubation and acceleration.

Over the first 16 months since its inception, the KIC enrolled 146 students in Master's programs, 28 engineers in PhD schools, and 21 professionals in Executive programs. A number of key features are integrated into each program design and curriculum. They include mobility between CLCs as an integrated element of the entrepreneurship training, business case–based teaching methods, skills training in the industry setting through internships, customer focus, and market orientation. From the earliest stages, industry partners are engaged in curricula design, the selection of candidates, and the teaching and coaching of innovation projects. In terms of technology, the KIC filed 11 patents at an average cost of 1 million EUR investment per patent and 23 new technological products and services. The KIC's business creation services helped nurture 52 ventures in incubators specialized in sustainable energy over the KIC InnoEnergy Highway.

The KIC leverages not only the existing resources and capabilities of its partners but also aligns its strategy with other European policy instruments designed or managed by EP, JRC, DG RD, and DG ENER. For example, KIC InnoEnergy is present in 12 of the 17 groups of the SET plan education initiatives and leads two of them. KIC has been awarded 9 million EUR in co-funding in 2012 under the Marie Sklodowska-Curie initiative. The KIC is represented at the Joint Research Center Advisory Board.

The KIC measures its "foreseeable impact," calculating that: "If we take as 100 the cost of any good produced/consumed in Europe, 27 is energy cost. Thus 1% of reduction in the cost of energy will represent 20 billion EUR of savings, thus of additional competitiveness of the European industry." When the KIC reaches maturity (with a target annual budget of EUR 400 million), KIC InnoEnergy will be producing 4% of master's degree engineers in sustainable energy in Europe, the objective being that they should become "game changers" of the energy sector by getting to the CXO and top research position levels.

Entrepreneurial Education

The KIC Master and PhD programs integrate education with innovation. The KIC offers a wide range of Master classes, each specialized in one of the thematic fields chosen as strategic focus. The KIC partners include leading universities and companies in each of the CLCs. They cooperate in designing curricula and teaching. Industry partners acknowledge that in the case of the KIC's educational programs there is a different level and quality of collaboration. The tendency of academia to disregard the value of such tight collaboration is replaced by partnership and appreciation of mutual benefits.

The degrees are attractive educational offerings for specific types of students, who are interested in the energy sector and at the same time considering an entrepreneurial career as their life choice, either upon graduation or at a later stage in life. Students go through an international learning experience, which gives them insight into the energy industry at the European level and at the same time a global perspective where engineering and technology solutions are applied to tackle grand challenges. They learn-by-doing and acquire entrepreneurial skills during hands-on action-based training in business creation. Entrepreneurship is an intrinsic part of the curricula and used in branding and marketing. Master classes use for marketing purposes the slogan: E2=MC ("Entrepreneurship in Energy needs a Master Class").

An example of a Master program is a degree in Clean Coal Technologies (CleanCoal), a joint program of five European universities. These academic institutions (AGH University of Science and Technology (AGH) in Kraków, Poland; Silesian University of Technology (SUT) in Gliwice, Poland; Royal Institute of Technology (KTH) in Stockholm, Sweden; Instituto Superior Tecnico (IST) in Lisbon, Portugal; and Karlsruhe Institute of Technology (KIT) in Karlsruhe, Germany) co-design a program that prepares students to engage in development and application of technologies related to efficient thermal and chemical conversion of coal with reduced pollutant emissions to air, water, and land with the focus on integration of chemical fuels and renewables to create sustainable and high efficiency solutions with a view on global environmental challenges.

Training in innovation and entrepreneurship is an integral part of the curriculum of this two-year, double-degree Master program with emphasis on multi-disciplinary education encompassing mechanical engineering, energy engineering and management, chemical engineering/technology, environmental engineering, communication, and law. An example of the showcase created by this different approach is a team of five KIC InnoEnergy master's students who won second place in the Hult Global Challenge. This challenge, sponsored by the Clinton Foundation, is a global competition that offers a prize of USD 1 million to the best business and technological solution. Business schools and technical universities worldwide participate every year with their best and brightest.

Ranking second in this prestigious Hult Global Challenge was a clear success for the KIC student team and a demonstration that top talent has no home country. The challenge is how to keep the talent in European companies and institutions, even if the professional career of the talent takes a student outside Europe. In 2011, approximately ninety percent of 190 students were non-Europeans.

Chapter 13

KNOWLEDGE AND INNOVATION COMMUNITIES: A KIC MODEL

In 2008 the EIT Regulation, which outlined the concept of a Knowledge and Innovation Community, was adopted by the European Parliament and the Council. KICs had already been nicknamed "five-legged animals" after four years of public consultations and discussions of their model. On a positive note, this statement reflected the novelty of the model, which as a concept was truly unique, even taking into consideration all other existing innovation networks in Europe and elsewhere.

However, it also was a clear expression of doubt that this original model of a Europe-specific innovation network developed in the environment of innovation policy makers could be translated into operational entities, attract substantial private sector investment, move the best European research universities to create joint degrees, and have academia and industry collaborate more closely on educational programs, research projects, and open innovation. The ultimate skepticism toward the KIC model was voiced by the leading excellence-driven academic institutions in Europe. The approach of industry also shifted from openness to a "waiting mode" in the face of financial crises, which started in 2008.

Additionally, a number of governments and stakeholders openly expressed concerns that this excellence-driven initiative would increase rather than bridge the divide and innovation gap between less developed countries and the rest of Europe. In this atmosphere, the three KICs were selected by the end of 2009 and incorporated in 2010. In the same year and in 2011, all three signed the Framework Agreement with the EIT, giving them access to public grants for at least seven years and thus establishing a stable, long-term base for complex, multidimensional research and innovation projects. Each of the KICs covers one of the interdisciplinary and intersecting thematic areas: Climate Mitigation and Adaptation, Sustainable Energy, and Future Innovation and Communication Society.

The concept of Knowledge and Innovation Communities, these "five-legged animals," is complex and multidimensional. They are network enterprises, which means that they operate as a portfolio of collaborative projects, in which different organizations or rather their specific units enter into strategic alliances for limited periods of time.

In terms of spatial articulation, these innovation networks have five or six nodes, or the so-called "co-location centers," which are distributed across Europe. Every node has a physical, brick-and-mortar presence in a large or medium-sized metropolitan area, where a significant part of an innovation value web has already been located. Each KIC has an organizational structure of a network of a few co-location centers; however, two of the KICs have parallel networks of different functions and structures. In the case of Climate-KIC and CLC, the network is complemented by a network of six Regional Implementation Centers. In the case of EIT ICT Labs, this is a network of six affiliate partners. The nodes are interlined through mobility schemes and virtual connectivity in the digital environment. In some cases, the nodes are placed in dynamic entrepreneurial ecosystems, which are also major nodes of the global networks, for example of venture capital.

The network members or partners are internationally distributed but thematically convergent parties representing three sides of the Knowledge Triangle: research, education, and innovation. In the legal and formal sense, the KICs are public-private-partnerships and include universities, industry, governments, research, and non-profit organizations.

As legal entities they have a governance structure and accountable management with executive power over all KIC resources. They are business-driven toward financial self-sustainability so that when the public EIT funding is withdrawn at a certain point, they will be able to further expand, having a sound customer-oriented value proposition and a business model. Although they have a long-term agreement with the EIT, the grand allocation decisions are taken on an annual basis following the KIC's business plans and meeting the milestones and satisfactory Key Performance Indicators.

The KICs search for optimal ways to implement the mission of the European Institute of Innovation and Technology, the founding institution. They are united around the EIT mission to become "a key driver of sustainable European economic growth and competitiveness through the stimulation of top-class innovations with a positive impact on economy and society."

To achieve this objective, the KICs develop mechanisms to catalyze processes in the innovation webs through a number of intersecting project-oriented activities. The projects pipeline is built and managed during a structured process specific to each KIC. This is a bottom-up approach open to a different degree to KIC and also non-KIC stakeholders. The ideas for joint projects are developed at the level of the CLCs and are coordinated and managed at the KIC level. The projects include specific activities in one of the three key areas: entrepreneurial and entrepreneurship-driven engineering and science education, interdisciplinary and transdisciplinary research and innovation, and new venture incubation and acceleration. Each KIC has a different approach to defining, structuring, and organizing its activities, which are targeted often to quite diverse groups.

The management of the KICs is modeled on the good practices of the private sector, including the incentive model and competitive remuneration. Each KIC is led by a CEO who heads a small executive team. The CEO controls all of the assets of the KIC as a legal entity, is accountable for its operations, finances, and results, and reports to the KIC's Governing Board. Each of the co-location centers has its own director, who is part of the KIC's executive team. KICs deploy different organizational structures to manage the network. The executive team is employed full-time by the KIC, while other employees often share their time between other projects.

The legal structure of the KICs differs. KIC InnoEnergy is a for-profit company incorporated as Societa Europea in the Netherlands. Two other KICs are not-for-profit associations. Climate-KIC is registered in Belgium and EIT ICT Labs is registered in the Netherlands. Partnership agreements are flexible in that they foresee exit/entry mechanisms for partners. The formal relationship between the KICs and their CLCs is a commercial or shareholding agreement, since CLCs are incorporated in their own right. The memberships in the KICs' networks or partnerships have a stratified structure. The core partners are usually quite limited in number and oscillated around 20 organizations. Associated or affiliated partners include a significant number of stakeholders ranging from 80 up to approximately 200.

In each consortia core partners include a few large multinationals or large companies, and also a few excellent European research universities and universities of science and technology. KICs find it quite difficult to engage small and medium-sized companies into their structure and so they are integrated at the level of projects rather than governance. In the case of Climate-KIC, local, regional, and national governments play a significant role as a partner or co-owner of entities involved in the KIC. The legal mechanisms of each KIC have provisions enabling the exit and entrance of partners. There is a record of both events happening on a dynamic basis, making KICs living and flexible structures, with the EIT ICT Labs opening the sixth node of its network in Italy.

The cooperation between the EIT and each KIC was to be formalized through a seven year Framework Partnership Agreement, with defining objectives, rights, and obligations of each party, and the nature of activities that a KIC is to perform. The long-term legal framework allows funding of value-added activities, activities that would not take place if there were no access to EIT grant funding. The EIT makes annual grant decisions for each KIC on a competitive basis depending on the KIC's business plans, a rolling triennial work program outlaying the activities planned for that period, and an estimate of financial needs.

The funding model of the KICs is based on a 4:1 leverage, whereby the EIT's annual contribution covers up to 25% of the overall KIC annual budget and is allocated to added value activities. KIC partners provide complementary 75% funding also in the form of in-kind contribution, their on-going projects, European grants, and national funding. This is a unique EIT feature and an attempt to develop a new governance model toward the KICs and within the KICs as public-private-partnerships.

The KICs also pioneer simplification mechanisms for grant monitoring. In the period of 2010-2012, the three KICs attracted a substantial and growing non-EIT contribution. It includes, from a variety of sources such as other EU instruments (Framework Program, Structural Funds), the cash or in-kind contribution of academic and industry partners, and the revenues generated from a KIC's activities. Within the first two years of operation, the KICs attracted 78.5% of the total budget from non-EIT sources: 38.5% from partners' contribution, 21.5% from national and regional governments, and 13.5% from other EU programs. The split shows that the EIT funding reached almost 21.5% and the total KICs budget from public sources, excluding members or shareholders, was at the level of 56.5%. This gives a balanced funding structure for a PPP.

Despite the crisis, the KICs have attracted significant industry commitment that is constantly growing, EU funds, and national resources, since the EIT grants cover up to 25% of their annual operating budgets, which range from 50 to 100 million EUR per year. From the beginning, the KICs have managed to access the global talent pool and students from outside Europe have constituted a significant percent of total enrollment.

The KICs catalyze changes in the national innovation systems offering an alternative to the traditional Framework Programs' research funding schemes. They are still in the experimental phase and they have embraced the model in a different way. While they have generated the first tangible results already within the first 18 months of their operation, it is premature to assess the viability of their different models, especially since each of them is also preconditioned by the industry sector in which it operates. Ownership, accountability, and personal risk-taking are considered to be positioned in the center of their open innovation-driven, entrepreneurial culture.

While all of the KICs are managed by a CEO, the background of the leadership epitomizes to a large degree the origins of a KIC's core partners, who formed the winning consortia. Consequently, Climate-KIC is driven by universities, and EIT ICT Labs and KIC InnoEnergy by industry, with the latter having a more entrepreneurial focus. Entrepreneurship as a key driver of multidimensional innovation processes in the Knowledge Triangle is a common area of exploration and experimentation.

The network approach of a KIC, together with its governance structure and the focus on exploitation of innovation, are distinctive features of the EIT approach to reinventing innovation (Expert Group 2007). According to this report, KICs "address long-term EU societal challenges offering new opportunities for innovation in Europe. The KICs' goal is to drive real impact through the training of entrepreneurs in higher education, through new business creation leading to new products and services for the existing EU industry, and through the creation of new businesses (including SMEs) in Europe." KICs are striving to be driven by entrepreneurial culture and are driven by common visions and goals expressed in a business plan. The KICs' innovative webs of excellence" should slowly spread across Europe and interconnect with global networks.

The KIC as a new type of operationalization of the EU innovation strategy represents value in itself as an experiment, as a learning environment, and as a public policy innovation. Through reiterations of the legal framework, the governance model, and the strategy, the KIC model can be enhanced and calibrated. Since their launch, the KICs have impacted other dominant models and have ultimately reinvented and accelerated the transformative processes in the innovation arena at the EU level at the level of the European Member States.

All three KICs have conceived quite different value propositions, which are partly dependent on the industry sector and structure in which they operate, and partly dependent on taking a different approach. The establishment process of the first three KICs demonstrated the complexity of a KIC concept in a number of stages and aspects. First, the partners did not share a common understanding of what a KIC and its CLCs are. They did not have unanimous views on legal framework, governance, value proposition, and management.

By nature, a partnership of competing companies in an innovation network with universities and research organizations has created a number of potential tensions and even deal-breakers, with IP policy being one area of potential disagreement. The overall issue across all of the forming partnerships was a question of how to build trust, align conflicting interests, and commit quality resources in a situation of multiple, often urgent needs, to address innovation challenges at the institutional level and embrace entrepreneurship as a driver of collaborative processes in the Knowledge Triangle of education, research, and innovation.

The sustainability of commitment has been a constant point of discussion among partners. The difficulty of the process sometimes weakened their dedication and in a few cases led to a withdrawal from the consortium. The KIC model has undoubtedly triggered with its distinctive features a new mode of strategizing and implementing a pan-European angle to the networked models. It can be argued that this qualitative rearrangement of resources along new processes and governance models converges into a new model of growth for Europe.

Innovation Policies Beyond the Crisis

The global financial crisis that started in 2008 shuttered a number of governments and large industries. Some countries and some companies are coping better than others with the challenges of returning to the growth path and retaining talent. Can public innovation policy help? Can corporate innovation policy change the negative dynamics of diminishing returns? Is "innovation policy" an oxymoron? Can policy make a better innovation?

If the approach to policy is limited to fund allocation the answer seems to lean toward policy as an inadequate medium. A policy should stimulate innovation in the environment, strengthen emerging trends, incentivize stakeholders to collaborate more effectively, and stimulate creativity in experimenting with the innovation models, meaning the qualitative processes in which quantifiable financial and non-financial resources stimulate the demand or supply side but do not pick winners or prescribe what to do.

While this may be a desirable approach, it is quite difficult to implement this kind of philosophy and trust-based approach to the ingenuity of bottom-up leadership. The policy makers are part of a bureaucracy, which tends to consolidate power through the control mechanisms of monitoring and auditing. There is a sound rational for this method since public institutions' ultimate role is to safeguard taxpayers' money.

Overall, budget thinking seems a more prudent and adequate approach than investment in creative solutions. The inertia of a bureaucracy and its culture, whether in the public environment, university setting, or a large multinational, has its own dynamics, making it more difficult to arrive at a consensus and implement and prove positive results of experimentation. This is particularly true in a turbulent market environment of economic crisis at all levels: micro, midi, and macro. Being entrepreneurial in the context of a crisis is particularly interesting since it means decreasing input per number of output—that is, having more impact with less resources over a limited period of time.

The role of small enterprises as drivers of growth in an innovation economy has been extensively researched. There are claims that small companies are more innovative than large business organizations. However, the research evidence on the relation between innovation and firm size is inconclusive (Acs and Audretsch 1988; Cohen and Levin 1989; Azoulay and Lerner 2010).

On the other hand, there is evidence that start-up companies are critical in stimulating growth in emerging industries. Thus, the role of small enterprises as drivers of growth depends on the condition of an industry and its structure. Their role is the greatest in immature industries where market is fragmented. This means that there is more competition based on time-to-market conditioned by speed of development and marketing of new offerings to customers.

There is research-based evidence that high-growth enterprises (not all small and medium-sized businesses, but those that are innovation-driven) and venture capital (that is, the capital and know-how necessary for taking weighted risks and providing assistance in a period of rapid growth) are critical for stimulating growth.

Entrepreneurial activity as such is not an isolated mean to value creation in itself. This can be proven if we compare GDP per capita growth over the long-term data provided by Global Entrepreneurship Monitor, OECD, and World Bank/IMF. The analysis shows that the entrepreneurial activity (number of start-ups created) is not necessarily positively correlated with the GDP per capita growth.

However, there is a correlation with a number of indicators such as effectiveness in growing early-stage ventures into full-fledged businesses (preconditioned for example by the availability of managerial talent), low barriers to growth of high-potential entrepreneurship (e.g. burden of complying with tax regulations, cost of managing IPRs), and the availability of venture capital and early stage financing (that is funds at the level of EUR 50,000-1 million to bridge a so-called "liquidity gap").

The conclusion would be that instead of generic policies, the specificity of the relations between entrepreneurship and economic growth requires support for the ventures with high-growth potential, which is a distinctive policy set from entrepreneurial policies as such. There are a number of interesting historical examples of innovations in innovation policy and novel policy initiatives. President Eisenhower established DARPA, a small laboratory, with a mission to deliver breakthrough solutions to the defense industry during the Cold War period. DARPA became famous for such inventions as GPS and Internet. This small organization uses a specific model of outsourcing transitional research and development to universities and research labs, focusing on generating radical ideas and testing prototypes. Other examples are Semintech, an agency established to enhance the semiconductor industry in the Silicon Valley, Small Business Investment Company (SBIC) and Small Business Innovation Research (SBIR) in the US, the Israeli Yozma Venture Capital Ltd., and the New Zealand Venture Investment Fund (NZVIF).

The lessons learned from these policy initiatives is that the essential issue for economic development is not only what is produced but also how it is produced. These questions gain a new dimension in a network society, in an open innovation environment, and in the era of wikinomics (Tapscott and Williams 2006, 2010).

Well-considered public innovation and entrepreneurship policies can profoundly influence the opportunities available to a nation in the mid and long-term. The key challenge is to keep the medium-term growth perspective high on the policy agenda. Faced with the crisis in the Euro zone, Europe's leaders are contending with urgent liquidity/solvency issues and must focus on the short-term perspective, predominantly postponing innovation again and again.

The paradox is that while it becomes even timelier to explore an innovation and entrepreneurship policy mix as a basis for smart, inclusive, and sustainable growth, again Europe's policies may not be implemented, which would mean a repeat of the Lisbon scenario. In a free market economy, a free enterprise is a vehicle for value creation. This enterprise, however, is also networked and the value is no longer expressed in terms of GDP at the macro level and market valuation at the micro level.

While the growth is created by entrepreneurial enterprises in the Schumpeter and Drucker tradition, the world has become too complex and too interlinked to follow only the legacy of Adam Smith, Stuart Mill, and David Ricardo. There remains, however, a simple fundamental relationship in the market economy: Value to a customer has to exceed price, and price has to exceed cost production or service delivery. Customers, who can be also embodied as a society-at-large, look for competitive value proposition.

A lot of innovation ends at one of the two points: Either there is not a critical mass of customers willing to pay a price, or a company is not able to solve the problems related to fixing externalities and drive the cost of production down. In many cases, this free market interaction requires a policy intervention. This is a case, for example, when an outdated solution supplied by the existing companies needs to be replaced with a new one. In the case of the energy sector, the question is: Should energy subsidies be directed toward more investment into batteries and smart grids, hydrogen, solar, wind, and biofuel? This is not the question a policy should answer.

However, the reality is that it often does. For example, in the US, the short-term policy linked to the presidential elections drives support for a particular technology. President Bill Clinton supported hybrid vehicles, President George Bush advocated fuel cell vehicles, and President Barack Obama supports battery electric vehicles. The sustained funding in the long-term is a very important driver for innovation, as it is often the case in Europe and in Japan, where there seems to be more sustained planning in terms of policy. Climate change and renewable energy are just two examples of industries where energy is being supplied at a price that is inexpensive for customers and profitable for the companies. As much as solar solutions or electric-plug vehicles are vital for greener growth, suppliers alone cannot meet the price points unless supported by public policies.

A well-intended electric vehicle as a choice of mass consumers faces a very difficult challenge, since it is more costly than a solution that has been around for more than one hundred years—the combustion engine. Initially, the electric car is more costly and also far less convenient than the combustion engine car, since the latter needs to refuel for a couple of minutes every 500 or so kilometers, while the batteries of the electric car need to be recharged for a few hours every 100 kilometers given the current state of technology. The infrastructure for recharging electric plug vehicles needs to be in place and governments should make sure that such public infrastructure is available before making political decisions in favor of electric cars. Once the infrastructure is mature it may make sense, taking the investment, price, and customer value proposition into account. The key role for policy is to develop the infrastructure and support multiple technologies rather than arbitrarily choose a solution.

When examining growth driven by innovation and entrepreneurship in the Knowledge Triangle, the value creation cannot be addressed in purely financial or economic terms. The perspective should be wide and should relate not only to economy, but to society-at-large, in terms of inter-generational solidarity. Redefining value has become an important variable of redefining growth in public policies and also a sign of corporate social and environmental responsibility.

The global financial crisis of 2008 fundamentally resulted in a loss of trust in the self-regulating mechanisms of capitalism. Trust, as a key asset and fundament of the free market economy, was conducive to redefining the role of state and governments in saving companies and safeguarding the measures balancing the short-term impact of crisis on companies' profits, shrinking demand and growing unemployment.

The austerity measures, in the context of the most severe monetary crisis in the Euro zone since the launch of the common currency, shifted the power of innovation from the private sector to the public sector. Unless there is creativity, innovation, and entrepreneurialism, the governments' impact will be limited. Innovation in public policy is urgently called for in the short-term, but also equally valid in the mid to long-term perspective.

Chapter 14

ENTREPRENEURSHIP: MISSING LINK IN THE KNOWLEDGE TRIANGLE

The role of small enterprises as drivers of growth depends on the condition of an economy, as well as of that of an industry and its structure. Evidence shows that in emerging markets and emerging industries growth comes from small entrepreneurial ventures. In developed economies and mature industries growth comes from large companies that are able to reinvent themselves and become innovative and entrepreneurial organizations.

New emerging industries transcend and blur the boundaries between developed and developing economies. In the emerging industries, growth is generated by small entrepreneurial ventures rather than established organizations. For start-up ventures and fast growing enterprises, growth depends on the availability of risk capital, as well as managerial talent able to manage growth, govern changing partnerships, and access global markets.

While in the emerging markets most growth comes from the sector of small or mid-sized businesses, entrepreneurial activity as such is not necessarily a means to value creation. The Global Entrepreneurship Monitor ranking (GEM 2014) supports this argument, when we look at the link between GDP growth and entrepreneurial activity. Lerner proves this point with the example of Jamaica and Singapore; the former, as the leader among 42 nations assessed in the category of entrepreneurial activity, is at the same time one of the lowest ranked in the category of effectiveness in growing early-stage ventures into full-fledged businesses (Cohen and Lerner 2011).

Klonowski outlines key aspects that make the SME sector a driving force for forward thinking economies (Klonowski 2010). Firstly, six out of every ten new jobs are created by the SME sector. Secondly, SMEs are spearheading the industrial transformation from traditional industries into high technology sectors. Thirdly, these firms are making significant inroads in developing global export markets. Fourthly, SMEs are at the forefront of developing innovations with a clear competitive advantage. It is estimated that over 90% of worldwide innovations come from the SME sector. Ninety-nine percent of enterprises active within the EU-27 in the non-financial business economy were SMEs, with over 20.9 million in 2011. They accounted for two out of every three jobs (66.7%) and for 58.6% of value added. More than nine out of ten were micro-enterprises that employed less than 10 people. Their relative share of workforce and value added was considerably lower. The contribution of the SME sector to total value added was lower than their contribution to employment, which points to the lower level of apparent labor productivity.

This pattern was dominant among activities such as manufacturing and ICT. SMEs seem to have difficulty in leveraging the potential of partnering with large enterprises to play a role benefitting from economies of scale: they have limited capital intensity and adopt or develop innovations at a slower rate. Although entrepreneurship and innovation are considered drivers of economic growth, it is the large enterprise in Europe that tends to manifest higher labor productivity ratios than SMEs. Entrepreneurship as a project-oriented practice is usually credited with being a major source of innovation and, consequently, of employment and wealth creation. There is mixed evidence, however, as to whether small and medium-sized enterprises generate a higher net growth rate and number of jobs than large industry. This argument holds strong especially in the developed economies, where established industry secures stability in terms of job creation and continuity of employment, which are often favored in the developed societies.

Entrepreneurship can be defined in a broader sense as a project-oriented integrative capacity to organize limited resources (people, capital, time). The Schumpeterian entrepreneur—the engine of "creative destruction"—operated within the logic of increasing economic returns. Taking into consideration the complexity and interrelations in today's world, this economic dimension does not seem to work in isolation. On the one hand, it is responsible to include social, environmental, and sustainable categories into the equation. On the other hand, the private sector is no longer the innovation leader, and also entrepreneurship can be well-defined in a number of different settings including the non-profit sector and public administration.

In the European Knowledge Economy, entrepreneurship has been a missing link of the Knowledge Triangle. Being entrepreneurial is an outcome of a system of incentives and disincentives to behave in an entrepreneurial way. The political choice of prior generations of Europeans, demonstrated for example by labor market policies, resulted in a society where risk-taking was penalized by the system and also by social ostracism.

In the United States, the labor market system rewards good choices (e.g. the choice of a college, field of study, mobility), and severely punishes bad choices, since it offers no welfare or quality medical care for the unemployed. By contrast, in Europe, comfort-driven choices or risk-averse decisions do not result in similar consequences as in the United States. There are limited incentives to becoming rich because of

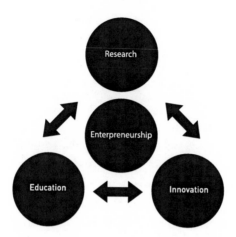

Figure 9. Entrepreneurship and Knowledge Triangle

high taxation of income and capital income or charges for capitalizing on options for shares, as well as punitive bankruptcy laws.

There is a huge desire in China and in India to become rich; the culture is very materialistic, and there is no shortage of people who simply want to earn a lot of money as a symbol of their social status and identity. In Europe, by contrast, there is a culture-based lack of social acceptance for becoming rich and a negative perception of both self-made millionaires and entrepreneurs who try to grow their fortunes with mixed luck. They arise suspicion in a society in which one can have a wonderful life without taking risks.

However, entrepreneurship has rarely been associated with industry, universities, and research. Siemens, Carlsberg, Behring, Citroen Merrieux, Nobel, and Reuter are names of great European entrepreneurs and innovators of the industrial revolution. The European enterprises that they established were to a large extent an outcome of effective collaboration between research, education, and innovation, collaboration driven by entrepreneurship and entrepreneurial people.

After a successful expansion of European enterprises into the global markets, during which they deployed the linear models of innovation rather than a web-based, networked Knowledge Triangle concept, the challenge is to reactivate the ability to generate spin-offs and spin-outs. European enterprises will die at their own pace if they do not embrace innovation and entrepreneurship conducive to research collaboration and the development of more creative and entrepreneurial people. Entrepreneurship is a human intensive activity: Entrepreneurs deliver solutions at a price, which is often higher than the cost of bringing the solution to the users and this margin, which gives an entrepreneur a return and allows the accumulation of capital for investment.

Creativity and entrepreneurship are at the core of processes in the Knowledge Triangle. Innovation depends on creativity—the production of new knowledge or new meaning. The meaning can be, for example, a symphony or a new architectural design that does not produce new knowledge as such, yet frames existing knowledge in a new context and by this act gives it new meaning. Creativity is the source of everything and innovation is a social or commercial application of human creativity.

Entrepreneurship is a missing link between creativity and innovation and the market with its consumers and users, and with society-at-large. It is the core of the processes in the innovation network, an indispensable element that integrates the network and accelerates the velocity of exchange, a catalyst leading to exponential growth and higher quality of outputs and impact. Creativity, innovation, and entrepreneurship can have diverse impact on the exchange in the innovation network. They can destabilize continuous flows, cause discontinuation, or rupture. The more creativity, innovation, and entrepreneurship in the system, the higher the probability of breakdowns of exchange between the actors and institutions. And a breakdown or discontinuation of one flow invariably has consequences for other flows in the network.

The issue is how to bring to the forefront and how to integrate entrepreneurship into the Knowledge Triangle. Entrepreneurship can add other criteria beyond efficiency of the system characterized by input indicators. Government policies geared toward activation of the flows and exchanges in the Knowledge Triangle depend on the priorities. For example, a policy may target the development of human capital by supporting education and research and thus enhance economic competitiveness.

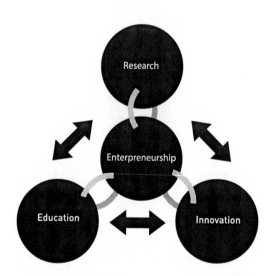

Figure 10. Entrepreneurship as an Integrator of the Knowledge Triangle

Entrepreneurship is an ability to combine different elements into a relationship in order to achieve a goal. Entrepreneurship is a project that can take the form of a profitable business, but also of a new institution improving the health or innovativeness of a country. There has been and can be more entrepreneurship in big corporations which are reinventing themselves, re-engineering their processes, decentralizing decision making, and fostering intrapreneurship, as in the case of Nokia, IBM, and GE. This process is often conducted by policies and strategies developed by the leadership of a company or its unit. Companies active in the Knowledge Triangle integrate knowledge generated within universities and research centers to create new units or new strategies to adapt to these new learning environments.

Decoupling the activity of entrepreneurship from business, since entrepreneurship has been defined beyond profit-making, can also support research and change academic institutions into new types of entrepreneurial universities. In all cases, entrepreneurship, in the traditional form of a start-up activity or in a broader framework, is always a risk-taking activity, usually linked to innovation and creativity. Since innovation and creativity are directly linked to competitiveness and thus to economic growth, as we know from economic literature, there is a correlation and self-perpetuating cycle: creativity, innovation, entrepreneurship, competitiveness, productivity. Entrepreneurship is central in this concept.

Strategic Shift: Toward an Entrepreneurial University

The increasingly global competitive market for higher education requires universities to develop a more strategic orientation, defining their identity, mission, and institutional strategy. In practice it means developing, branding, and marketing their value proposition in order to attract the best students and faculty out of the global talent pool. Research universities have to face the dilemma of whether they should remain focused on excellent research and education, or embrace the "third mission"— that is, stimulate and become proactively involved in the creation of an infrastructure for economic development.

There are a number of interlinking elements that foster the "third mission" of universities. They include Technology Transfer Offices, entrepreneurship courses and degrees, different models for business incubation and acceleration, mentoring and business coaching, and even university venture capital funds to finance university spin-offs.

The bigger the competitive pressure on the local job market, the more that university stakeholders expect the academic institution to bridge the gap between knowledge and society. Students assume that a university education will increase their opportunities for a fulfilling professional career. Faculty looks for more research funding. Industry hopes that academia will provide quality graduates and help drive innovations. Governments assume that public funding for education should generate growth and jobs in the country, not elsewhere, and that universities have a role to play in building an innovation ecosystem. A university can create "value" in a number of ways.

The key question, though, is: What is value? How do different players in the value net or the innovation ecosystem perceive "value?" What does it mean for individuals and organizations collaborating or competing in a university's innovation networks?

Globally, an increasing number of excellent research-driven academic institutions have decided to undertake a strategic shift and embrace the "third mission" of a university, the fostering of economic development. Initially, universities were religious schools, value-producing institutions endowed with a mission to foster the dominant values of the society—the doctrine of the Catholic Church—and preserve accepted knowledge.

Many great universities have a monastic origin, including Oxford, Cambridge, Sorbonne, Leuven, Jagiellonian University, or even Harvard. The second function of the university was elite formation. Universities educated social elites, which stratified societies, cascading the correlation: the top tier universities produced top elites, the second tier universities produced the next tier of elites.

Until the beginning of the twenty-first century, this elite formation function had been preserved and demonstrated by the fact that, for example, 70% of French leaders in the public domain graduated from the Grandes Écoles, 80% of British elites graduated from Oxford or Cambridge, and Yale University produced more US presidents than all other American universities combined. An entrepreneurial university induces a culture of entrepreneurialism as an institution. Taking this strategic path, it also creates an infrastructure for knowledge commercialization and sharing, supports spin-offs, fosters entrepreneurial culture on campus, and offers programs in entrepreneurial education.

On the path to the strategic shift toward an entrepreneurial institution, a university becomes more tightly-knit not only in its local innovation ecosystems, but also across globally distributed innovation networks, under the realization that it has a large captive audience all over the world, including its alumni. This captive audience can be analyzed using the value net model, which helps one to understand the different roles of stakeholders and their interactions in value creation processes or a value net of a university.

The stakeholders in the value net model for an organization include customers, suppliers, complimentors, and substitutors. A university, even as a private institution, has a mission beyond profit making. Therefore, its multiple actors in the value net include students and faculty, private companies and non-profit organizations, government agencies, national and local governments, and alumni. The students are the customers. The tuition and other revenues they generate, such as public funding, amounts usually to the university's largest revenue stream. Companies are customers in two ways.

Firstly, they bring value to the quality of education offered for students as potential future employers. If there are not enough companies recruiting on campus, students perceive the university as less competitive. It is important to reach out to companies and invite them to visit the campus and approach students with recruitment offers.

There is a second aspect of companies as customers and that is on the supplier side. Companies in many cases become partners in research projects. The funding from research and consulting projects commissioned by the industry is in many cases the second largest portion of a university budget. Companies are customers because they hire students; at the same time, they are also suppliers because they provide research projects.

The third customer is the government in that it provides public funding for research and higher education. Different departments on campus are complimentors offering joint degrees, exchanging staff, and providing expertise in interdisciplinary research projects. Companies are another type of complimentor. They become engaged in classes. Some classes are entirely funded by companies, and include internship and co-operation programs. The university can attract students by having a sound network of complimentors, as in the case of Stanford, where the main complimentors are on the entrepreneurial side of a network of big and small companies and of venture capitalists. Taking the focus on undergraduate and graduate education, the key node in the value net is a department offering a degree or a program. Students are the "products" of the educational service provided by the university.

However, in terms of research, the value net may divert from the department and the unit to analyze the research project team, a polycentric, project-oriented network. It is a very different unit, since unlike the department, with its organizational structure and administrative capacity, knowledge and not students is the "product."

Foremost and for all stakeholders in the value net of a university, "value" means students. It is difficult to measure "students" as "value." A proxy used most often is their starting salary upon graduation. In the case of engineering education, industrial advisory groups usually prepare a qualitative judgment on students' value. It is more difficult in the case of the liberal arts environment.

The value proposition for university professors is considered more competitive in the United States than in Europe. Talent is searched for and selected out of the global pool. Professors and young researchers are more empowered and their initiative starting at the bottom of the university hierarchy allows them to work faster and more effectively.

While there are cases in some European countries such as Germany or Switzerland where universities employ professors for whom the national language is non-native, at the best American research universities most faculty are non-Americans. In general, there is little internal competition between the departments at US universities, which take a pragmatic approach to structural organization. Departments specialize in different fields, and if there is low demand for a particular department, it most likely will be dissolved. Once in a while, the profitability of departments is discussed and as a result some are merged or liquidated. Departments are predominantly organizational structures to support educational services rather than conduct and organize research projects. If a researcher wants to change a department, because it is easier to write research proposals from a different unit, it can be done with little hurdle.

This is quite different from a European university, where a vast majority of funding is distributed top-down, and the funding model solidifies the departments and the staff. The division of research funding is decided higher up in the university hierarchy and trickled down. This administrative approach freezes internal competition between professors and departments since there is usually a group that does not want to change the status quo. As a result, the process, rather than strategic and customer-focused, becomes more political and bureaucratic.

There is little structural incentive to stop projects or units that do not yield expected returns in terms of value creation. In the United States, the research group resembles a team of entrepreneurs. Each researcher brings research money, so in general the group is independently funded. Many professors have tenure, but their core income comes from research funding, which they share with the university. In this way, each researcher makes money for the university as students do with their tuition.

Researchers need to reach out through writing proposals and collaborate with governments and companies. It is their obligation; the university offers a support structure but the responsibility for generating revenue rests with the researchers. They need to be agile and alert to provide their services at market demand, which can arise at any moment. For example, the earthquake in Japan in January 2011, which destroyed nuclear plants, created an urgent demand for researchers and an opportunity to deploy solutions or develop research projects. In this sense, the research strategy of American universities is bottom-up, market-driven, and entrepreneurial in that it exploits opportunities, is customer-focused, and follows market demand and interest.

Branding of a university as an entrepreneurial institution is one of the key elements of a successful strategic shift. Even in such places as Silicon Valley, there are different brands and different mindsets between universities. For example, while Stanford University is a reference point for a research-intensive academic institution with an entrepreneurial brand, Santa Clara, a Jesuit university, makes efforts to strengthen the role of engineering education and to recognize the importance of technology in bringing change to the lives of people around the world. In the 1950s, Stanford University was an insignificant academic institution. A number of converging factors, including breakthrough innovations, spectacular success stories, and government funding for research, helped build up the university name. Most of the innovations Stanford is credited for, including HP and Google came out from its graduate students. Notably, Yahoo! was started by an undergraduate student.

However, there are fundamental differences between universities in Silicon Valley in terms of branding research and teaching commitment. At Stanford, research is valued first and foremost and faculty members have guaranteed time for research activities. It is expected that a faculty is sufficient in teaching and excellent at research. The teaching is condensed in the morning so that the afternoon hours are reserved for research activities. One day per week is devoted to research only. Publishing in top academic journals is a must. The cost of supporting graduate or PhD students at Stanford amounts to about 85,000 USD including tuition, stipend, and an overhead. Professors are expected to raise funds to support their students in conducting research.

This is the market-oriented and market-financed model. Administrative functions or service, for example deanship or chairmanship, do not mean so much at Stanford. By contrast, Santa Clara University, located in the heart of Silicon Valley in San Jose, does not have a similar brand despite being part of the Valley. While Stanford's graduate program attracts the top 5% of the best students in the world and 50% of the graduate programs at Stanford are in engineering, the reputation of this oldest Jesuit university in California is built on its undergraduate program, which fosters involvement with global agenda challenges and community service, and also has a public mission for its engineering programs. Solving problems in the emerging markets and the developing world creates conditions for boosting students' creativity. For example, an innovative design for cleaning water developed at the

Santa Clara Social Benefit Incubator is focused on filtering water at the last tap, not at reservoirs in the traditional way.

The prevailing image is that while Stanford's graduates start technology companies, Santa Clara's graduates become business administrators, lawyers, accountants, engineers, or social entrepreneurs. They all feed into the vibrant ecosystem of Silicon Valley and beyond. While often neglected, the graduates of universities like Santa Clara are one of the crucial ingredients of the Valley innovation ecosystem as very good employees, medium level managers, technicians, and support staff. This talent is the essential element of the success of the Silicon Valley economy and ecosystem.

A strategic decision to turn a research university into an entrepreneurial university requires top-down and bottom-up converging forces. The University of Michigan is one of the top ten research universities in the United States and has a long tradition of fostering entrepreneurship. The Zell Lurie Institute for Entrepreneurial Studies at the Ross Business School is highly recognized for its comprehensive model of business-school driven entrepreneurship education. The Institute experiments with action-based learning and has pioneered collaboration with venture capital in the Midwest. It manages three university venture funds, one of them focused on financing social entrepreneurship, which provides students with an opportunity to understand the VC industry in a learning-by-doing mode.

In 2009, the College of Engineering was given a mandate to create a program for its students by a newly created position—Associate Dean for Entrepreneurial Programs. In-the-field customer surveys revealed that a large fraction of engineering students were interested in entrepreneurship, with half of them interested in social entrepreneurship. The key challenge was the implementation of a massive personnel-intensive program for 4000 students interested in taking at least one course on new business creation. It turned out that the business school model of entrepreneurial education did not match the needs of students interested in technology start-up. Science and engineering students had to focus on understanding market demand and customer needs and quit the technology driven mindset.

In order to achieve this, a new model of entrepreneurship education had to be designed. Taking advantage of their technology-savvy, the students were interested in taking courses enhancing their creativity and business mindset rather than participating in business plan competitions. They expected the college to help them accelerate business ideas on campus through networking, coaching, and mentoring. The College of Engineering had a profitable Technology Transfer Office with commercial innovations coming out of labs. However, there was no entrepreneurial ecosystem or support infrastructure. The construction of such infrastructure posed a significant implementation challenge for the college. Both the support from the dean and the clearly outspoken plan helped the strategic shift bring early results.

An incentive structure in academia is not suited to stimulate and reward a new type of entrepreneurial researcher, the quintessence of an entrepreneurial university. On the one hand, the motivation of an individual to undertake risks is a personal, intrinsic motivation independent of the external environment. However, in a number of academic settings, these choices are punished and discarded by colleagues rather than rewarded and respected. Rather than single metrics, such as quotation index and impact factor, a balanced incentive structure rewarding dual career tracks helps foster institutional shift. It includes a portfolio of human resources management solutions such as leave of absence, re-entry mechanisms, and the recognition of innovation and entrepreneurship accomplishments in the tenure track record along with purely academic achievements.

However, the global academic rankings system, notably the Shanghai List prepared by Shanghai Jiao Tong University in China, shapes university policies using six indicators: the number of alumni and staff awarded Nobel Prizes and Fields Medals; the number of highly cited researchers selected by Thomson Scientific; the number of articles published in the journals Nature and Science; the number of articles indexed in the Science Citation Index—Expanded and Social Sciences Citation Index; and per capita performance with respect to the size of an institution.

The Academic Ranking of World Universities ranks more than 100 universities on an annual basis and the top 500 are published on the web. The brand of a research university in the academic community depends purely on research performance indicators. It is a challenge for a university to remain focused on academic excellence and at the same time be an entrepreneurial institution. However, two emblematic universities of this type, Stanford University and the Massachusetts Institute of Technology, were both in the top three of the worldwide rankings in 2011.

From a company's point of view, there are two key aspects of fostering collaboration with academia. Leading research universities attract companies if they provide not only a big pocket of fundamental research, but also a pool of innovations and potential innovations and, foremost, top quality graduates.

The ease of interaction between business and academia preconditions good collaboration. For example, the Stanford University and the University of Berkeley, although located only an hour's drive from each other, are like day and night. The former is more open and more transparent, and thus it is easier to navigate across the hierarchy, gain access to the network, find superstars, and understand how innovation comes out of research labs. Many excellent universities struggle with the scope and quality of industry collaboration. They try to mitigate the problem by putting processes in place, for example by setting up Technology Transfer Offices.

However, Stanford is considered a pretty "messy" place; yet its success in partnering with companies is a function of how much knowledge, expertise, and excellence there is, multiplied by how easy it is to get access to this knowledge. Often great universities have much less industry interaction than they should, and the University of Michigan is a good example[18]. It is not easy to interact with, from the perspective of a company, which is partially due to its culture—too administration-driven and bureaucratic. It is not that there are different kinds of researchers working at Stanford, but it is part of the specific culture that, in its environment, the same people do not allow things to become a problem. The cultural problem is the key challenge, and in fostering industry–academia collaboration, the key question is how to change and what values to foster to bring the change.

Finland is an interesting example of how a university culture can shift toward entrepreneurship. The country leads international rankings as the most innovative state. Its innovation system includes excellent education, a number of funding agencies such as Tekes, Finnish Funding Agency for Technology and Innovation (with a 700 million EUR yearly budget), and VTT, Technical Research Center for Finland, the largest multi-technological applied research organization in Northern Europe with an annual budget of 300 million EUR. Traditionally, entrepreneurship has not been embedded in Finland's higher education institutions. A movement started by students of Aalto University has initiated a new trend.

---

(18) Having an opportunity to examine for one year (2010-2011) the University of Michigan and in particular the campus-wide efforts to turn this academic institution into a more entrepreneurial organization, I agree with this opinion expressed by Professor Thomas Zurbuchen, Associate Dean for College of Engineering.

Aalto Entrepreneurship Society was launched on Facebook in 2009. It is an independent, private, not-for-profit association financed through private donations. It receives 20,000-30,000 EUR funding from private foundations to do ad hoc projects selected by its teams. The Aalto Entrepreneurship Society Board as well as its working team changes each year. The tradition is to leave very little money in the beginning of the year, so not to erode the creativity of the new upcoming team. The Society partners with the Aalto Entrepreneurship Center at Aalto University and co-owns Venue Garage and Startup Sauna.

Venture Garage is located in an old industrial building on the university campus. It is designed as an open creative space similar in character to the IDEO offices in Palo Aalto, California. There is, however, a real sauna in the middle of the open working spaces. This sauna is actually one of the meeting rooms and is especially appreciated as a brainstorming environment. This is a sort of tribute to the Finnish tradition and the origin of the idea for the Aalto Entrepreneurship Society, which actually originated during a typical Finnish sauna ritual. Venture Garage space was given to the Aalto Entrepreneurship Society initially as a temporary arrangement, but the keys to the premises were simply never returned.

Startup Sauna is a student-led business accelerator located on the premises of Venture Garage. Startup Sauna was founded in 2010 for incubating, seeding, and accelerating start-ups. In 2012 Startup Sauna had four full-time employees, 54 teams of alumni ventures, and a six-week acceleration program run twice per year, a brand also recognized in Northern Europe, including the Baltic countries and Russia, where they source ventures. Startup Sauna staff recruits the best local teams for their program during Warm-ups, cyclical networking events. Every week they celebrate entrepreneurship by organizing all sorts of events: speed dating, the Slush conference, keynote lectures, and a National Day of Failure, launched for the first time in 2011. The walls are covered with photos of famous Finnish entrepreneurs including Ulf Michael Widenius (called Monty), the founder of MySQL AB, and Linus Torvalds, the founder of Linux, who are the role models of Venture Garage students.

One of the programs is Startup Life. Students are sent to the Silicon Valley with a mission to internationalize the program, network, and invite Stanford and also MIT students to come to Helsinki to work over the summer during the Summer of Startups, a two-month program for ventures that are either in their very early stages, pre-prototype, or still just an idea and a team. They receive EUR 5000 seed funding and the support of an experienced mentor.

A vast majority of Aalto University students do not know whether they want to be entrepreneurs. Some want to try, yet doubt whether they can succeed. The experience at the Venture Garage and Startup Sauna is often life-changing because of the day-to-day work with the Garage's entrepreneurs-in-residence who mentor students. They devote their time free-of-charge in order to "give back." At the same time, while working with smartest students-entrepreneurs, they have access to the best teams and best projects in which they can potentially invest.

This nascent entrepreneurial ecosystem seems to work because of freedom, openness, and the University's policy "not to disturb."[19] The money given has no strings attached. Public money is called "dumb money" by student entrepreneurs, in juxtaposition to "smart money," funding provided by seasoned investors such as venture capital or business angels, whom they try to attract to their Garage.

(19) The policy "Not to Disturb" was how Professor Tula Teeri, President of Aalto University, explained to the author of this book her approach in support of students' entrepreneurship movement on campus, ACES Awards 2012, Brussels, .

Fostering Open Innovation

Effective management of intellectual property is crucial for capturing the value of internal and external knowledge. Close IP regimes were predominantly used when IP was generated internally and internally exploited. Patenting activity was often used as quite a costly defensive strategy preventing competitors from moving into certain markets.

Creating a proactive intellectual property strategy, and sharing technologies rather than keeping IP in-house, is increasingly recognized in different industries. There are cases when the classic low cost defensive strategy of opening the results via publications is turned into a valuable part of the core asset. For example, owners like MySQL AB opened and shared its IP as an OSS project, under the use of General Public License (GPL), which protects the rights of the original copyright.

Companies increasingly create value by granting licenses for unused technologies or by selling the patents themselves. They also enter into cross-licensing agreements and organization patent pools, which facilitate technology collaboration. Under these circumstances, especially in areas that are densely populated with patents, an unintentional patent infringement may be unavoidable. Establishing an OSS project can be an alternative way to turn a potentially costly legal dispute into mutual success. This was the case in telecom infrastructure equipment and mobile devices.

There are different aspects of openness related to intellectual property issues and policy. IP policy should promote trade and investment by granting patents of highest quality, lowering costs and time of filing, and changing and renewing patents.

However, effective IP policy should also give incentives for sharing opportunities with others, thus avoiding a waste of IP, for example by creating a secondary market and usage charges. In practice, there is limited sponsorship to open innovation at the policy level, since quite often the beneficiaries are existing incumbents. They take advantage of the existing IP regime to protect the wealth they already possess. There are examples of a major breakthrough. For example, Taiwan has taken a radical approach and has transformed itself from a "pirate kingdom" to an advocate of a better global intellectual property protection system (Sun 1998).

One of the key issues during the due diligence process is to consider the dependence of the product on a specific patent, competing patents, and the strength of the protection. Most managers think of innovation in a sustaining technology context, a more or less stable competitive environment, with known competitors and customers. The behavior of market players (consumers, firms/ suppliers, elected officials/ politicians, and administrators/bureaucrats/professional employees/ public servants) undermines the interaction and the flow of knowledge. Finding balance between free competition and open cooperation between various players in the innovation networks is of strategic importance for industry leaders, academics as well as policy makers. Open innovation increases competition on ideas and execution rather than product lock-in and OSS projects often lead to the establishment of industry standards. Thus, open innovation serves all stakeholders in the innovation process, as well as customers.

This big picture of economy through the lenses of the global innovation network brings concrete implications for innovation policies in intellectual property protection and the fostering of open innovation. The emerging global innovation economy is different from the knowledge economy. It is a complex system constituted by local, national, and regional innovation systems. Public policies recognizing the dynamics and underlying drivers of the global innovation economy will lead in the long-term to establishing new kinds of interventions and tools.

The future prosperity of nations lies not in building their innovation capacity but in their ability to explore the global innovation potential and leveraging locally the opportunities it offers. Low patent application is often used as a benchmark to assess the low competitive position of a country. Intellectual capital management is a process by which research results from laboratories turn into commercial products or services. Technology transfer portfolios may include patents, copyright material, software, and biological material. There are two main mechanisms of the ICM process. One is intellectual property licensing; the other is commercialization of technology via business ventures. The latter may create substantially higher financial benefits for stakeholders and an upside potential reflecting high risk associated with setting up a venture rather than technology licensing.

Patenting activity is highly concentrated geographically and specialized in terms of technology (OECD, 2008). In 2005, California and the northeast regions contributed 34% of patents filed in the US; Tokyo filed 28% of Japanese patents; in the European Union, patenting activity was distributed between the Ile de France region, Stuttgart, Oberbayern, Noord-Brabant, and the South East of England. ICT-related patenting originates mainly in Tokyo, San Jose/San Francisco, CA, and the region of Noord-Brabant. Out of the top ten regions for biotechnology patenting, seven come from the US, two from Japan, and one from Denmark, which also held the largest number of patents in renewable energy technologies. German regions show their strength in patenting automobile equipment for reducing car emissions.

In 2004, almost 80% of patents originated from the private sector, and half of these related to high-technology industries; universities owned 4% and the government sector owned 2% of patents filed. Setting the legal framework for patenting activity is crucial for accelerating innovation as evidenced by the Bayh-Dole Act (US Public Law 96-517).

Under this Act, universities may elect to retain the title to inventions developed under federally funded research programs, while at the same time they must grant a royalty-free, non-exclusive license to the government. If a company holds an exclusive license, it is obliged to manufacture the product in the US to a large extent. When marketing and licensing an innovation, universities must give preferences to small companies (less than 500 employees). The Act specifies that universities must share with the inventor(s) a portion of any revenue received from licensing. At Stanford, for example, the royalty distribution policy indicates that 1/3 of net royalties goes to inventors, 1/3 to the inventors' department, and 1/3 to the inventors' university.

The legal framework for patenting activity in the EU is embodied in the negotiations over the European Community Patent. In 2012, European Patents were still granted under the European Patent Convention, which is a bundle of nationally enforceable patents, which need to be carried out through national courts in individual countries. This process creates disadvantage both in terms of financial costs and, most importantly, time-to-market.

Innovation is an open system where organizations interact with their environment, and so we will place our analytical focus on the process rather than on input or output. The basic model consists of input, then value-added (that is, lean) processes leading to output, and support systems assist this sequence. This linear model is yet too simplistic. A waterfall model, which includes a multiple feedback loop, is still quite mechanistic with a set of points of contact where knowledge is passed from one team to another with feedback loops leading to reiterations only at the end of the value chain. A typical example is in production when a manufacturing team tells another manufacturing team that it is not possible to produce an item at a given cost without simultaneous consultations with other teams in marketing, sales, or logistics.

Another emerging element is the new approach to cooperation among different components of production and service processes. While ICT allows even small enterprises to cooperate vertically (e.g. with suppliers), it does not help in developing their collaboration horizontally, for example with universities or relevant external actors of the innovative value chains. Big enterprises are in general much stronger in this sense (Leitner 2007).

However, the capability to exploit local and tacit knowledge, as well as the cooperative attitude, has a much wider importance for new innovation models, which include or are based upon non-technological components. It challenges the stakeholders to redefine complementary chains among different actors and can have strong advantages for local economies with weak technological R&D. Defensive IPR strategies and public investment in scientific excellence are no longer sufficient to prevent newcomers from entering the emerging markets or industry sectors from gaining market share. The diversity of stakeholders participating in this process as a whole and in particular stages or phases is a limiting factor to effective communication between them. Each of the participants of the innovation process is biased depending on their origin and background.

These biases prevent understanding of what is innovation, how it happens, and how it is being managed in the networked world. These cognitive biases limit the potential impact of individual innovators and their capacity to innovate as a team or an innovation network. The insight into the nature of science, research, invention, innovation, development, translation, and commercialization helps create a common basis for further discussion on the interrelations between these areas, and the impact of innovation on individual enterprises and people. Fostering a culture of trust and open communication may turn out to be more conducive to open innovation and more effective than top down strategies.

Venture Capital and Intrapreneurship

The role of the venture capital industry is well-suited to nurture high-risk, high-potential-reward businesses. Lerner proves that a single dollar of VC funding generates as much innovation as three dollars of traditional corporate research and development (Lerner 2010). However, it should be understood that it is complimentary and can never substitute other sources of innovation such as universities and corporate research laboratories.

While it cannot substitute other sources of innovation, it is a critical element of a healthy innovation ecosystem as the concentration of all these actors leads to spillover effects through positive externalities, so in an ideal situation all these stakeholders of an innovation milieu would benefit from operating in physical proximity. Venture capital—as a private or corporate investor—is too often a missing link in Europe's innovation test beds. It should not be neglected as it is a funding gap as well as a know-how shortage. Even among experienced venture capitalists and business angels, there are not sufficient competences and/or mentoring capacity to help young businesses pass through the "death valley."

The development of a successful and flourishing innovative entrepreneurship sector faces two major problems: access to finance and access to know-how. It is often found that access to finance is one of the major problems that firms from the SME sector face, as it is a particular constraint on their ability to increase the level of technology in their enterprises. This constraint comes from equity, debt markets, and informal markets (i.e. business angels). In terms of equity provision, the existing venture capital firms are growing in size and, consequently, aim to employ capital in larger increments in order to improve deal economics.

As a result, they are increasingly disinterested in pursuing smaller transactions. This phenomenon has been termed "the liquidity gap." Evidence suggests that the liquidity gap is most pronounced in the range of $500,000-$2,000,000. In terms of debt provision (i.e. commercial banking), private entrepreneurial firms are not attractive candidates for financing from the banking sector. European banks are broadly considered as risk-averse to funding smaller, private firms if they lack a track record, have small amounts of collateral, or have insufficient credit ratings. These credit constraints result in a sizeable pool of entrepreneurial projects being precluded from possible financing.

The existing business angels and their organizations in the EU are not as active as in other countries. They also partner less with other capital providers. The second problem concerns access to "know-how." This lack of "know-how" prevents firms from ultimately converting business ideas into credible business plans, and then into viable enterprises. Newly created enterprises with entrepreneurs inexperienced in a commercial environment may possess shortcomings in their managerial skills and abilities.

There are two fundamental areas where assistance is required. Firstly, in the early stages, beginner enterprises are often "virtual" in their development. The key problem for these enterprises is survival. Secondly, more mature enterprises require different assistance, as the key concern is management of growth.

The problems of access to finance and the provision of know-how are closely related and pose a major challenge for European ventures because of the shortage of venture capital. Since access to finance may be necessary for addressing liquidity and growth capital, the know-how of a venture capitalist is vital for helping the companies deal with sales, and operational challenges and effective managerial skills are needed to ensure proper utilization of capital provided to the enterprise.

Providing finance without managerial assistance is likely to translate into developmental stagnation for the firm (lack of know-how often leads to limited investments, which, in turn, leads to limited employment growth), increased sensitivity of the firm with respect to external factors, and a business potential that is unlikely to be captured. Research confirms that underdeveloped human capital is a key deterrent for venture capital development.

Providing know-how without finance is likely to lead to an immediate downfall of the firm, a "freeze" of the private initiative, and a lack of propensity for taking business risk. In both circumstances, the unintended consequences of these two challenges are the possible chain reaction for business failure.

There are numerous challenges for the growth of venture capital, best demonstrated on a comparative basis with the leading markets, most notably the USA.

Firstly, private equity in the EU represents a relatively small proportion of total assets allocated for investment purposes by institutional investors. Secondly, the allocation of venture capital funds toward the seed and start-up firms, firms in the SME sector, is low and investors tend to choose private equity investments. Thirdly, the development of the venture capital markets in Europe is disproportionate in terms of differences among countries. The most developed private equity markets in the EU, as measured by fundraising and investment, are the United Kingdom, Germany, and France. Fourthly, venture capitalists perceive an apparent shortage of viable investment opportunities. In certain countries such as Poland, they chose to search for deals elsewhere, for example in Berlin or Prague, due to excessive valuations, which is also true for Western European financiers, who look for investment opportunities globally in the USA, Israel, and China. Fifthly and most importantly, venture capital investments in Europe are relatively low as benchmarked against other markets for most attractive industries and sectors such as biotechnology.

Intrapreneurship is a specific form of entrepreneurship characteristic of some large companies and multinationals. New business creation in Europe is characterized by a relatively large degree of intrapreneurship as compared to the US (Audretsch 1995, among others). Gromb and Scharfstein show that the prevalence of intrapreneurship in Europe may be determined to a large extent by bankruptcy rules (Gromb and Scharfstein 2001).

However, intrapreneurship becomes increasingly important for big corporations. Examples include Nokia reinventing itself from a forestry company to one of the largest mobile phone companies in the world, IBM from a computer company to an information services company, and GE diversifying from a manufacturing conglomerate into a company deriving large part of its value from offering financial services. That is also entrepreneurship and it is at times conducted from the top of the company and sometimes from a unit of a company.

Companies active in the Knowledge Triangle integrate some of the knowledge generated within universities and research centers rather than create new units or new strategies to adapt to this new knowledge environment. An example could be further development of fusion energy, electrical cars, intelligent grids, or a new model of innovating in the pharmaceutical industry by purchasing young innovative biotech companies.

Thus entrepreneurship becomes an alternative strategy for keeping up the company's competitiveness, which is a "sink or swim" competence for large corporations. In all of these cases, entrepreneurship in the traditional form of start-up activity is widened into a broader innovation framework as a risk-taking activity, usually linked to innovation and creativity.

The way to finance innovation is through profits, equity, and debt. If the equity markets do not support industry, then the industry needs to rely on either debt, government subsidies, or profits. Except for such sectors as biotech, cleantech, or nanotechnology, companies cannot be taken public through Initial Public Offering until they become profitable. Silicon Valley has always relied upon equity, while Japan has relied on debt and China has relied on government subsidies and protective policies.

It is difficult to grow companies based on profit and impossible in most of the emerging technology-driven sectors because it takes a long time for an industry to become profitable. For example, the accumulation of the semiconductor industry, which began in the late 1950s, was not profitable as an industry until the mid-1980s. The pattern of funding innovation in Silicon Valley is quite specific not only to the extent that there are less walls between people and institutions, and between research labs and industry. The time from "lab-to-market" tends to be shorter and shorter as there is a catalyst in the middle in the process.

The combination of venture capital industry and thousands of small companies has become a Silicon Valley mechanism for speeding up the innovation process. Venture capital usually benefits from wealth accumulated in a given industry or in a territorial milieu of innovation because its investment requires specific knowledge of the industry and working closely with the start-ups. This consolidates the territorial milieus of innovation, the nodes in the global innovation networks, when risk capital and know-how are accumulated.

Women Entrepreneurs

In general, women lag behind men in terms of entrepreneurial activity, especially in the context of innovation-driven entrepreneurship.[20] This is also the case in Europe, although a lack of common definition and gender specific data in many cases makes it difficult to assess the scope of the issue. In such a case it is difficult to assess the effectiveness of policy instruments in raising entrepreneurship rates among women, especially women in science and technology. In contrast to the US, where an annual survey monitors entrepreneurship by women, there is still limited statistical evidence on the impact of women innovators and entrepreneurs in Europe.

Nevertheless, there are a number of sources delineating the problem. Available data shows that only 8.3% of patents are awarded to women by the European Patent Office (EPO). Only 20.3% of businesses financed with venture capital are owned by women (EVCA). A lower percentage of women-led businesses versus those led by men are innovative. There is no evidence that innovativeness or entrepreneurialism is gender specific. There is limited evidence that women have fewer entrepreneurial skills than men. Nevertheless, when compared with men, women create fewer jobs, less women are self-employed, fewer start their own businesses, and fewer have the intention or ambition to do so; if they do, they tend to chose sectors that are not as competitive and innovation driven as those chosen by men (Eurostat). The OECD report on the gender gap concludes that access to finance and support for existing businesses, not only start-ups and small enterprises, are key

(20) This chapter is a revised version of an article written by the author of this book entitled "Women Entrepreneurs: Key to Solving the Crisis," published by Lisbon Council in a report: "SMEs in the Single Market: A Growth Agenda for the 21st Century," Brussels, 2012. Available at http://www.lisboncouncil.net/publication/publication/85-smes-in-the-single-market-a-growth-agenda-for-the-21st-century.html.

to boost economic growth by tapping on this unused potential (OECD 2012).

While various forms of women-led economic activities are important to the growth agenda, the most potential impact can be delivered by increasing the number of women-funded and women-led high-growth enterprises. These innovation driven ventures are often linked to university graduates, and to the research and innovation coming out of universities and labs. They are essential nodes in the innovation networks since they attract and integrate knowledge communities and try to bridge the gap between academia, business, and governments. Universities attract and develop talent for innovation and play a pivotal role in shaping the attitudes, skills, and long-term support networks necessary to foster innovation and entrepreneurship among women students.

The policies aiming to exploit the potential of women not only in business but also in academia, public institutions, and society-at-large need to be anchored in policies integrating the Knowledge Triangle, that is research, education, and innovation, as well as entrepreneurship. Labor market policies, social inclusion, and policies related to women in the e-economy should be integrated into a comprehensive policy framework for women's empowerment.

Women face specific barriers to participation in innovation processes, and their participation in science, technology, and entrepreneurship lags behind men (OECD 2010). The challenges of leveraging the potential of women innovators and entrepreneurs lie in this specificity of the obstacles they face. The report assessing policy instruments targeted toward promoting entrepreneurial activity among women at the European and at the Member States levels classifies obstacles faced by women into three categories: contextual, economic, and soft (EEC 2008).

The contextual obstacles are rooted in the traditional perception of the role of women in many European societies. Stereotyping social roles leads first to educational choices and then to career preferences resulting in horizontal and vertical segregation. Women are less likely to specialize in science and technology and are less recognized in these fields. They are more risk averse and find it more difficult to combine different social roles when working in high-stress competitive environments requiring long, flexible working hours and constant training.

This social context requires much more persistence, resilience, and struggle for a woman innovator and entrepreneur to succeed whether she chooses high growth sectors or self-employment, lifestyle business, or new business creation out of economic necessity. The economic obstacles partially result from the social context and are specifically linked to access to finance and to risk capital in particular. Women are seen as less credible by investors, which limits the growth potential of their ventures in capital-intensive sectors. The soft obstacles originate in motivations, self-perception, skills, and training.

On the one hand, the lack of adequate business skills and knowledge discourage women from making risky career choices. On the other hand, the lack of a sufficient number of successful role models and mentors limits their progress as they are often excluded from high profile networks in business and academia, where knowledge is shared and decisions are made.

These obstacles do prevent growth and limit the potential impact of women. However, on the positive side, the OECD points out that women entrepreneurs do contribute to the economy by creating new jobs for themselves and for others and also by bringing diversity, which stimulates innovativeness, especially in the non-technological aspects of process innovation, business management, organization, and culture.

Women constitute over 60% of university graduates in Europe (EUROSTAT). The major shift in consumption patterns shows that over 50% of purchase decisions are made by women. For every ten men in the developed economies, there are nine women who have entrepreneurial training, although women are less likely to volunteer for such training (GEM 2014). In the developed and the emerging economies of Europe, 80% of women believe that their role is changing for the better and 90% of those expect that it will change for the better in all aspects from gender equality to politics to opportunities in the marketplace as women continue to benefit from the Internet economy and social networking.

However, women in Europe are of an opinion that they have reached a progress plateau. They do not foresee that their daughters will have more opportunities than they had (Nielsen 2011). Indeed, most likely the new generation of women will need to create social and economic opportunities for themselves.

That is, unless the low innovative and entrepreneurial activity of women is tackled by public policies. These policies could be designed to help the next generation of women innovators and entrepreneurs create high-growth, innovation-driven, sustainable enterprises in the single European market. However, how can policy makers design policies that influence foremost human motivations, attitudes, and culture?

Over the last ten years, Member States have developed and tested a wide range of initiatives to promote innovation and entrepreneurship among women. Finland has developed a public venture capital fund dedicated to innovative service sectors. In Sweden, a national train-the-teacher program was launched to train business advisors on how to deal with needs specific to women entrepreneurs. In France, a women's business angel network was established. In Germany, the National Agency for Women Start-ups and Power for Female Entrepreneurs launched programs for supporting women entrepreneurs specifically in science and technology. In Poland, structural funds were used to train women from economically deprived regions or social groups in entrepreneurship.

Policy initiatives at the European level were also explored in a number of ways. They originated in a number of policy making institutions and included data analysis and dissemination; creation of pan-European women's business networks; mentoring schemes; promotion of women's role in the economy and society; and the facilitation of access to information on EU funding schemes, the promotion of digital inclusion, and specifically entrepreneurship, for example through the European Network of Mentors for Women Entrepreneurs and Erasmus for Young Entrepreneurs.

Promotion of gender equality or equality of opportunity is not sufficient to stimulate innovativeness and entrepreneurship among women. A separate policy objective supported by targeted actions and programs complemented with activities that help overcome obstacles is needed (e.g. targeting women networks and business associations, women-friendly information packages, support with child care, etc.).

There are no cases where a comprehensive policy response has been designed and deployed to tackle all categories of the specific challenges women face: contextual, economic, and soft. These existing policies can be gradually enhanced or continued in the current shape and scope. Empowering women is fundamental in both the economic and social dimension for Europe to overcome the crisis. Changing motivations, attitudes, values, and behaviors of decision makers and women innovators and entrepreneurs themselves would catalyze and could become one of the drivers for the growth agenda for Europe.

Chapter 15

ENTREPRENEURIAL INSTITUTION: ROLE OF

THE EUROPEAN INSTITUTE OF INNOVATION

AND TECHNOLOGY

There have been a number of references to the European Institute of Innovation and Technology throughout the text of this book, especially in the sections related to the Knowledge and Innovation Communities. It is worthwhile to focus for a moment on the Institute in order to understand and recognize its role in developing the Communities and the new model of innovation management and financing in Europe.

The European Institute of Innovation and Technology was established in 2008. It has a status of a European Union agency (EC 294/2008). Its key mission is to establish and fund with annual grants a new type of pan-European innovation network, bringing together research, education, and innovation.

The regulators granted an unprecedented level of autonomy in terms of strategy and governance to this new institution. This was manifested by the leeway left to the Institute's Governing Board and derogations from the EC rules. The members of the Board, appointed in their personal capacity for a non-renewable four-term tenure, were to shape the strategy of the EIT and design and monitor the KICs.[21] The founding

---

(21) The first and second Governing Board of the Institute included eighteen members appointed in their personal capacity by the European Commission. Additionally there were four so-called representative members selected by the KICs and appointed by the Board. The Board was headed by a Chairperson and supported by a four-person Executive Committee. The proceedings of the Board were monitored by a Commission observer. Over the period of 2008-2014 I served on the EIT's Governing Board as an Executive Member leading the entrepreneurship agenda and shaping its policy through the Strategic Innovation Agenda and the Calls for KICs.

Board of the EIT (2008-2012) was responsible foremost for establishing the first three Knowledge and Innovation Communities, awarding the first annual grants to the KICs, and preparing the EIT's long-term strategy in a formal document to be accepted by the European Commission, the Parliament, and the Council as a basis for its funding beyond 2014. It was also tasked with establishing the EIT Foundation as a first of its type, an independent instrument capable of raising private funding and attracting other forms of industry commitment in order to support the EIT and its KICs.

The discussions in the early meetings of the founding Board were a laboratory for learning how to translate the EIT regulation into a new operational model that could increase Europe's limited capacity to exploit its innovation potential.[22] The Board members represented research, education, and business, and so all the sides of the Knowledge Triangle were represented. Initially the main strategy was to bring together big European companies with the best research universities and research centers in order to establish a set of productive interfaces similar to the one already existing in Europe.[23] The traditional engineering and research culture developed in the industrial economy required continuous efforts to stimulate the process of redefining the innovation processes and their essence in the knowledge-driven economy, where innovation and entrepreneurship are key drivers of growth. However, the Board went beyond this phase into a more radical and daring model.

The Board agreed that Europe has all-important components to innovation such as great research, excellent education, and

---

(22) I am very grateful for the opportunity to listen to and to participate in the Board discussions. This was a fascinating learning environment because of the wisdom, experience, and passion of my Board colleagues. We sought to conceptualize a new model and thus help Europe more quickly overcome the unfolding economic crisis.

(23) Europe has some leading global innovation hotbeds such as, for example, Cambridge in Great Britain (Kirk and Cotton 2012). However, during the Board discussions, we realized to what extent the Knowledge Triangle is disintegrated in most innovation nodes in Europe and started looking for a missing link.

accomplished industry. It recognized however that successful strategies for the Knowledge Triangle depend not only on how well universities and companies collaborate. The strategic debate reached three strategic conclusions. Firstly, the key components of a new system of how innovation should be managed in Europe represent a new type of governance as compared to the existing innovation networks. Secondly, there is a need to induce entrepreneurship as the missing link in the Knowledge Triangle and a catalyst of value creation processes. Thirdly, the EIT cannot be a funding agency in order to accomplish its ambitious goals but must define itself as an entrepreneurial institution, a sort of investor in a KIC and a manager of a KIC portfolio rather than a traditional agency.

Based on these broad assumptions, the EIT established the first three Communities with unprecedented speed, within only 18 months of its inception. Climate-KIC, EIT ICT Labs, and KIC InnoEnergy were selected in an open Call for proposals, which broadly defined three themes. The themes were defined in the EIT Regulation (EC 294/2008) as climate change, renewable energy, and ICT. They directly linked to the meta-theme of Europe's innovation strategy, the so-called Grand Challenges. These major areas were identified as key challenges to the wellbeing of the European and the global society. They had a significant role as vectors aligning multiple strategies of the EU and national governments toward tackling a limited number of complex and critical issues.

While the legislator proposed the themes, the Board re-conceptualized them, showing its thought leadership in delimiting specific areas where Europe can still make a significant difference in the global arena. Climate change was addressed more specifically as climate mitigation and adaptation. Renewable energy was changed to sustainable energy. ICT gained a new focus in its rephrasing as information and communication society, shifting the meaning from industry to people and communities.

Gradually since 2009, the EIT's headquarters have been established in an office space donated by the Hungarian government in Infopark, a newly opened science park in Budapest. In time, its young administration grew to a team of about 40 people. This team is headed by a director responsible for all operational activities including the monitoring of the KICs. The director is endowed with the sole financial responsibility for the sound management of public money, including the management of the agency as well as the grants to the KICs.

By 2014, the EIT had issued a number of documents, which shed some light on the strategy of what has been maturing into a new type of this comprehensive policy instrument. The two most important include the Call for KICs (2009) and Strategic Innovation Agenda (2011). They defined the nascent identity of the Institute in a quite unique frame as a seed investor and later as an impact investment institute. Both notions resonate strongly as being drawn from the language of the venture capital industry. Indeed such terms used in a context of a Community body sound radical and provoke a question: Can the notion of entrepreneurship as a missing link in the Knowledge Triangle also relate to an agency managing public funds for innovation?

The EIT as a Seed Investor

There are some examples of successful public policy instruments to stimulate entrepreneurship by being entrepreneurial institutions themselves. This is the case, for instance, with Yozma Fund, an Israeli government initiative to boost the venture capital industry (Senor and Singer 2009). The EIT seems unique in this respect in Europe by introducing "an investment logic" into the research-education-innovation policy landscape and by doing so through leveraging of the specificity of the fragmented yet networked innovation environment.

In April 2009, the European Institute of Innovation and Technology published a Call for proposals to establish the first Knowledge and Innovation Communities (EIT 2009). The Call for KICs was anchored in the EIT Regulation, a legal basis for establishing the EIT and the KICs. The Regulation was quite general in defining the framework and specifying the role, activities, field areas, and funding sources of future KICs. It left a lot of flexibility to the EIT to address these diverse aspects of future KICs. As the outcome of the strategic discussions of the EIT Governing Board and the support of the European Commission observers of the Board meetings, the Call text was developed, conceptualizing the KICs, their spatial articulation, governance, management and operational models, and funding structure.

The Call reflected a conceptual model integrating diverse views of the EIT Governing Board, which converged into a unique and ambitious translation of Regulation into the EIT and its operational units—the KICs. The Call text, a nine-page document, in its form, language, and level of detail, reflected a new approach breaking with the traditional elaborated documents prevailing in the European framework programs and made a statement toward a new "empower-trust- incentivize" rather than "prescribe-monitor-control" mode. During the discussion preceding the publication of the Call, some EIT Governing Board members started to conceptualize the Institute's role toward the KICs as a "seed investor."[24]

The term "seed investor" is used in the venture capital industry to define a provider of funding at a very early stage of venture growth. The investment is usually made in return for a substantial equity stake at low valuation. It reflects the risk of passing through "the valley of

---

(24) The concept of the EIT as a seed investor came from the discussions within the Entrepreneurship Working Group that I presided. A presentation prepared with my colleague, Professor Alexander von Gabain, who supported me from the beginning in my role as the leader of the entrepreneurship agenda, provoked a vivid discussion in the Board, and eventually a number of concepts coming from the investment industry were induced into the Call. This direction was strongly supported by Professor Martin Schuurmans, the founding Chairman of the EIT Governing Board, who understood well the value of learning from the entrepreneurial markets, having established R&D organizations and a biomedical institute and school in a university in China. His successor, Alexander von Gabain, the founder of biotech enterprises, as well as two other Governing Board colleagues—Professor Julia King and Mr. Linnar Viik, as well as Director General Ms. Odile Quintin and Ms. Lucia Recalde of the European Commission—actively participated in these early discussions and eventually both the Governing Board and the Commission endorsed the direction for the Call for KICs.

death," that is, the first few critical years before a company gains its first paying customers.

In precise terms the EIT was not and even from a legal perspective could not be a seed investor in the KICs. The EIT has not taken equity in the KICs. The Institute does not even have a formal representation in the governance structures of the KICs. The KICs themselves are not expected only to maximize value for the shareholders. It is not possible that a consortium would return the grants to the EIT in any form. No return on investment (ROI) was taken into account when choosing the first consortia.

However, on a conceptual level, the seed investor was a sort of metaphor epitomizing the logic of the Call. There appears to be some resemblance to the investor's thinking, especially if the EIT and its role toward the consortia are contrasted with the role of other EU funding agencies. The shift was marked along the lines of public funding redistribution toward adding value with public funding.

Consequently, the EIT proposed a governance model quite different from that of a traditional public institution. The terms used in the Board discussions included such concepts as "investing in KICs," "portfolio of KICs," "failure of a KIC," "weighted economic and social returns on investment in KICs," and "self-sustainability of a KIC."

A business model and a business case of a KIC were to rely on the transfer from research lab to the markets and to the society. They were to include all three sides of the Knowledge Triangle: education, research, and innovation. The education related activities were to be planned as new schemes of innovation-focused programs through EIT-branded master, doctorate, and post-doctorate degrees and diplomas. The business related activities, technology transfer, commercialization, and societal applications were to target the ultimate objective of a KIC, that is to stimulate innovation in large firms, create spin-offs and start-ups, and support innovative SMEs with high growth potential. The innovation related activities, by definition, were to be excellence driven and cutting edge, and thus enticing enough to attract, keep, and work with top class partner organizations and top-class talent from around the world. In business terms these activities were the product or service offering of a KIC to internal and external customers. The former were partners in the consortium. The latter were to be acquired over time.

An interesting novelty related to the investment framework was the concept of the business plan to be included with the proposals. This financial plan was to reflect a vision toward financial self-sustainability based on a value proposition and a business model. New business creation through spin-offs and start-ups, licensing of technology and patents, and offerings of products and services were part of the self-sustainability plan. The Board believed that the robustness of the plan to raise 75% of the KIC funding, especially from industry, and keep the commitment of the partners was a decisive success factor for a KIC. The business plan was an integral part of the proposals.

The Call attracted twenty consortia, eighteen of which fulfilled the eligibility criteria. A ranking prepared in a blind review process shortlisted six proposals. Representatives of the six consortia were invited for a hearing at the Governing Board of the EIT. In a secret vote, the Board selected winning applications. The Climate-KIC consortium was selected for the theme of "Climate Mitigation and Adaptation," while the consortium of EIT ICT Labs was selected for "Future Innovation and Communication Society," and the KIC InnoEnergy proposal was selected for "Sustainable Energy." The final score of a proposal was to be the sum of the scores of a two-step evaluation procedure. The maximum score possible was 200 points. The first part of a KIC proposal was to include the originality, competitiveness, and feasibility of the proposal.

The evaluation of quality of the first part of the proposal was based on seven criteria, which added up to a maximum of 100 points.

Table 1: Selection Criteria for the First Knowledge and Innovation Communities Source: The EIT Call for KICs (2009).

Criteria Stage 1 (maximum score)	Comments
Novelty and attractiveness of the proposal (20 points)	The innovativeness of the proposal was assessed in terms of the innovation model and the level of pioneering of the declared research projects to be undertaken and commercialized.
Economic, environmental, societal, and innovation impact of the KIC in the context of European challenges and policies and potential to make a major contribution to the aims of the EIT (20 points)	The Institute has changed the approach to the assessment of grant effectiveness. Subsequently, rather than on inputs such as investment in research, education, and innovation activities, the KICs were to be assessed based on outputs and eventually impact. These assessment indicators were to be proposed by the KICs themselves so that they would reflect the strategy of a consortium. The proposals that pointed toward how to leverage existing recourses and align their actions with other existing policy instruments and available funding were awarded higher scores.
Internal coherence of the KIC strategy and activities (10 points)	The integration of the Knowledge Triangle was judged in terms of uniqueness of interpretation of the KIC model and propensity to experiment with the model as such.
Criteria Stage 2	**Comments**
The quality of the co-location plan (20 points)	This was a feasibility assessment of an operational aspect of the KIC as a network, a new model of organizing partners across Europe for the purpose of collaboration according to a new pattern. The point of scrutiny was the degree of completeness of the co-location plan, the complementarity of nodes, and the plan of operation within each node and between them. This was in fact a plan for the management of people innovating in an integrated yet geographically widespread network.
Planning for the management and use of intellectual property (10 points)	The intellectual property plan was to reflect the EIT IPR Guidelines, a separate document published by the EIT as a policy framework (EIT 2009). The effectiveness of the IPR policies included transfer, licensing, and industrial value creation and consistency with KIC objectives, mechanisms to reflect the EIT guidelines with respect to remuneration and reward schemes taking into account the role of the SMEs. This difficult point of negotiation was to be agreed upon between partners before entering into formal collaboration, so not to delay the implementation process of a KIC's strategy.

Completeness and credibility of the KIC business plan (10 points)	The business plan was evaluated in terms of completeness of tools and resources of partners and the level of integration between them to form new innovation value chains, planned investments activities involving the private and financial sectors, SMEs, start-ups and spin-offs, and new partners. It was to include a market analysis and competitive benchmarks for the completeness and credibility of the financial plan including identification of the responsible actors, short/medium/long-term milestones, key performance indicators (KPIs), and sensitivity analyses (risk-assessment). Finally, it was to predict a potential return on investment over a 10-year period, including financial and non-financial indicators.
Quality of the plans for dissemination of best practice and public outreach activity (10 points)	As beneficiaries of public funding, KICs were to consider the need to disseminate their learning and share best practices within the EU community. Therefore, effectiveness of plans for outreach including research, education, and business communities were part of the assessment score.

The assessment of the proposals posed a specific challenge. When an investor makes an investment decision, it is to a large extent taken on the belief in the management team, secured technology, business model, and market potential; most often the investment decision is very subjective and intuitive. In the public setting, a transparent, "equal level playing field" and objective selection process had to be put in place for compliance reasons. With all rules observed, some degree of flexibility was embedded into the selection process in line with the EIT Regulation. The experts prepared their evaluation opinions, which served as a basis for an informed grant awarding decision. But it was ultimately the Board's collegial decision on the winning consortia, based on experts' judgments and evaluation of proposals including the business plans and face-to-face interviews with consortia leaders and in the Board discussions.

In order to pass the first step of the evaluation, proposals must have obtained at least 30% of the maximum points for each of the seven criteria listed above and at least 50 points in total for this evaluation stage. The five highest-scoring proposals from each priority area were to pass on to the next step of evaluation. The second stage of assessment took under scrutiny the commitment, capability, and combined strength of the partners involved in a partnership. This could give candidates a maximum total score of 50 points. The management, governance, and organization of the partnership and co-location, covering also the financial and legal aspects of the KIC, could bring up to 50 points. The maximum score for the second part of the proposal was 100 points.

The distribution process of public funding to the consortia is structured as an annual competitive process based on consortium business plan assessment as well as its progress report, its assessment report and the recommendation of the EIT director, and a hearing of consortium management at the EIT Governing Board. The business plan is a tool for monitoring operational activities of a KIC and its long-term progress toward financial self-sustainability.

While the business plan with its milestones and KPIs was a tool to assess the effectiveness of a KIC in the short to mid-term, their long-term impact was to be measured also in economic and social dimensions such as job creation.

The robustness of the plan to raise 75% of a consortium's funding was one of the decisive factors in the assessment process during the Call for KICs. The Board believed that the ability to attract external funding was a good prediction of the commitment of partners and eventually of the future success of a consortium. The proposals were to include proof of the long-term commitment of the partners, and the reputation of the partners, especially of those coming from the business sector, was part of the scrutiny. The point concerning the sustainable and long-term self-supporting financing mechanism was related to the concept that consortia should become financially independent from the EIT in the long term and become innovation powerhouses generating revenue from their activities.

The Board estimated that in order to achieve a significant impact at the European level, a KIC's operating budget should reach between 50-100 million EUR per year. Only up to 25% is funded by the EIT, and the rest of the KIC's global expenditure comes from other sources, with the KIC being responsible for raising the remaining 75%. The EIT contribution was not expected to fund new infrastructure but instead leverage existing infrastructure by covering costs of establishment, administration, and coordination of a KIC as well as its value-added activities in education, innovation, and entrepreneurship. The full 75% from non-EIT sources was not expected to be in place on the day of the application. The application was to include a roadmap for how a consortium planned to ensure substantial contribution from businesses.

Impact Investment Institute

The EIT expressed its mission as "To become the catalyst for a step change in the European Union's innovation capacity and impact." The KICs, with the new innovation model, were to become the drivers of change. But could the EIT become a change agent with a modest budget of 308 million EUR and its nascent history in the midst of the economic crisis?

In 2011, the EIT prepared its Strategic Innovation Agenda (SIA) (EIT SIA 2011). This document presented the vision of the young institution and a road map for the period of 2014-2020. The document was sent to the European Commission and served as the basis for a draft of the SIA that was sent to the Parliament and the Council as a foundation for the discussion over the EIT's future budget. The SIA remains the point of reference for understanding this emerging institution.

Firstly, the document emphasized that the EIT believes in the concept of networked innovation in the Knowledge Triangle. The SIA also reconfirmed the KIC model as a template for the current as well as the future KICs. It reiterated that KICs should remain autonomous, independent legal entities, transnational public-private partnerships with a Seven-Year commitment of partners. The KICs were given the freedom to decide on their legal structure, governance model, organization, and strategy, which validated the EIT approach to managing and financing innovation. This approach is marked by empowering bottom-up initiative and encouraging business thinking expressed for example by the reference to the KIC's business model and business case, private funding (co-investment), effective governance structure, clear IP rules, and operational efficiency. It proposed the establishment of six more Communities, which justified the projected budget of 2.9 billion EUR.

Secondly, the text referred to building an entrepreneurial culture in Europe. Entrepreneurship has become a vector in the Knowledge Triangle capable of overcoming the silos of industry and academia through entrepreneurship education, support of new business creation, and growth of existing innovation-driven ventures. The SIA also introduced an EIT-labeled diploma for educational programs at the KICs, ensuring that the programs would comply with the EIT Handbook. It also showcased the EIT Entrepreneurship Award for ventures coming out of the KICs and the EIT Roundtable of Entrepreneurs as a way to establish a link between the EIT entrepreneurial community and venture capital industry.

Thirdly, the SIA explained the existing governance and monitoring system as well as grant management. Among other issues, it described how the cooperation between the EIT and each KIC was formalized through a Seven-Year Framework Partnership Agreement defining objectives, rights, and obligations of each party, and the nature of activities to be funded by the EIT grants. It elaborated that the EIT made annual grant decisions for each KIC based on the KIC's business plan and rolling triennial work program. The former presents an estimate of financial needs, resources, and funding sources; the latter outlays the activities planned for that period, and lists risks related to the execution of the work plan and strategies to mitigate them. It also displays general information on the operation and administration of a KIC.

Fourthly, the SIA stated the intention to introduce a competitive funding process. The rational for testing a mechanism for stimulating competition between the KICs was to maximize the return on investment in the KICs. Since 2012 a portion of the annual funding awarded by the EIT has been based on an assessment of each KIC's individual performance and a competitive review between the KICs. The business plan is a tool to monitor the strategic development on annual bases. The annual business plan presentation at the EIT Governing Board meeting, which ultimately takes funding decisions, is preceded by a structured process of business plan formulation. The competitive funding process is expected to increase the KICs' balance sheet over time as a consequence of a growing portfolio of tangible and intangible assets.

Fifthly, the document commented on the EIT itself as an institution capable of adding value and acting as a change agent in the context of the existing European innovation system. The change is induced by bringing an alternative proposition to the stakeholders in the Knowledge Triangle. This value proposition creates an opportunity to reallocate resources to areas of higher productivity, and in this sense introduces an entrepreneurial culture in Europe.

Table 2: EIT Strategic Innovation Agenda (EIT SIA 2011).

Strategic Goal	Tools and Programs
Consolidation of the Knowledge and Innovation Communities and launching the next KICs in strategic thematic areas	EIT Scoreboard; Annual competitive grant giving process based on business plans and a hearing at the Governing Board meeting; Management mechanisms such as the EIT Forum with the KICs' management and progress reports
Launch of the next Knowledge and Innovation Communities	Call for KICs
Fostering entrepreneurship as a driver of innovation processes in the Knowledge Triangle	EIT-labeled diplomas for KICs' educational degree and non-degree programs; EIT Entrepreneurship Award for ventures nurtured within the KICs' ecosystems; EIT Roundtable of Entrepreneurs as a sounding board to link the EIT community with the venture capital industry
Understanding the different KICs' experimental models and their dynamics	Research, case studies, and independent evaluations and stakeholders consultation
Integration, dissemination, and communication of practices and learning on transnational business creation to stakeholders beyond the KICs by sharing learning on new business innovation models, processes, and ways in Europe	Outreach programs and stakeholder meetings across Europe
Verification and alignment of the EIT policy impact of the KICs to international world class innovation experiences	Reiterations of the Triennial Work programs and Annual Reports
Attracting industry to the KICs and supporting cross-KIC agendas	EIT Foundation

Delivering results rapidly in the midst of the crisis and testing new innovation models with limited funding has been considered a successful experiment. This is manifested by the scope of the increased budget. When established in 2008, the EIT's budget was 308 million EUR for the period 2008-2013. In 2013 the Council and Parliament agreed on a budget for the EIT of 2.4 billion EUR. It represented

3.52% of the Horizon 2020 budget, which was decreased in the process of negotiation by 12.25% (from the EUR 80 billion proposed by the Commission down to EUR 70.2 billion). In this context, the ambitious original proposal in the Strategic Innovation Agenda of 2.8 billion EUR was decreased by only 14.4%. This revised EIT budget should be looked upon in the context of the overall limits to the entire 2014-2020 European Union budget with respect to the 2007-2013 period due to fiscal constraints in the Euro zone and the economic crisis.

The new resources allow the transition of the EIT from its infancy into a fully-fledged impact investment institute. Taking into account the available budget and the need to preserve the KIC model and still gather critical mass for impact across all of Europe, the co-legislators (the European Parliament and the Council) agreed to launch five new KICs during the period 2014-2020, rather than six as proposed in the SIA.[25] They will be launched in three tranches in the following thematic areas: Raw Materials and Healthy Living and Active Aging (in 2014); Food4Future and Added Value Manufacturing (in 2016); and Urban Mobility (in 2018).

Taking into consideration the set up of the EIT, it can be considered as an accomplished institutional innovation. The new budget is no doubt tangible proof that the young Institute has induced new innovation processes across Europe and there is political consent to scale up its activities. Its investment in the KICs has made an impact by creating an opportunity for entrepreneurial people and organizations—both universities and businesses—to develop ventures and to foster new entrepreneurial culture in Europe. The laboratory of learning for the existing KICs will be extended beyond a few locations with the new resources and support of national and regional governments.

---

(25) The original proposal of the SIA additionally included the "Smart and Secure Societies" KIC, which was eventually abandoned.

Limits of the EIT Experience

The mission of the European Institute of Innovation and Technology is to design, build, and help grow Knowledge and Innovation Communities, the Europe-specific entrepreneurial innovation networks that experiment with new operational models for transnational innovation and business incubation at a pan-European level. The main challenge in the short-term to achieving this goal comes from high expectations for delivering results under the necessity of acting decisively in the context of the economic crisis in Europe. In efforts to achieve this goal, the EIT has faced particular challenges in the first years of its operations. While the main challenges are on the radar of the Institute's management as outlined in the Strategic Innovation Agenda—including the consolidation of the existing KICs, the establishment of new KICs, and the growth of the institutional capacity of the EIT headquarters—there are some limits of the EIT experience that require more specific policy actions.

1. Attracting, growing, and retaining talent in Europe

Over the last decade, the war for entrepreneurial talent has intensified and Europe is now suffering from a painful brain drain. Some 400,000 European science and technology graduates now live in the US and thousands more leave each year. A survey released in 2007 by the EC found that only 13% of European science professionals working abroad intended to return home. Because of increased global competition and strategy of growth by investment in research, innovation, and entrepreneurship, the mobility of knowledge workers and demographic changes will only intensify the brain drain.

Early evidence coming out of the KICs shows the necessity of making more orchestrated efforts to reach people with entrepreneurship potential and unite this diverse talent under the EIT brand. For the time being, the EIT has only begun making efforts to build an EIT community of the KICs' alumni, faculty, and collaborators. It would be wise to consider a more proactive role of the Institute in building the community, tracking individual talent, spotting high potential individuals, and offering support by connecting to opportunities such as, for example, potential investors in the Roundtable of Entrepreneurs.

A specific case of tapping on Europe's talent relates to students coming from the Central and Eastern European countries and from regions considered as less innovative although sometimes characterized with a high level of entrepreneurial activity, as in the case of Greece. They are hardly represented in the bulk of first admissions to the KICs. The mission of the EIT is to make a pan-European imprint. EIT Passports, fellowship programs that are planned for the future, may be one of the ways to tackle this issue.

An additional aspect of attracting talent to the EIT community is related to gender issues. There is no policy at the EIT level for stimulating more diversity. The cornerstones of the EIT actions directed toward the KICs could be simple monitoring and reporting tools. Additional impact could be achieved by sponsorship of best practice sharing, promoting women's social networks across the KICs, and launching mentoring programs. A radical change though can be introduced only if a European policy to deploy quotas as transition instruments to increase the number of women in leadership positions by 2020 is accepted, as advocated by Viviane Reding, Vice-President of the European Commission in charge of Justice, Fundamental Rights, and Citizenship (April 2012). The EIT could take a pronounced position in this Europe-wide debate, especially with the KICs and their partners, and lead by example.

2. Assessing effectiveness through the EIT Scoreboard

Validation of the EIT's innovative model can be documented only by quality results, delivered quickly and defined as a next generation of entrepreneurial Europeans, new products, and services for industry partners in the KICs, and new, high-growth companies incubated and accelerated in the innovation networks of the KICs and its nodes, which create value and jobs. The KIC model is based on an entrepreneurial culture induced in institutions in the Knowledge Triangle, which partner to form the consortia.

The EIT has put in place a system for monitoring and assessing the effectiveness of the KICs in the form of reporting and business plan assessment. The success of the KICs surely means the success of the EIT. However, there is an additional dimension to be surveyed and eventually assessed. It is the effectiveness of the institution as such, of its governance mechanism and administration.

The EIT has undertaken a number of efforts to develop a tool to assess its effectiveness: the EIT Scoreboard. The tool was initially based on strategic objectives considered critical for the success of the EIT and the KICs, which included the following areas: development of the EIT brand and label; creation of new businesses; growth of existing businesses; recruitment of and collaboration with top-class talent; development of an educational ecosystem for entrepreneurship; production of research and innovation breakthroughs; organization of people's mobility across co-location centers; aggregation of partners and people; and contribution from third parties. The challenge came from matching particular quantitative and qualitative indicators with these strategic objectives.

The lack of templates for assessing this type of a pan-European networked, entrepreneurial institution such as the EIT has been a trial and error process of defining from scratch the monitoring of the EIT administration and the KICs' activities and grant management in a new trust-driven way. The long-term direction and future impact will be visible only after substantial time due to the nature of innovation activities. The EIT impact will then be reflected in fostering the cross-KIC agenda and dissemination of learning to the stakeholders outside the EIT community. Based on the Scoreboard, the EIT can amend its strategy to support a KIC, and reward the ones that meet their objectives as well as the EIT mission.

3. Outreach, dissemination, and best practice sharing: Tapping the potential of the less innovative regions in Europe

As a public body, the role of the Institute is to develop a model, test it, learn from mistakes, and then share the learning with institutions and organizations that can benefit from its knowledge. Dissemination of knowledge and best practice sharing needs to be an inherent part of the EIT's activities but also incorporated into the strategy of the KICs. The challenge is to maintain the market-driven orientation of the KICs while at the same time putting in place a motivation mechanism so that they undertake this sort of action.

Outreach is a different issue from that of dissemination and best practice sharing. It is related to reaching out to resources that could potentially bring value to the KICs as well as to Europe at-large.

The EIT is an instrument fostering excellence and is not designed to deal with issues related to inclusion and social cohesion. This excellence-focused strategy resulted in the placement of only one of seventeen existing co-location centers in Central and Eastern Europe. Lack of effective outreach mechanisms limits the Institute's ability to tap into the existing reservoir of talent and entrepreneurship in that particular region as well as in other regions in Europe that are traditionally less advanced. There can hardly be a compromise on excellence since the EIT is meant to help Europe compete globally, a goal for which excellence is a condition sine qua non. Yet, at the same time it diminishes the EIT's potential by wasting resources available in less innovative regions in Europe. Moreover, excellence as a selection and assessment criterion should be defined by the EIT in a specific sense relevant for innovation-driven knowledge triangle strategy rather than as strictly excellent science.

In line with the EIT's status as a European Community body, it should also facilitate cross-fertilizing interaction with existing and new EU programs. Over time, the EIT should also take a proactive role toward regional and national bodies in Europe involved in innovation, so that the character of formal arrangements and informal interactions leads to the accumulation of knowledge, talent, and capital within, around, and beyond existing co-location centers.

4. Fostering entrepreneurship, entrepreneurial education, and access to funding

It has been argued throughout this book that one of the most effective ways to exploit Europe's innovation capacity is through entrepreneurship. But the question is: What in practice does entrepreneurship mean for the Institute? It can be argued that the EIT should foremost foster entrepreneurial culture and that it does so through its diplomas for entrepreneurial education programs, its entrepreneurship award, and its roundtable of entrepreneurs.

However, part of the challenge is not only about "soft" actions but also about how to build collaboration with small and medium-sized enterprises. How can SMEs be included into the structure of the Knowledge Triangle? Successful collaboration models between industry, universities, governments, and the not-for-profit sector in the KICs are in most cases an outcome of a bottom-up and top-down approach. Yet for small businesses, such collaboration often appears costly and time-consuming and so they in practice are excluded or their impact is limited in this kind of innovation network. One could argue that the EIT could help by forming more explicit policies toward the KICs. It also could experiment with programs and tools to foster this type of structural inclusion as part of the cross-KIC agenda, including partnership with the EIT Foundation.

Another aspect is revisiting incubation models in Europe. The KICs experiment with building their own models. There can be a number of actions in this context undertaken by the EIT. The Institute, through the KICs and the Foundation, has good connections with industry. This could become a channel to scale up ventures and give them access to global distribution channels, as well as access to the pool of experienced managers.

Finally, getting the EIT alumni ventures on the radar of the venture capital industry could be one important contribution of the EIT through its Roundtable of Entrepreneurs. Extending its contacts to business angels and family offices would create a unique platform for networking and sharing. Another solution-oriented action could be to establish a goal-specific finance facility within the EIT Foundation and, for example, the European Investment Fund, in order to provide funding for KICs' start-ups and their international expansion.

Chapter 16

LESSONS FOR EUROPEAN INNOVATION POLICY

Over the last decade, the European Union has been implementing systemic reforms and making incremental steps in order to boost its economic growth and preserve the social model. There have been important structural changes introduced by research, education, and innovation policies as well. These include the establishment of the European Research Area and European Higher Education Area, the growth of Community funding provided within Framework Programs for Research and Technological Development, and new institutions such as the European Research Council and the European Institute of Innovation and Technology.

These policy efforts however did not manage to close the innovation gap between Europe and the United States and Japan. The economic crisis made this goal even more challenging, if at all realistic. While many European countries are known for their systemic approach to innovation, new ideas, new dynamics, and more effective implementation of policy instruments are urgently needed. Horizon 2020 responds to these needs as a new opening for European innovation policy designed in the times of crisis.

This book has been an attempt to provide insights into how innovation and entrepreneurship can be stimulated in Europe. Here are key lessons based on the experience of the European Institute of Innovation and

Technology and its Knowledge and Innovation Communities. They can be useful to calibrate existing policies and design new instruments in the hope of overcoming the "European paradox": the inability to exploit research and innovation potential.

1. Use crisis as the time for accelerating systemic change

2. Stimulate collaboration in the Knowledge Triangle

3. Recognize entrepreneurship as the missing link in the Knowledge Triangle

4. Encourage a strategic shift toward a model of an entrepreneurship-driven Knowledge Triangle

5. Foster open innovation in a global networked environment

6. Acknowledge the importance of venture capital and reward serial entrepreneurship

7. Experiment with institutional framework, governance, and incentive systems

A commentary on these lessons is provided below:

1. Keep innovation policy high on the political agenda

The global economic crisis challenged and at the same time offered an opportunity for European governments to consolidate efforts to redesign innovation policies. But in the adversity of crisis, keeping innovation high on the policy agenda can be considered a success in its own right. Called to help deal with liquidity problems and prevent bankruptcies, governments tend to sacrifice the measures that pave the road to growth in the mid-term. These emergency solutions come at the price of shrinking budgets for research and education. Facing reality means that new strategies are needed to restart economic growth with limited resources. This means not more of the same but a qualitative change in how innovation is managed and financed.

2. Stimulate collaboration in the Knowledge Triangle

The Knowledge Triangle model brings into an innovation network environments where research activities, education, and innovation take place. The Knowledge and Innovation Communities have created templates that have brought competitors together to collaborate in the development of technology, products, services, and processes. They have brought the best research universities together to offer joint degrees under the EIT label. The KICs experiment with business incubation and acceleration models by channeling entrepreneurial talent into its multimodal, multidimensional networks of innovation networks. The early evidence shows that such collaborative partnerships can successfully deliver results if structured upon certain principles such as internationally distributed but thematically convergent parties representing institutions from all sides of the triangle; long-term commitment of partners to finance and support the projects; effective governance of a suitable legal entity; and the inclusion of entrepreneurship as the missing link in the Knowledge Triangle. This KIC paradigm can be used for designing and calibrating innovation instruments and their governance mechanisms.

3. Recognize entrepreneurship as the missing link in the Knowledge Triangle

Evidence shows that the speed and effectiveness of change in the Knowledge Triangle networks are conditioned to a large extent by how entrepreneurship, entrepreneurial culture, and entrepreneurial education become an integral part of the model. The cornerstone is culture that encourages students, faculty, and network managers to take calculated risks. This objective should be reached through projects that shorten the time from labs to markets, stimulate creation and growth of new born-global companies, and develop entrepreneurial students. Efforts to copy the Silicon Valley in Europe have failed since the vitality of the American model to a large extent comes from the switching capacity of its multilayered networks. Investment in establishing more structural links between clusters, Technology Transfer Offices, business incubators and accelerators across Europe, and mobility of students and faculty involved in new business creation and transnational peer-to-peer learning environments seems to be the way for Europe to move forward.

4. Encourage a strategic shift toward a model of an entrepreneurship-driven Knowledge Triangle

An important aspect of creating value that is generated within a Knowledge Triangle with the involvement of students is the knowledge and technology that is translated into industrial applications or commercialized. In part, the process of knowledge creation is through standard academic processes, such as the publishing of academic papers and filing for patents, but increasingly it is through the outcome of the economic and social activity of students and alumni and the impact they bring as individuals, innovators, entrepreneurs, and leaders. A relationship between university spin-off activity and economic growth may be too simple a measure to reflect the conflicting priorities of universities and businesses. Policy makers can encourage such a strategic shift by providing funding, changing the governance of universities and incentive systems in academia, and acknowledging entrepreneurs as role models and leaders.

5. Foster open innovation in a global networked environment

The European Patent is an important milestone toward the harmonization of IPR legislation in Europe, lowering patenting costs and speeding up the patenting process. A unified intellectual property law favors commercial exploitation of ideas and facilitates venture capital investment in Europe. But protecting IP is just part of the equation. Another part is the company's ability to innovate and exploit its innovation capacity also through intrapreneurship. This ability is increased by operating in an open innovation environment where knowledge flows freely among innovation network members. An opportunity for policy makers in Europe is to enhance industry involvement in the Knowledge Triangle. It can be achieved by governance mechanisms and incentive structures that stimulate a "challenger mentality." Economic crisis and disruptive innovations unexpectedly change the logic and consequently the business models of whole industries, the telecom market being but one example. Open innovation platforms and creative learning environments for collaborative partnerships such as the Knowledge and Innovation Communities are possible models to adapt.

6. Acknowledge the importance of venture capital and reward serial entrepreneurship

Lack of proper regulation may have a detrimental effect on the cost of financing entrepreneurial activities. Availability of venture capital is critical for stimulating growth and increasing chances of commercial success for innovative companies. Since young, innovative, born-global companies are key driving forces for growth and job creation, creating favorable conditions for venture capital in Europe is critical. Approximately 40% of early stage and venture capital in Europe is financed with public money (EVCA 2010). This public funding helps bridge the shortage of risk capital in Europe. But supply of public funding distorts the market and leads to overvaluation of companies. Policy makers often neglect an important component of an entrepreneurial ecosystem: the presence of business angels and serial entrepreneurs. Some countries, such as the United Kingdom, have introduced tax incentives that allow for 100% tax relief on up to 100,000 pounds invested in a start-up. In Germany, the European Investment Fund has introduced a pilot facility to co-invest with individuals ("super-angels"). However, while young companies complain about the shortage of risk capital, venture capitalists and business angels are often of the opinion that the quality of ventures remains low in Europe. Policies should focus on mitigating risk of venture capital by providing financing and increasing the quality of start-ups. This can be done for example by stimulating the renewal of business incubation and acceleration models in Europe. Another method is deployment of incentives for experienced (often retired) managers to invest their time and develop young talent. Gender-specific policies are usually missing, which leaves untapped the talent of women entrepreneurs.

7. Experiment with institutional framework

Arguably, the most interesting lesson for the European innovation policy resulting from the analysis presented in this book is the encouragement to experiment in the institutional sense. The entrepreneurial innovation networks—the KICs—seem to provide early evidence for the benefits of experimentation. Setting up the European Institute of Innovation and Technology appears to be a promising way to change how innovation is managed and financed in Europe, achieved by allocating a relatively small budget and giving a mandate to the EIT Governing Board to innovate. This entrepreneurial institution shifted the logic of public money from budget spending to investing. This requires however a new type of governance and new competences in public administration. The public innovation policy tools are usually designed from a bureaucratic, control-based perspective. A new trust-based approach is needed for innovation in a public institutional context.

These are key lessons for the policy makers, drawn upon the experience of designing and establishing the first three entrepreneurial innovation networks in Europe by the European Institute of Innovation and Technology. Trust is a common denominator underlying all of them as a prerequisite for creating value in an entrepreneurship-driven Knowledge Triangle.

Conclusion

Creative Destruction and Value Creation: A Question of Identity

Europe's prosperity has originated in its creativity, innovativeness, and entrepreneurial talent. The surnames of great European entrepreneurs—Behring, Citroen, Daimler, Lafarge, Reuter, and Siemens—are now associated with large European brands. With few exceptions, iconic entrepreneurs may still be born in Europe, but to fulfill their dreams, they usually must leave the Old Continent. Actually, because of the economic crisis, some immigrant entrepreneurs have even decided to re-emigrate in search of better opportunities elsewhere.

In the global networked economies of the twenty-first century, creativity, innovation, and entrepreneurship are the source of growth. Creativity drives innovation and allows an organization to scale up solutions and diminish costs, redesigning value chains and business models. The analytical grid presented in this analysis defines innovation in a networked environment as a multi-channel, collective learning process. Myriad small entrepreneurial firms, service providers, freelancers, and social entrepreneurs connect locally in the space of places and act globally across the virtual space of flows. Their owners brainstorm in Silicon Valley garages, Chinese coffee shops, and Finnish saunas. They originate concepts for start-ups, develop an impulse to internationalize, and expand existing projects.

The intellectual landscape of this book is a reflection on innovation and entrepreneurship in a networked global reality. The author has strategized how Europe can embrace innovation-driven entrepreneurship in order to develop a new model of growth beyond the crisis. The analysis aims to provide an answer to this question by scrutinizing how innovation creates wealth in a networked environment out of the synergy generated by combining production factors in the production process and how entrepreneurship manages and finances the entry of new products and processes into the market and into the society, thus creating economic and social value.

The assumption that underlies the whole analytical premise of this framework is that in order to enable collective capacity to develop innovation, it is necessary to understand networked environments that are conducive to innovation. Therefore, observations of diverse innovation settings helped define innovation as an ever present, self-perpetuating system of information exchange and knowledge sharing that takes place often beyond formal educational institutions. Countless, emergent, and ephemeral learning environments are created by people who live in real time in two worlds: in the physical one and in the virtual one, where they learn by "hanging out," "messing around," and "geeking out." Consequently, innovation was understood as a collective distributed open learning process in a constantly changing world enabled by information and communication technologies.

In order to propose a theory explaining how value is created in a networked environment, the author examined innovation settings in Europe, the United States, and China, among other places. This geographical spread allowed for a better understanding of how, where, and when knowledge is produced, disseminated, and translated. This examination disclosed existing and emergent structures, dynamics, architecture, and management practices of various types of innovation networks. The network theory provided tools for analyzing the logic, dynamics, structures, management practices, and business models of the various innovation networks: social networking sites, process networks, and creation networks. It explained why resources are accumulated in some industrial clusters so that certain metropolitan areas emerge as innovation nodes and gain importance.

The analysis of diverse innovation networks led to a proposal of a model specific for collaborative partnership of business and academia. The model proposition for this sort of innovation network includes three components: research, education, and innovation. The model is called a Knowledge Triangle. This is a concept of an innovation network constructed of institutions engaged in knowledge production and dissemination. A Knowledge Triangle is represented by variation of structured, formal contractual collaboration, as well as informal linkages and temporary alliances. There has been evidence that, unless goals are aligned, a network ceases to exist, since the commitment of members decreases and erodes network value. It was recognized that production and diffusion of knowledge occur within institutional settings, such as research institutes, universities, and businesses, but they also take place beyond their boundaries. Consequently, the Knowledge Triangle concept remains as a proxy of a more complex model that is in fact a sphere woven by countless, diverse innovation network actors in creative environments where the innovation process takes place, led by individual or collective agents who coordinate and orchestrate the process using different types of power.

It was further contended that the effectiveness of collaborative partnerships characteristic of business and academia was a function not only of innovation per se but also of innovation-driven entrepreneurship. Entrepreneurship was recognized as an integrator of such networks and a catalyst of value creation processes. It integrates networks and creates synergies between the research, education, and innovation activities. Specifically, it was observed that innovation creates wealth out of the synergy generated by recombining knowledge, while entrepreneurs manage and finance exploitation of the outcomes of the innovation process. There was a practice-based proposition that bridging the gap between innovation and markets can be done through a diverse set of entrepreneurial entities operating for-profit and in some cases not-for-profit.

Ultimately, the conceptual framework proposed in this book included four components: research, education, innovation itself, and entrepreneurship. The framework is useful for analyzing strategic issues in business and in policy setting. It allows an investigation of how collaborative partnerships of academia, business, government, the not-for-profit sector, users, and customers create value, value being defined in economic and social terms. This is where a strategic management model proposed by John Hagel III and John Seely Brown is used to analyze a shift in managing such networks from transaction culture and tightly-knit connections to trust-based culture and an organizational structure that is tightly-knit locally and at the same loosely-coupled globally.

The next step was to look into different kinds of flows that could be observed in a Knowledge Triangle. They were divided into three categories: knowledge, talent, and capital. Taking into consideration the four-component model of the entrepreneurship-driven Knowledge Triangle, it was detected that the resources flowing in the networks are not of generic type. They are specific kinds of knowledge that can be deployed and/or commercialized; certain types of people who are prone to take risks and who aspire to build ventures; and capital that is provided by investors with expectations of high profits in return for high risk.

Next, the author described three newly established organizations operating under the organizational arrangement of Knowledge and Innovation Communities. These pan-European innovation partnerships of institutions representing research, education, and innovation are a specific type of an innovation network. The author has taken an active role in the conceptualization of the KIC model in practice and has participated in its experimental deployment.

Empirical evidence on Climate-KIC, EIT ICT Labs, and KIC Innoenergy was presented in the form of case studies. To the extent of the material available, the Communities were analyzed in four dimensions: legal and governance structure, organization set-up and management, business model, and activities related to integrating research, education, and innovation through entrepreneurship. While each of the Knowledge and Innovation Communities differs, they converge in these four categories, as each has been designed to effectively achieve network goals. It led to conceptualization of a KIC model that is in essence a network enterprise interlinked and codependent on other innovation networks.

The observation of international experiences of innovation, particularly in the United States, informed the design of the KICs and the practice of the EIT. This new European undertaking inspired a broader reflection on innovation policy, and the lessons learned were presented. They called for a shift from a control-based to a trust-based governance model. The bottom line of the policy recommendations was to apply the concept of the entrepreneurship-driven Knowledge Triangle as a starting point for designing innovation policies. Fostering open innovation environment and clear IP regime was considered to attract industry commitment and venture capital investment. The latter, in the light of the lessons learned, should be supported not only by providing public funding but also by rewarding serial entrepreneurship and business angel investment. After all, they both should be targeted to rekindle the European economy since stimulating innovation-driven entrepreneurship through novel management and financing as tested in the KIC model has been proposed as a model of growth for Europe beyond the crisis.

In summary, the core argument put forward in this book suggests that the European innovation-driven economy needs both a structural as well as a cultural transformation: structural, in the sense that it needs new governance, management, and financing practice; cultural, in the sense of its return to the entrepreneurial origins of European prosperity in the twentieth century. The economic crisis evolving since 2008 is a good opportunity to accomplish such a "cultural revolution." Growth beyond the crisis must be based on entrepreneurship and not only on further investment in the innovation capacity of Europe. Let it not be entrepreneurship by necessity due to lack of other opportunities for the crisis generation. Let the creative destruction prompted by the crisis lead to value creation. Well-designed innovation policies are certainly conducive to the achievement of this goal.

After all, the next chapter of European history belongs to a generation who will have to create opportunities for themselves. Will they be able to innovate, take risks, fail, learn fast, and start all over again? Will they choose to become born-global entrepreneurs and yet stay in Europe?

ACKNOWLEDGEMENTS

There is a historic context and a personal story behind every book and this one is no exception. Its concept was born out of my intellectual curiosity, aroused in the midst of fascinating discussions between my colleagues from the European Institute of Innovation and Technology (EIT). This book was conceived during the most severe economic crisis in Europe since the Great Depression and tries to answer the "how" question, which many policy makers and business leaders are asking today in Europe: "How do we return to the path of growth and job creation?" It is in some sense a document reflecting the sort of discussions that took place in the early phase of forming the EIT and its Knowledge and Innovation Communities.

The EIT was initially thought to be a new European university for the 21st century, a concept put forward by José Manuel Barroso, the President of the European Commission. Founded in 2008, the EIT became one of the most daring policy experiments of the European Union: ultimately not a university but dynamic and integrated yet open, collaborative environments called Knowledge and Innovation Communities (KICs), interlinking the best European research institutes, universities, and companies. They were based on a novel intellectual framework developed by Professor Manuel Castells as a Europe-specific innovation network of networks, an engine for Europe's innovativeness and competitiveness.

I had the privilege of working with Professor Castells on the EIT Board and on a number of research projects. This book would be quite different if not for our intellectual exchange and his much needed encouragement to continue the work. I want to thank him for acknowledging my right to be what he called "a new type of academic," commuting between the world of academia, business, and policy-making. I am most grateful for his attentive and careful review of the text and his respect for my ideas. I feel honored that he endorsed this book by writing such a positive preface.

This book has benefited largely from the intellectual stimulation of the various academic milieus I visited or worked for over the past years. They include foremost two great schools at the University of Michigan in Ann Arbor: The College of Engineering and The Stephen M. Ross School of Business.

First, I am most grateful to my host Professor Larry Seiford, former dean of the IOE Department at the College of Engineering and co-Director at the Tauber Institute for Global Operations at the University of Michigan. We met during a Research Assessment Exercise at Aalto University in Helsinki in 2009 and shortly after Larry offered me an opportunity to come to Michigan and work on my book project. I started writing this book in 2010 in my guest office at the IOE Department and coincidentally finished writing it there in 2014. While Larry's intellectual stimulus was essential, I would like to extend my warmest gratitude to Larry's wife Beverly, whose most caring friendship manifested itself on so many occasions.

I would also like to thank Professor Radoslaw Michalowski, Chair of the Dekaban Foundation, for kindly offering me the Dekaban Fellowship. I extend my thanks to Professor Thomas Zurbuchen, Vice Dean for Entrepreneurship, College of Engineering, for the invitation to join the Center for Entrepreneurship as a Faculty Affiliate. Dozens of discussions with my colleagues at the University of Michigan shaped my research. My notes from that period document how privileged I was to conduct research on entrepreneurial universities at a time when the University of Michigan was undergoing such a transformation. I was there at a special moment in which the top down strategy of the University President and deans of various colleges synergized with students' initiatives to form a vibrant entrepreneurial ecosystem around the university. Let me take this opportunity to especially thank Professor David Munson, the Dean of the College of Engineering, as well as my colleagues, Professors Jeffrey Liker and Larry Burns from IOE, Aileen Huang-Saad and Doug Neal from the Center for Entrepreneurship, and Richard Chylla of the Office of Technology Transfer, for a number of our conversations and interviews which helped me reflect on engineering education for to-be entrepreneurs.

I would like to thank Professors Thom Kinnear and Tim Faley for inviting me to the Samuel Zell & Robert H. Lurie Institute for Entrepreneurial Studies at the University of Michigan's Ross Business School. At the ZLI I met many wonderful colleagues including Peter Adriaens and Tom Porter. Ross Business School offered me a complementary perspective to entrepreneurship education with comparison to the model developed at the College of Engineering and this dual perspective greatly enriched my understanding of how to teach students to grow successful ventures. My special thanks goes to Professor Jeff Degraff, my role model in combining great research, consulting practice, and teaching. I want to thank many other colleagues at Ross including Professors Jerry Davis, Roman Kapuscinski, Aneel Karnani, Bill Lovejoy, Leonard Middleton, and Corey Seeman, Director of the Kresge Business Administration Library. I also appreciate insights from Professors Victor Rosenberg of the School of Information and Eve Kerr of the VA Center for Clinical Management Research.

This book has also greatly benefited from my stay at the Santa Clara University in San Jose, in spring 2010. I would like to thank Professor Jim Koch for his kind invitation, which gave me a chance to experience the heart of the Silicon Valley. It was at Santa Clara that I started a process of recording or videotaping interviews with outstanding people I had a chance to meet along my intellectual quest.

I owe a special thanks to John Seely Brown, whose research and ideas so greatly shaped my thinking about the model I present in this book. My warmest thanks go Professors Warren Bennis, Regis McKenna, William T. Coleman III, Charly Kleissner, John Kohler, Doug Solomon, and Prabhakar Raghavan, all of whom I met during my stay at Santa Clara, as well as to Professor Godfrey Mungal, Dean of the School of Engineering, students and staff at the Center for Science, Technology and Society, and Radha Basu at the Global Social Benefit Incubator at Santa Clara Univeristy I am truly thankful to Professor Martin Carnoy for an opportunity to hold a seminar at The Stanford Graduate School of Education in 2010, as well as Paul Marca, Andy DiPaolo, Mike Lyons, Irv Grousbeck, Lisa Winter Sweeney, and Richard Dasher, who showed me different facets of Stanford University. I also appreciate the interest in my work and the invitation from Professor Ernest J. Wilson III, Dean of the Annenberg School for Communication and Journalism at the University of Southern California, Los Angeles, and his colleagues Professors Jonathan Aronson, Sarah Banet-Weiser, Paolo Sigismondi, Jonathan Taplin, and Helena Yli-Renko.

I extend my thanks to Cornelia S. Huellstrunk and Javier Garcia Martinez from the Keller Center at Princeton University. As an advisor at the center, I had an opportunity to coach Arielle Sandor and Christine Blauvelt, co-founders of DUMA Works, and experience the global aspect of education that I researched. Let me also thank the researchers at the Internet Interdisciplinary Institute at the Universitat Oberta de Catalunya in Barcelona, foremost Josep Lladós-Masllorens and Mireia Fernández-Ardèvol, for their comments on the direction of my research. Likewise, I want to thank colleagues of ESADE Business School, Luisa Alemany, Elena Bou, and Alfred Vernis Domènech, for sharing their insights.

While this book is to a large degree an outcome of my "intellectual pilgrimage," I would also like to thank colleagues at my home institution. My special thanks go to Professor Rajmund Bacewicz, Vice-Rector for Research at Warsaw University of Technology, and to Dr. Zbigniew Turowski, Director of the Warsaw University of Techology Business School. I would also like to thank my colleagues with whom we shared passion for entrepreneurship foremost, Dr. Agnieszka Skala and Dr. Janusz Zawiła-Niedźwiedzki.

I would like to thank Professors Luc Soete, André Sapir, and Reinhilde Veugelers, as well as Andrew Wyckoff, Alessandra Colecchia, Mariarosa Lunati, and Karen Wilson of the OECD, Ann Mettler and Paul Hofheinz of the Lisbon Council, and my friends at Science|Business, a Brussels-based media company, especially Richard Hudson and Peter Wrobel. Let me also extend gratitude to the amazing world shapers and thought leaders I had the privilege of collaborating with at the World Economic Forum, including Paola Antonelli, Lina Boren, Tim Brown, Brian Collins, Nicholas Davis, and Mark Turrell. I want to cordially thank Maria Pinelli for inviting me to join the EY Strategic Growth Forum in Palm Springs and Shanghai and for introducing me to top performing global entrepreneurs. Meeting members of the Telefonica Disruptive Council in Sao Paolo and visiting a Campus Party of 4000+ entrepreneurs was yet another impulse to explore the dynamics of start-up communities. I also thank Fan Dong for sharing her PhD thesis on social media entrepreneurs in China and for facilitating contacts with some of them. This book in some aspect draws on their comments, reviews, ideas, and work.

My deep acknowledgment goes to every single person from the extraordinary group of colleagues whom I met on September 15, 2008 in Budapest. This was the day President Barroso announced the formation of the EIT, and I had the privilege of being one of 18 nominated EIT Governing Board members. It was an honor for me to be invited to form the EIT with such distinguished colleagues. This public service over six years was my way of giving back to the European

Union community in gratitude for a historic turnaround so fortunate for Poland and for my generation. I would like to thank Mme Androulla Vassiliou, Commissionaire for Education, Culture, Multilingualism and Youth. I owe special thanks to her also for her kind recognition of my "instrumental role" in setting up the EIT and championing the entrepreneurship agenda.

I owe a special credit and thankfulness for backing my work to the Chairmen of the EIT Board Professors Martin Schuurmans and Alexander von Gabain, as well as colleagues of the Executive Committee Giovanni Colombo, Professor Anders Flodström, Professor Yrjö Neuvo, Professor Karen Maex, Bruno Revellin-falcoz, Jeroen van der Veer. While I want cordially to thank all my EIT Board colleagues, my special thanks go to Professor João Caraça, who also reviewed this book, as well as Bertrand Collomb, Ellen De Brabander, Professor Wolfgang Herrmann, Professor Dame Julia King, Professor Erna Möller, Peter Tropschuh, Linnar Viik, Christine Patte, Professor Alfons Sauquet, Peter Olesen, the current Board Chairman, and Gábor Bojár. I am equally thankful to colleagues from the DG EAC, Commission observers to the EIT Board Mme Odile Quintin, Mr. Xavier Prats Monné, and Mr. Jan Truszczyński, as well as colleagues, foremost Lucia Recalde and Jordi Curell Gotor. I wish to broaden my thanks to colleagues from the EIT Headquarters in Budapest especially to Jose Manuel Leceta, Director of the EIT, and Mathea Fammels. My cordial recognition goes to the CEOs of the three Knowledge and Innovation Communities: Mary Ritter of Climate-KIC, Willem Jonker of EIT ICT Labs, and Diego Pavia of KIC Innoenergy as well as their colleagues. I appreciate the working relationship and the creative tension that made me reconsider my theories after the "sanity check," thanks to their pragmatic approach to deploy concepts on the ground.

Since this book was written during my term as a member of the EIT Board, I had to be especially careful to respect the confidentiality of information to which I had access. This is why in certain cases I decided to limit the data strictly to publicly available information, as in the case of the KICs, so not to abuse my function and breach confidence. I published parts of this book earlier in Poland for the sake of my academic tenure. I want to thank professors Wiktor Askanas and Manuel Castells who formally reviewed my thesis, which appeared under the title "Entrepreneurial Innovation Networks: Knowledge Triangle and Emerging Business Models" (Warsaw University of Technology Publishing House 2013). My warmest thanks and acknowledgements go to Dr. Ewa Halicka, who was also the first reviewer of my research findings.

The quality of this book would not be such if not for the work of my editor Melody VanWanzeele, whom I cordially thank for her meticulous work that enhanced this book to its current state. The production and global distribution of this book is managed by my New York book agent, Ken Gillet, whom I thank for navigating me through the publishing and who holds the commercial success of this book in his hands.

My last but most important expression of true gratitude goes to my family. Foremost, I would like to thank my husband and my daughters, to whom I dedicate this book. Their patience and respect for my creative passion gave me the freedom and courage to pursue this intellectual quest.

Daria Tataj

Ann Arbor, July 2014

Documentary Annexes(26)

Climate-KIC

Table 3: Core partners of Climate-KIC.

Business partner	Public partner	Academic partner
Electricité de France S.A. GDF Suez SA Bayer Technology Services GmbH DSM Schiphol Nederland B.V.	Netherlands Organisation of Applied Scientific Research TNO Stichting Deltares Institute for Sustainability	ETH Zurich Imperial College London Technische Universität Berlin Forschungszentrum Jülich GmbH Potsdam Institute for Climate Impact Research PIK GFZ German Research Centre for Geosciences Commissariat à l'énergie atomique et aux energies alternatives CEA l'Institut national de la recherche agronomique INRA L'Université de Versailles Saint-Quentin-en-Yvelines UVSQ Delft University of Technology Utrecht University Wageningen University

(26) Source: websites of Climate-KIC, EIT ICT Labs, KIC Innoenergy (2013)

Table 4: Four themes for Climate-KIC activities and programming.

Key Themes	Description
Assessing climate change and managing its drivers	Climate-KIC facilitates entrepreneurship in a new business entity forming across multiple sectors of the economy which offers novel systems and services to measure and manage CO2 and other greenhouse gas emissions, to predict the future state of the climate system, to detect its response to mitigation, and to develop adaptation actions.
Transitioning to resilient, low-carbon cities	Activities under this theme focus on transforming urban mobility and traffic management systems, improving waste management and recycling systems, and ensuring smart and cost effective building technologies—areas that offer enormous business opportunities.
Advancing adaptive water management	Reliable water provision to existing urban and rural environments will become increasingly difficult in a warming world, posing challenges on science, technology, policy, and the economy. Climate-KIC will explore commercial opportunities by developing sustainable solutions in adaptive water management.
Developing zero-carbon production systems	Climate-KIC will help deliver the significant climate change mitigation and job growth potential of low carbon production systems, focusing on bio-renewables—i.e. chemicals, materials, liquid fuel, and energy that use biomass as their feedstock—and on integrated energy production and consumption.

Table 5: Components of the Climate-KIC education model.

Contextual Learning Journey	Five-week summer course prepared by key universities including Imperial College and ETH
Training	It is a program for executives, managers, and employees in business and government who want to address the climate change challenge in their own professional environment by learning about the highest standards of sustainable practice in Europe and beyond. It is designed as tailored climate change solutions in focus groups, in workshops, and at thought-leadership retreats. An option for a customized training includes a range of time-sensitive options, including short courses, e-learning, and learning in the workplace.
Short Courses	Climate-KIC short courses run over a two-day period in various locations across Europe including France, Germany, Netherlands, Switzerland, Spain, Italy, UK, and Poland. It is a professional education option for becoming familiar with climate change basics, the risks and economic impacts of climate change, and practical mitigation and adaptation strategies.
Corporate L&D Solutions	Large corporate clients must roll out climate change awareness education. Rather than in the form of a traditional course, Climate-KIC deploys options for education via electronic media such as VLEs, webinar, interactive video, DVD, podcast, community forums, and blended learning solutions.
Climate Innovation Winter Journey	It is a five-week intensive climate innovation school based in three Climate-KIC nodes. Students and professionals from organizations which are not part of the KIC and who come from Slovakia, Slovenia, Bulgaria, Romania, Hungary, Czech Republic, and Poland, are invited to this program. Selected participants for the Winter Journey have some of their costs covered.
Climate-KIC Alumni Association	The Association is a way to build a peer-to-peer lifelong learning program, to strengthen and maintain professional networks of excellence, stay connected to fora discussing the most recent climate innovation developments, and co-design innovation workshops and entrepreneurship programs as a coach or mentor. Alumni Association spreads the culture of "giving back" or "giving forward."
Contextual Learning Journey	A five-week intensive summer course organized in three co-location centers for a group of 25-30 Master's and PhD students chosen on a competitive basis in an open international call.

Table 6: Climate-KIC Incubation Program.

Stage 1
Attracts entrepreneurs who have validated their business idea and want to start a company. Helps entrepreneurs translate inventions into business plans, deliver a prototype or demo, receive industry feedback, develop a team competence assessment, and put a basic business plan in place including IP. It includes a grant up to €20k, access to the Business Coach Network, and Access to Climate-KIC Masterclasses.
Stage 2
Helps entrepreneurs translate a business plan into a value proposition and a business case with a business model. At this stage teams with a business plan, a prototype or demo, substantial industry and user references, and a management team in place can receive a grant up to €25k and access to the Venture Competition, the Business Coach Network, and Climate-KIC Masterclasses.
Stage 3
Helps entrepreneurs turn ideas and proof of concept into fundable business opportunities. It is open to incorporated (or in process) start-ups with a detailed business plan, early customers, and partners. In order to qualify for a grant up to €50k and access to the Incubation Network, Venture Competition, Business Coach Network, and Masterclasses, a firm should deliver a proof-of-concept and have manufacturing and distribution partnerships signed, IP secured, and a customer or investor feedback mechanism in place.

Table 7: Climate-KIC Incubators Network.

Country	City	Incubator
France	Paris	IncubAlliance
Germany	Berlin	Grundungshaus
The Netherlands	Delft Utrecht Wageningen	Yes!Delft UtrechtINC StartLife
Switzerland	Zürich	VentureLab VentureKICK
United Kingdom	London	Imperial Innovations

EIT ICT Labs

Table 8: Industry dominated representation on the EIT ICT Labs Executive Steering Board.

Co-location Center	Representatives
Berlin Node	Deutsche Telecom AG and DFKI
Eindhoven Node	Philips and 3TU.NIRICT
Helsinki Node	Nokia and VTT
Paris Node	Alcatel-Lucent and Inria
Stockholm Node	Ericsson and KTH
Trento Node	Telecom Italia, Trento Rise

Table 9: EIT ICT Labs Partners.

Industry	Universities	Research Organizations
Deutsche Telekom Laboratories SAP Siemens Philips Nokia Alcatel-Lucent France Telecom Ericsson Telecom Italia	TU Berlin 3TU / NIRICT Aalto University UPMC - Université Pierre et Marie Curie Université Paris-Sud 11 Institut Telecom The Royal Institute of Technology, KTH Trento RISE / University of Trento	DFKI Fraunhofer INRIA Novay VTT SICS Trento RISE / FBK CWI TNO

Table 10: EIT ICT Labs specialization of co-location centers.

Name of the co-location center	Geographic location of the CLC office	Specialization
Berlin Node	Germany	Education - EIT ICT Labs Education Catalysts and Master School Activities (e.g. Cloud computing) Business - Business coordination and EIT ICT Labs Business Catalysts development Smart Energy Systems (lead) Intelligent Mobility and Transportation Systems (lead) Research – "Internet Technologies & Architectures" and "Computing in the Cloud"
Eindhoven Node	The Netherlands	Physical meeting & project spaces for EIT ICT Labs activities, connected to the other nodes through state-of-the-art and beyond ICT infrastructure; Facilities and services for mobility across CLCs and organizations, including "virtual mobility" (e.g. video café); Space for local and KIC-level workshops; Soft landing pads for SMEs expanding their operations in other EU countries
Helsinki Node	Finland	Enabling mobile data expansion smart spaces and ubiquitous interaction Green ICT for ecological sustainability Big data and service design & engineering Games and gamification ICT for wellbeing and active aging
Paris Node	France	Digital cities of the future
Trento Node	Italy	Digital cities Smart spaces Smart energy systems Intelligent mobility and transportation systems Healthcare & wellbeing Future media & content delivery
Stockholm Node	Sweden	EIT ICT Labs Master School Networking solutions for future media Cloud computing

KIC InnoEnergy

Table 11: KIC InnoEnergy CLCs and the area of their core competency.

Geographic location of the CLC office	Core competency
Grenoble/France	Sustainable nuclear and renewable energy convergence
Eindhoven/Holland	Intelligent, energy-efficient buildings and cities
Munich/Germany	Energy from chemical fuels
Barcelona/Spain	Renewables
Krakow/Poland	Clean coal technologies
Stockholm/Sweden	European smart electric grid 5 electric storage

Table 12: Services offered by KIC InnoEnergy Highway.

Technology	due diligence, mapping vs. competing products/services, positioning, patenting (if necessary), proof of concept with customer/industry, piloting, industrialization
Market	market assessment, market positioning, business case, business plan
Team	team assessment, training, team completion, legal constitution (of start-up or spin-off)
Finance	seed money, VC rounds (brokerage)

Table 13: Distribution of KIC InnoEnergy shareholders and partners.

	Shareholders/ Formal Partners	Associated & Network Partners	Total Partners
Industries	9	35	44
Research Centers	7	8	15
Universities	11	17	28
Business Schools	2	0	2
Total partners	29	60	89

List of Figures

List of Tables

Bibliography

1. Aalto Design Factory. (2012). *Aalto Design Factory, Annual Report 2010-2011*, http://www.designfactory.aalto.fi
2. Acs, Z. J., and Audretsch, D. B. (1988). "Innovation in Large and Small Firms: An Empirical Analysis," *The American Economic Review*, Vol. 78, No. 4 Sep. 1988, pp. 678-690.
3. Adamson, L. (2012). *Quality for Learning: EIT Quality Assurance and Learning Enhancement Model Handbook for Planning, Labelling and Follow up Reviewing of EIT Master and Doctoral Programmes* (handbook). Budapest: EIT.
4. Abrahamson, M. (2004). *Global Cities*. New York, New York: Oxford University Press.
5. Agars, M.D., Kaufman, J.C., and Locke, T.R. (2008). "Social influence and creativity in organizations: a multi-level lens for theory, research, and practice," in M.D. Mumford, S.T. Hunter, and K.E. Bedell-Avers (eds), *Multi-level Issues in Creativity and Innovation*. Elsevier JAI.
6. Ahmad, N., and Hoffman, A. (2008). "A Framework for Addressing and Measuring Entrepreneurship," *OECD Statistics Working Paper*, no. 2008/02, http://dx.doi.org/10.1787/243160627270
7. Ahmad, N., and Seymour, R. (2008). "Defining Entrepreneurial Activity," *OECD Statistics Working Paper*, no. 2008/01.
8. Aho Group Report. (2006). *Creating an Innovative Europe*, http://ec.europa.eu/invest-in-research/action/2006_ahogroup_en.htm/
9. Akamatsu, K. (1962). "A Historical Pattern of Economic Growth in Developing Countries," *Developing Economies*, vol. 2, pp. 3-25.
10. Amabile, T.M. (1983). *The Social Psychology of Creativity*. New York: Springer-Verlag.
11. Amin, A., and Thrift, N. (2002). Cities: Reimagining the Urban. Polity Press and Blackwell Publishers.
12. Amoros, J. E., Bosma, N., Global Entrepreneurship Research Association (2014). GEM Global Entrepreneurship Monitor 2013 Global Report. Babson, Universidad del Desarrollo, Universiti Tun Abdul Razak,
13. Arnold, E., Mahieu, B., Stroyan, J., et al. (2011). *Understanding the Long Term Impact of the Framework Programme: Final Report to the European Commission*. DG Research.
14. Arnoldo, H., Dean, C., and Wilde, L. (2001). *The Delta Project: Discovering New Sources of Profitability in a Networked Economy*. Palgrave.
15. Arthur, W.B. (2009). *The Nature of Technology: What It Is and How It Evolves*. New York: Free Press.
16. Asheim, B. T., and Gertler, M. S. (2005). "The Geography of Innovation: Regional Innovation Systems," in: J. Fagerberg, Mowery, R.R. Nelson (eds), *The Oxford Handbook of Innovation*. Oxford: Oxford University Press, pp. 292-317.
17. Askanas, W. (2008). "Management Education in Turbulent Times: Context, Content and Delivery," *Master of Business Administration*, vol. 3

(92), pp. 3-8.

18. Audretsch, D. B., & Thurik, A. R. (2001). *Capitalism and Democracy in the 21st Century: From the Managed to the Entrepreneurial Economy* (pp. 23-40). Physica-Verlag HD.

19. Aydalot, P. (1986). "Presentation," in P. Aydalot (ed.), *Milieux innovateurs in Europe.* Paris: Gremi.

20. Azoulay, P., & Lerner, J. (2010). "Technological Innovation and Organizations," *Handbook of Organizational Economics.* Princeton: Princeton University Press.

21. Baczko, T., Kacprzyk, J., and Zadrozny, S. (2010). "Towards Knowledge Driven Individual Integrated Indicators of Innovativeness," *Knowledge-Based Intelligent System Advancements: Systemic and Cybernetic Approaches.* pp. 129-140.

22. Bakhshi, H., and McVittie, E. (2009). "Creative Supply-chain Linkages and Innovation: Do the Creative Industries Stimulate Business Innovation in the Wider Economy?," *Innovation: Management, Policy & Practice,* August, pp. 169-189.

23. Bar, F., Cohen, S., Cowhey, P., Delong, J., and Kleeman, M. (2001). "The Next Generation Internet: Promoting Innovation and User-experimentation," in *BIRE-IGCC Economy.*

24. Bartlett, C., and Ghoshal, S. (1990). "Matrix Management: Not a Structure, a Frame of Mind," *Harvard Business Review.*

25. Becattini, G., and Rullani, E. (1996). "Local Systems and Global Connections: the Role of Knowledge," *International Institute for Labour Studies,* pp. 159-174.

26. Bennis, W. (1997). *Organizing Genius: The Secrets of Creative Collaboration.* New York: Basic Books.

27. Berghel, H. (1998). Who Won the Mosaic War?. *Communications of the ACM, 41*(10), 13-16.

28. Berners-Lee, T. (2000). *Weaving the Web: The Original Design and Ultimate Destiny of the World Wide Web by Its Inventor.* New York: Harper Collins.

29. Blank, S. (2005). *Four Steps to the Epiphany: Successful Strategies for Products to Win.* Cafepress.com.

30. Blank, S., and Dorf, B. (2012). *Start-up Owner's Manual: The Step-By-Step Guide for Building a Great Company.* K&S Ranch Inc.

31. Borras, S. (2003). *The Innovation Policy of the European Union: From Government to Governance.* UK: Edward Elgar Publishing Ltd.

32. Bou, E., Saz-Carranza, A., Collet, F., and Moreira Ottani, S. (2009). *SUCCESS Report. Model Design: Creating a New Collaboration Model,* http://www.knowledgetriangle.eu/index.php/kb_22/kb.html.

33. Bower, J.L., and Christensen, C.M. (1997). "Disruptive Technologies: Catching the Wave," in J. S. Brown (ed.), *Seeing Differently: Insights on Innovation.* Boston: Harvard Business School Press.

34. Boyce, C., and Neale, P. (2006). *Conducting In-depth Interviews: A Guide for Designing and Conducting In-depth Interviews for Evaluation Input.* Pathfinder International Tool Series 2.

35. Boyd, D., & Ellison, N. B. (2007). "Social Network Sites: Definition, History, and Scholarship," *Journal of Computer-Mediated Communication* 13(1), 11.

36. Brandenburger, A.M., and Nalebuff, B.J. (1995). "The Right Game: Use Game Theory to Shape Strategy," in J. S. Brown (ed.), *Seeing Differently. Insights on Innovation.* Harvard Business Review.

37. Brandernburget, A.M., and Nalebuff, B.J. (1997). *Co-Opetition: A Revolution Mindset That Combines Competition and Cooperation: The Game Theory Strategy That's Changing the Game of Business.* Currency Doubleday.

38. Breznitz, D., and Murphree, M. (2011). *Run of the Red Queen: Government, Innovation, Globalization, and Economic Growth in China.* Yale University Press.

39. Brown, J.S., and Duguid, S. (2000). *The Social Life of Information.* Boston: Harvard Business School Press.

40. Brown, J.S., and Hagel III, J. (2005). "Innovation Blowback: Disruptive Management Practices from Asia," in *The Only Sustainable Edge: Why Business Strategies Depends on Productive Friction and Dynamic Specialization.* Boston: Harvard Business School Press.

41. Brown, T. (2009). *Change by Design: How Design Thinking Transforms Organizations and Inspires Innovation.* Harper Collins.

42. Bruton, G.D., Ahlstrom, D., and Obloj, K. (2008). "Entrepreneurship in Emerging Economies: Where are We Today and Where Should the Research Go in the Future," *Entrepreneurship Theory and Practice, 32*(1), 1-14.

43. Cabo, P. (1997). *The Knowledge Network: European Subsidized Research and Development Cooperation,* PhD thesis, Rijksuniversiteit Groningen.

44. Caloghirou, Y., Vonortas N.-S., and Ioannides, S. (2004). *European Collaboration in Research and Development: Business Strategy and Public Policy.* Cheltenham (UK) and Northampton, MA (USA): Edward Elgar Publishing Ltd.

45. Camagni, R. (1991). "Local 'Milieu', Uncertainty and Innovation Networks: Towards a New Dynamic Theory of Economic Space" (Chapter 7), in R. Camagni (ed.), *Innovation Networks: Spatial Perspectives.* London: Belhaven Press, 121-142.

46. Carvalho, da Graça M. (2012). *Opening speech at the Horizon 2020 working panel on Industrial Leadership and Small and Medium-Sized Enterprises.* European Parliament.

47. Castells, M. (2008). *Notes on Creativity and Innovation.* Personal manuscript.

48. Castells, M. (1996, 2000, 2010). *The Information Age: Economy, Society and Culture: Volume I The Rise of the Network Society.* UK: John Wiley & Sons.

49. Castells, M. (2009). *Globalisation, Networking, Urbanisation: Reflections on the Spatial Dynamics of the Information Age.* Urban Studies 08/10/2009.

50. Castells, M. (2011). "A Network Theory of Power," *International Journal*

of Communication, vol. 5, 773-787.

51. Castells, M. (ed.). (2004). *The Network Society: A Cross-cultural Perspective.* UK, US: Edward Elgar Publishing Ltd.

52. Castells, M., and Hall, P. (1994). *Technopoles of the World: The Making of 21st Century Industrial Complexes.* Routledge.

53. Castells, M., and Himanen, P. (2002). *The Information Society and the Welfare State: The Finnish Model.* Oxford: Oxford University Press.

54. Castells, M., and Koch, J. (2009). *Inducing Social Entrepreneurship in Poor Communities: Some Preliminary Thoughts for Barcelona Roundtable. Center for Science, Technology, and Society.* Santa Clara University.

55. Castells, M., and Koch, J. (2010). *On Analyzing Social Entrepreneurship: A Methodological Note Prepared for the Santa Clara University.* Workshop on global social entrepreneurship, May 10-11, 2010.

56. Caves, R.E. (2000). *Creative Industries: Contracts Between Art and Commerce: Cambridge, Massachusetts, and London.* Cambridge: Harvard University Press.

57. Chesbrough, H. (2003). *Open Innovation.* Cambridge: Harvard University Press.

58. Chesbrough, H. (2005). *Open Business Models: How to Thrive in the New Innovation Landscape.* Boston: Harvard Business School Press.

59. Chesbrough, H. (2011). *Open Services Innovation: Rethinking Your Business to Grow and Compete in a New Era.* Jossey-Bass.

60. Chesbrough, H., and Vanhaverbeke, W. (2011). *Open Innovation and Public Policy in Europe: Science and Business.* ESADE Business School.

61. Chesbrough, H., Vanhaverbeke, W., and West, J. (2006). *Open Innovation: Researching a New Paradigm.* Oxford: Oxford University Press.

62. Chesbrough, H., and Teece, D. (1996). "Organizing for Innovation: When is Virtual Virtuous?" *Harvard Business Review.*

63. Chesbrough, H. (2003). *Open Innovation: The New Imperative for Creating and Profiting from Technology.* Boston: Harvard Business School Press.

64. Christensen, C.M. (1997). *The Innovator's Dilemma: When New Technologies Cause Great Firms to Fail.* Boston: Harvard Business School Press.

65. Christensen, C.M., and Raynor M.E. (2003). *The Innovator's Solution: Creating and Sustaining Successful Growth.* Boston: Harvard Business School Press.

66. Christensen, C.M., Anthony, S.D., and Roth, E.A. (2004). *Seeing What's Next: Using the Theories of Innovation to Predict Industry Change.* Boston: Harvard Business School Press.

67. Cieślik, J. (2009). "Zintegrowany model wsparcia innowacyjnej przedsiębiorczości akademickiej," *Zeszyty Naukowe Uniwersytetu Szczecińskiego,* Seria: *Ekonomiczne Problemu Usług,* vol. 525/2009, 121-140.

68. Cieślik, J., Tyszka, T., Macko, A., and Domurat, A. (2011). "Motivation, Self-efficacy, and Risk Attitudes Among Entrepreneurs During Transition to a Market Economy," *The Journal of Socio-Economics,* vol. 40, 124-131.

69. Clark, B.R. (1998). *Creating Entrepreneurial Universities: Organizational Pathways of Transformation* (1st ed.). Oxford and New York: Published

for the IAU Press by Pergamon Press.

70. Clark, B.R. (2004). *Sustaining Change in Universities: Continuities in Case Studies and Concepts*. Open University Press.

71. Clayton, P. (1997). *Implementation of Organizational Innovation: Studies of Academic and Research Libraries*. San Diego: Academic Press.

72. Climate-KIC. (2009). *Climate-KIC Proposal for Knowledge and Innovation Community of European Institute of Innovation and Technology (Part A, B and C)*. Climate-KIC internal document.

73. Climate-KIC. (2012). *Climate-KIC Business Plan*. Climate-KIC internal document.

74. Clydesdale, G. (2006). "Creativity and Competition: The Beatles," *Creativity Research Journal*, vol. 18 (2), pp. 129-139.

75. Cohen, W., and Levin, R. (1989). "Empirical Studies of Innovation and Market Structure," in R. Schmalensee & R. Willig (ed.), *Handbook of Industrial Organization*. Elsevier, ed. 1, vol. 2, no. 2.

76. Cohen, S., and Zysman, J. (1987). *Manufacturing Matters: The Myth of Postindustrial Economy*. New York: Basic Books.

77. Cossentino, F., Pyke, F., and Sengenberger, W. (1996). *Local and Regional Response to Global Pressure: The Case of Italy and its Industrial Districts* (Vol. 103). International Labour Office.

78. Council of the European Union. (2008). *Conclusion on the Definition of a "2020 Vision for the European Research Area."* http://www.consilium.europa.eu/ueDocs/cms_Data/docs/pressData/en/intm/104434.pdf

79. Coyne, K., Clifford, P., and Dye, R. (2007). "Breakthrough Thinking From Inside the Box," *Harvard Business Review*, vol. 85, pp. 70-78.

80. DiStefano, J.J., and Maznevski, M.L. (2000). "Creating Value with Diverse Teams in Global Management," *Organizational Dynamics*, vol. 29, issue 1.

81. Csikszentmihalyi, M. (1996). *Creativity: Flow and the Psychology of Discovery and Invention*. Harper Perennial.

82. *CTIT Progress Report 2010-2011*. (2011). Centre for Telematics and Information Technology, University of Twente.

83. Dâmaso, J. (2012). *Repensar a Universidade na Europa: O contributo das Comunidades de Conhecimento e Inovação - um estudo de caso* (Master's thesis).

84. Davenport, T.H. (1993). *Process Innovation: Reengineering Work though Information Technology*. Boston: Harvard Business School Press.

85. De Jong, J. P., & Den Hartog, D. N. (2007). "How Leaders Influence Employees' Innovative Behaviour," *European Journal of Innovation Management*, 10(1), pp. 41-64.

86. Dong, F. (2012). *Digital Creativity and Innovation in Chinese Social Networking Sites*, a dissertation presented to the Faculty of the USC University of Southern California, August 2012.

87. Drucker, P.F. (1986). *Innovation and Entrepreneurship: Practice and Principles*. Harper & Row Publishers.

88. Drucker, P.F. (2003). "The Discipline of Innovation," in *Harvard Business Review on the Innovative Enterprise*. Boston: Harvard Business School Press.

89. Dyer, J. (2002). *Effective Interfirm Collaboration: How Firms Minimize Transaction Costs and Maximize Transaction Value.* MIT Libraries.

90. ECORYS. (2011a). *External Evaluation of the European Institute of Innovation and Technology Framework Contract on Evaluation and Related Services.* European Commission (EAC 03/06), DG Education and Culture.

91. ECORYS. (2011b). *Study on the Concept, Development and Impact of Co-location Centers Using the Example of the EIT and KIC.* Commissioned by the European Commission, DG Education and Culture.

92. ECORYS. (2011c). *External Evaluation of the EIT-Framework Contract and Related Services.* European Commission (EAC 03/06), EC DG EAC, DG Education and Culture.

93. ECORYS. (2011d). *Study on the Concept, Development and Impact of Co-location Centers Using the Example of the EIT the KIC.* European Commission, DG Education and Culture.

94. Edler, J., Meyer-Krahmer, F., & Reger, G. (2002). "Changes in the Strategic Management of Technology: Results of a Global Benchmarking Study," *R&D Management* 32(2), pp. 149-164.

95. Edquist, C. (2005). "Systems of Innovation: Perspectives and Challenges. in J. Fagerberg, D.C. Mowery, and R.R. Nelson (eds), *The Oxford Handbook of Innovation.* Oxford: Oxford University Press.

96. EEC GHK, Technopolis. *(2008). Evaluation on Policy: Promotion of Women Innovators and Entrepreneurship.* European Commission, DG Enterprise and Industry.

97. *EFER Seminar Conference Materials.* (2012). Center for Entrepreneurial Learning, University of Cambridge, Judge Business School.

98. Egan, T.M. (2005). "Creativity in the Context of Team Diversity: Team Leader Perspectives," *Advances in Developing Human Resources,* vol. 7, pp. 207-225.

99. Eisenhard, K.M. (1989). "Building Theories from Case Study Research," *Academy of Management Review,* vol. 14. no.4, pp. 532-550.

100. Eisenhard, K.M., and Graebner, M.E. (2007). "Theory Building from Cases: Opportunities and Challenges," *Academy of Management Journal,* vol. 50, no. 1, pp. 25–32.

101. EIT ICT Labs. (2011). *EIT ICT Labs: Annual Report 2011.* http://www.eit.ictlabs.eu/ict-labs/all-news/article/.

102. Engelen, E., et al. (2011). *After the Great Complacence: Financial Crisis and the Politics of Reform.* Oxford: Oxford University Press.

103. Enkel, E., Gassmann, O., and Chesbrough, H. (2009). "Open R&D and Open Innovation: Exploring the Phenomenon," *R&D Management,* vol. 39 (4).

104. Ernst, D., & Naughton, B. (2007). "Insights from the IT Industry", in Christopher A. McNally (ed.), *China's Emergent Political Economy: Capitalism in the Dragon's Lair.* Routledge Studies in the Growth Economies of Asia.

105. Ernst&Young. (2011). *Next Generation Innovation Policy: The Future of EU Innovation Policy to Support Market Growth.* http://www.ey.com/GL/

en/Industries/Government---Public-Sector/Government-innovation/.

106. Erramilli M.K., and Rao P. (1993). "Service Firms' International Entry-mode Strategies of Service Firms: A Contingency Perspective," *Journal of the Academy of Marketing Science* 26(4), pp. 274–292.

107. Estrin, J. (2009). *Closing the Innovation Gap: Reigniting the Spark of Creativity in a Global Economy* McGraw-Hill.

108. European Cluster Policy Group. (2010). *Final Recommendations - A Call for Policy Action*. http://www.proinno-europe.eu/ecpg/newsroom/ecpg-final-recommendations/.

109. Commission. (2005). Mobilising the brainpower of Europe: Enabling universities to make their full contribution to the Lisbon strategy. Brussels: COM(2005) 152 final. http://eur-lex.europa.eu/LexUriServ/LexUriServ.do?uri=COM:2005:0152:FIN:EN:PDF

110. European Commission. (2006). *Delivering on the Modernisation Agenda for Universities: Education, Research and Innovation*. http://europa.eu/legislation_summaries/education_training_youth/lifelong_learning/c11089_en.htm/..

111. European Commission. (2007). *Towards a Post-carbon Society*. DG Research—Socio economic sciences and humanities. http://ec.europa.eu/transport/themes/strategies/studies/doc/future_of_transport/2009_02_transvisions_task2.pdf/.

112. European Commission. (2008). *Towards World-class Clusters in the European Union: Implementing the Broad-based Innovation Strategy*. http://eur-lex.europa.eu/LexUriServ/LexUriServ.do?uri=COM:2008:0652:REV 1:en:PDF/.

113. European Commission. (2008). *Mobilising ICT to Facilitate the Transition to an Energy Efficient, Low Carbon Economy*. Staff working document. http://www.europarl.europa.eu/sides/getDoc.do?language=EN&reference=A7-0120/2010/.

114. European Commission. (2009). *Making Public Support for Innovation in the EU More Effective: Lessons Learned from a Public Consultation for Action at Community Level*. Commission Staff Working Document. http://ec.europa.eu/enterprise/policies/innovation/files/swd_effectiveness_en.pdf/.

115. European Commission. (2010). *An Integrated Industrial Policy for the Globalisation Era Putting Competitiveness and Sustainability at Centre Stage*. Available at: *An Integrated Industrial Policy for the Globalisation Era Putting Competitiveness and Sustainability at Centre Stage*. http://ec.europa.eu/enterprise/policies/industrial-competitiveness/industrial-policy/files/communication_on_industrial_policy_en.pdf.

116. European Commission. (2010). *Europe 2020 Flagship Initiative Innovation Union*. http://ec.europa.eu/research/innovation-union/pdf/innovation-union-communication_en.pdf/.

117. European Commission. (2010). *Flash Eurobarometer 283: Entrepreneurship in the EU and Beyond*. The Gallup Organisation. http://ec.europa.eu/public_opinion/flash/fl_283_en.pdf/.

118. European Commission. (2010). *Regional Policy Contributing to Smart*

Growth in Europe 2020. http://ec.europa.eu/regional_policy/sources/docoffic/official/communic/comm_en.htm/.

119. European Commission. (2011). *Commission Opinion of 30.11.2011 on the Independent Expert Evaluation on the EIT* . COM(2011) 816 final. http://eit.europa.eu/fileadmin/Content/Downloads/PDF/EC_SIA/commission-opinion-on-the-external-evaluation_en.pdf/.

120. European Commission. (2011). *Horizon 2020—The Framework Programme for Research and Innovation.* COM(2011) 808 final. http://eur-lex.europa.eu/LexUriServ/LexUriServ.do?uri=COM:2011:0808:FIN:en:PDF/.

121. European Commission. (2011). *Regulation of the European Parliament and of the Council Amending Regulation (EC) No 294/2008 Establishing the European Institute of Innovation and Technology.* COM(2011) 817 final. http://eit.europa.eu/about-us/key-documents/.

122. European Commission. (2011). *Supporting Growth and Jobs—an Agenda for the Modernisation of Europe's Higher Education Systems.* COM(2011) 567 final. http://eur-lex.europa.eu/LexUriServ/LexUriServ.do?uri=COM:2011:0567:FIN:EN:PDF/

123. European Commission. (2012). *Report from the Commission to the European Parliament and the Council on the Evaluation of the Union's Finances Based on the Results Achieved.* COM (2012) 675 final. http://eur-lex.europa.eu/LexUriServ/LexUriServ.do?uri=COM:2012:0675:FIN:EN:PDF/

124. European Institute of Innovation and Technology. (2009). *Report of Governing Board Working Group on Research.* EIT internal document.

125. European Institute of Innovation and Technology. (2009). *Call for Knowledge and Innovation Communities.* http://www.eit.europa.eu/

126. European Institute of Innovation and Technology. (2010). *Intellectual Property Guidelines.* http://www.eit.europa.eu/

127. European Institute of Innovation and Technology. (2011). *Report on Visits to Co-location Centers.* EIT internal document.

128. European Institute of Innovation and Technology. (2011). *Strategic Innovation Agenda: Investing in Innovation Beyond 2014.* Report submitted by the European Institute of Innovation and Technology to the EU Commissioner for Education, Culture, Youth and Multilingualism. EIT internal document.

129. European Institute of Innovation and Technology. (2011). *Information Note on Business Involvement in the Activities of the EIT and its Knowledge and Innovation Communities (KICs).* EIT internal document.

130. European Institute of Innovation and Technology. (2012). *Annual Reports: 2008; 2009; 2010; 2011.* http://www.eit.europa.eu/

131. European Institute of Innovation and Technology. (2012). *Annual Work Programmes: 2012; 2013.* http://www.eit.europa.eu/.

132. European Institute of Innovation and Technology. (2012). *Rolling Triennial Work Programmes: 2010-2012; 2011-2013; 2012-2014; 2013-2015.* http://www.eit.europa.eu/

133. Eurostat. (2011). *Key Figures on European Business with a Special Feature*

on SMEs. http://epp.eurostat.ec.europa.eu/cache/ITY_OFFPUB/KS-ET-11-001/EN/KS-ET-11-001-EN.PDF/.

134. Eurostat. (2012). *Key Figures on Europe.* http://epp.eurostat.ec.europa.eu/cache/ITY_OFFPUB/KS-EI-12-001/EN/KS-EI-12-001-EN.PDF/

135. Etzkowitz, H. (2008). *The Triple Helix: University-Industry-Government Innovation in Action.* Taylor & Francis.

136. Etzkowitz, H., and Leydesdorff, L. (2000a). "The Dynamics of Innovation: From National Systems and 'Mode 2' to a Triple Helix of University-Industry-Government Relations," *Research Policy,* vol. 29 (2), pp. 109-123.

137. Etzkowitz, H., et al. (2000b). "The Future of the University and the University of the Future: Evolution of Ivory Tower to Entrepreneurial Paradigm," *Research Policy,* vol. 29 (2), pp. 313-330.

138. Expert Group to the European Commission. (2007). *Taking European Knowledge Society Seriously.* http://ec.europa.eu/research/science-society/document_library/pdf_06/european-knowledge-society_en.pdf/.

139. Expert Group to the European Commission. (2009). *The Role of Community Research Policy in the Knowledge-Based Economy.* http://ec.europa.eu/research/era/pdf/community_research_policy_role.pdf/.

140. Expert Group to the European Commission. (2011). *Final Report of the Expert Group on Synergies between FP7, the CIP and the Cohesion Policy Funds.* http://www.era.gv.at/attach/seg-final_en.pdf/

141. Fagerberg, J., Mowery, D.C., and Nelson, R.R. (eds). (2005). *The Oxford Handbook of Innovation.* Oxford: Oxford University Press.

142. Fairlie, R.W. (2014). *Kauffman Index of Entrepreneurial Activity 1996-2013.* http://www.kauffman.org/~/media/kauffman_org/research reports and covers/2014/04/kiea_2014_report.pdf.

143. Fernandes, A., Vieira, S., Medeiros, A., and Jorge, R. (2009). "Structured Methods of New Product Development and Creativity Management: A Teaching Experience," *Creativity and Innovation Management,* vol. 18, pp. 160-175.

144. Fey, C., and Birkinshaw, J. (2005). "External Sources of Knowledge, Governance Mode and R&D Performance," *Journal of Management,* vol. 31, no. 4, pp. 597- 621.

145. Florida, R. (1995). "Toward the Learning Region," *Futures,* Volume 27, Number 5, June 1995, pp. 527-536(10).

146. Florida, R. (2002). "The Economic Geography of Talent," *Annals of the Association of American Geographers,* vol. 92 (4), pp. 743-755.

147. Florida, R. (2004). The Rise of the Creative Class: And How It's Transforming Work, Leisure, Community and Everyday Life. Basic Books.

148. Florida, R. (2005). "The World is Spiky," *The Atlantic Monthly,* October 2005.

149. FORA. (2010). *New Nature of Innovation.* http://www.newnatureofinnovation.org/full_report.pdf/.

150. Forbes, N., Wield, D. (2002). *From Followers to Leaders: Managing Technology and Innovation in Newly Industrializing Countries.* London and New York: Routledge.

151. Ford, C.M., Sullivan, D.M. (2004). "A Time for Everything: How the Timing of Novel Contributions Influences Project Team Outcomes," *Journal of Organizational Behavior*, vol. 25, pp. 279-292.

152. Ford, C.M., and Sullivan, D.M. (2008). "A Multi-level Process View of New Venture Emergence', in M.D. Mumford, S.T. Hunter, K.E. Bedell-Avers (eds), *Multi-level Issues in Creativity and Innovation*. Elsevier JAI.

153. Frambach, R. (1993). "An Integrated Model of Organizational Adoption and Diffusion of Innovation." *European Journal of Marketing*, vol. 27 (5), pp. 22-41.

154. Freeman, C. (1988). "Japan: A New National Innovation System?," in G. Dosi, C. Freeman, R.R. Nelson, G. Silverberg, L. Soete (eds), *Technology and Economy Theory*. London: Pinter.

155. Furman, J.L., Porter, M.E., and Stern, S. (2002). "The Determinants of National Innovative Capacity," *Research Policy*, vol. 31, pp. 899-933.

156. Gadrey, J., Gallouj, F., and Weinstein, O. (1995). "New Modes of Innovation: How Services Benefit Industry," *International Journal of Service Industry Management*, vol. 6 (3), pp. 4-16.

157. Gallouj, F. (2002). *Innovation in the Service Economy: The New Wealth of Nations*. Cheltenhan: Edward Elgar Publishing Ltd.

158. Gartner, W.B. (1985). "A Conceptual Framework for Describing The Phenomena of New Venture Creation." *Academy of Management Review*, vol. 10 (4), pp. 696-706.

159. Gartner, W.B. (2001). "Is There an Elephant in Entrepreneurship? Blind Assumptions in Theory Development (Business research)," *Entrepreneurship Theory and Practice*, Summer 2001.

160. Gedajlovic, E., Neubaum, D.O., and Shulman, J.M. (2009). "A Typology of Social Entrepreneurs: Motives, Search Processes and Ethical Challenges," *Journal of Business Venturing*, vol. 24 (5), pp. 519-532.

161. Georghiou, L. (2001). "Evolving Frameworks for European Collaboration in Research and Technology," *Research Policy*, vol. 30, pp. 891-903.

162. Georghiou, L. et al. (2008). *Challenging Europe's Research: Rationales for the European Research Area (ERA). Report of the ERA Expert Group*. Brussels: European Commission, Directorate General for Research.

163. Gerchenkron, A. (1962). *Economic Backwardness in Historical Perspective: A Book of Essays*. Cambridge: Harvard University Press.

164. Giarini, O. (1994). "The Service Economy: Challenges and Opportunities in Business Firms," in M.M. Kostechki (eds), *Marketing Strategies for Services*. London: Pergamon, pp. 23-40,.

165. Godeke, S., and Pomares, R. (2009). *Solutions for Impact Investors: From Strategy to Implementation*. Rockefeller Philanthropy Advisors.

166. Gołębiowska-Tataj, D. (2008). *Entrepreneurship and Venture Capital: Key Challenges and Tasks*. Position Paper for the EIT 2nd Governing Board Meeting in Budapest.

167. Geiger, R.L., and Sá, C.M. (2008). *Tapping the Riches of Science: Universities and the Promise of Economic Growth*. Cambridge: Harvard University Press.

168. Gibbons, M. et al. (1994). *The New Production Of Knowledge*. London: Sage Publications.

169. Gompers, P.A., and Lerner, J. (2004). *Venture Capital Cycle*. Massachusetts Institute of Technology.

170. Gompers, P.A., and Lerner, J. (2000). "The Origins of Ownership Structure: The Determinants of Corporate Venture Capital Success: Organizational Structure, Incentives, and Complementarities," in R.K. Morck (ed.), *Concentrated Corporate Ownership*. University of Chicago Press, pp. 17-54.

171. Graham, P. (2012). *Startup=Growth*. http://www.paulgraham.com.

172. Granstrand, O., Bohlin, E., Oscarsson S., and Sjöberg, N. (1992). "External Technology Acquisition in Large Multi-technology Corporations," *R&D Management*, vol. 22 (2), pp. 111-133.

173. Gromb, D., & Scharfstein, D. (2001). "Entrepreneurial Activity in Equilibrium," *draft, Sloan School of Management*.

174. Grönroos, C. (1990). *Service Management and Marketing: Managing the Moments of Truth in Service Competition*. Lexington, MA: Lexington Books.

175. Gupta, P.K. (2007). *Business Innovation in the 21st century*. Accelper Consulting.

176. Guseynova, N. (2011). *Aalto on Waves*. http://www.aaltoonwaves.com.html.

177. Gurteen, D. (1998). "Knowledge, Creativity and Innovation," *Journal of Knowledge Management*, vol. 2, pp. 5-13.

178. Haegeman, K., and Cagnin, C. (2011). *Priority Areas for the Next Waves of Knowledge and Innovation Communities: Exploration of Critical Success Factors, Alternative Options and Characteristics for Design*. JRC-IPTS Report. http://ipts.jrc.ec.europa.eu/publications/pub.cfm?id=4479/.

179. Hagedoorn, J. (2002). "Inter-firm R&D Partnerships: An Overview of Major Trends and Patterns since 1960," *Research Policy*, vol. 31, pp. 477-492.

180. Hagel III, J., and Brown, J.S. (2008). *From Transactional Markets to Relational Networks: Amplifying the Innovation Potential of High Tech Regions*. Stanford Project on Regions of Innovation and Entrepreneurship.

181. Hamel, G., and Prahalad, C.K. (1994). *Competing for the Future: Breakthrough Strategies for Seizing Control of Your Industry and Creating the Markets of Tomorrow*. Boston: Harvard Business School Press.

182. Hargadon, A. (2003). *How Breakthroughs Happen: The Surprising Truth about How Companies Innovate*. Boston: Harvard Business School Press.

183. Hartigan, P., and Elkington, J. (2008). *The Power of Unreasonable People: How Entrepreneurs Create Markets to Change the World*. Harvard Business Press.

184. Heap, S. H. (1989). *Rationality in Economics*. B. Blackwell.

185. Heath, C., and Sitkin, S.B. (2001). "Big-B versus Big-O: What is Organizational about Organizational Behavior?" *Journal of Organizational Behavior*, vol. 22, pp. 43-58.

186. Hemlin, S., Allwood, C.M., and Martin, B.R. (2008).

"Creative Knowledge Environments," *Creativity Research Journal*, vol. 20 (2), pp. 196-210.

187. Henderson, R., and Clark, K. (1990). "Architectural Innovation: The Reconfiguration of Existing Product Technologies and the Failure of Established Firms," *Administrative Science Quarterly*, vol. 35, pp. 9-30.

188. Herstad, S., Bloch, C., Ebersberger, B., and van de Velde, E. (2008). *Open Innovation and Globalisation: Theory, Evidence and Implications*. Vision ERA-NET.

189. Higgins, J. (2005). *101 Creative Problem Solving Techniques: The Handbook of New Ideas for Business*. New Management Pub.

190. Himanen, P., Castells, M., and Torvalds, L. (2001). *The Hacker Ethic: A Radical Approach to the Philosophy of Business*. New York: Random House.

191. Hoelscher, M. (2010). "Measuring creativity and innovation," in H. Anheier, and Y.R. Isar (eds), *Cultures and Globalization: Cultural Expression, Creativity and Innovation*. London et al.: Sage Publications.

192. Hofstede, G. (1984). *Culture's Consequences: International Differences in Work-Related Values*. California, UK, India: Sage Publications.

193. Hughes, A. (2003). *Knowledge Transfer, Entrepreneurship and Implications for Growth: Some Reflections and Implications for Policy in the Netherlands, ESRC Centre for Business Research*. University of Cambridge, Working Paper No. 273, Centre for Business Research.

194. Hollanders, H., and van Cruysen, A. (2009). *Design, Creativity, and Innovation: A Scoreboard Approach*. Pro Inno/Inno Metrics. http://www.proinno-europe.eu/sites/default/files/EIS_2008_Creativity_and_Design.pdf/.

195. Howkins, J. (2006). "The Mayor's Commission on Creative Industries," in J. Hartley (ed.), *Creative Industries*. Blackwell Publishing.

196. Husser, Ph., Lemola, T. (2010). EIT SCOREBOARD: Strategic Objectives and Measures Summary report, in cooperation with the EIT Scoreboard Working Group (Chair: Yrjö Neuvo; EIT GB participants: Karen Maex, Daria Tataj, Ellen de Brabander, Giovanni Colombo, Morten Loktu; Georgi Dimitrov). European Commission, DG EAC/A2.

197. Iansiti, M. (1998). *Technology Integration: Making Critical Choices in a Dynamic World*. Boston: Harvard Business School Press.

198. INNO Grips studies. (2012). *Analysis of Innovation Derivers and Barriers in support of Better Policies. Economic and Market Intelligence on Innovation. Social Attitudes to Innovation and Entrepreneurship*. Available at: http://ec.europa.eu/enterprise/policies/innovation/files/proinno/innovation-intelligence-study-4_en.pdf/

199. Innovation Union Scoreboard 2010. (2011). *The Innovation Union's Performance Scoreboard for Research and Innovation*. http://ec.europa.eu/research/innovation-union/pdf/iu-scoreboard-2010_en.pdf/

200. IPREG. (2011). *Entrepreneurship and SME-policies across Europe. The Cases of Sweden, Flanders, Austria and Poland*. http://www.ipreg.org/Rapport_2011_03,%20the%20case%20of%20Sweden,%20Flanders,%20Austria%20and%20Poland.pdf/

201. Ireland, R.D., Reutzel, C.R., and Webb, J.W. (2005). "Entrepreneurship Research in AMJ: What has been Published, and What Might the Future Hold?," *Academy of Management Journal*, vol. 48 (4), pp. 556-564.

202. Ito, M. (2009). *Hanging Out, Messing Around, and Geeking Out: Kids Living and Learning with New Media.* Cambridge: MIT Press.

203. Jacobs, D. (2007). *Adding Values: The Cultural Side of Innovation.* ArtEZ Press.

204. Jack, R., As-Saber, S., Edwards, R., and Buckley, P. (2008). "The Role of Service Embeddedness in the Internationalization Process of Manufacturing Firms," *International Business Review,* 17(4), pp. 442–451.

205. Jackson, R.W., Neidell, L.A., and Lunsford, D.A. (1995). "An Empirical Investigation of the Differences in Goods and Services as Perceived by Organizational Buyers," *Industrial Marketing Management* 24(2), pp. 99–108.

206. Janssen, O., van de Vliert, E., and West, M. (2004). "The Bright and Dark Sides of Individual and Group Innovation: A Special Issue Introduction," *Journal of Organizational Behavior*, vol. 25, pp. 129-145.

207. Jaussi, K.S. (2008). "Do Levels and Phases Always Happen Together? Questions for Considering the Case of New-venture Emergence," in M.D. Mumford, S.T. Hunter, and K.E. Bedell-Avers (eds), *Multi-level issues in creativity and innovation.* Elsevier JAI.

208. Jeffcutt, P., and Pratt, A. (2002). "Managing Creativity in the Cultural Industries," *Creativity and Innovation Management*, vol. 11 (4), pp. 225-233.

209. Karnani, A. (2011). Fighting Poverty Together: Rethinking Strategies for Business, Governments, and Civil Society to Reduce Poverty. New York: Palgrave Macmillan.

210. Ketels, C.H.M., and Memedovic, O. (2008). "From Clusters to Cluster-Based Economic Development: Special Issue on Global Value Chains and Innovation Networks: Prospects for Industrial Upgrading in Developing Countries. Part 1," *International Journal of Technological Learning, Innovation, and Development,* Vol. 1, No. 3, pp. 375-400.

211. Kharas, H. (2010). *The Emerging Middle Class in Developing Countries.* OECD. http://www.oecd.org/dev/44457738.pdf.

212. KIC InnoEnergy. (2011). *KIC InnoEnergy Business Plan 2012.* KIC InnoEnergy Internal Document.

213. King, N. (2002). *Managing Innovation and Change: A Critical Guide for Organizations.* London: Thomson.

214. Kirk. K., and Cotton, Ch. (2012). *The Cambridge Phenomenon: 50 Years of Innovation and Enterprise.* Center for Entrepreneurial Learning, University of Cambridge, Judge Business School.

215. Klonowski, D. (2007). "The Venture Capital Investment Process in Emerging Markets: Evidence from Central and Eastern Europe," *International Journal of Emerging Markets*, 2(4), pp. 361-382.

216. Klonowski, D. (2010). "The Effectiveness of Government-sponsored Programmes in Supporting the SME sector in Poland," *Post-communist Economies*, 22(2), pp. 229-245.

217. Klonowski, D. (2010). "Business Incubation and Its Connection to

Venture Capital," in Cumming, D. J. (ed.) Venture Capital: Investment Strategies, Structures, and Policies, John Wiley & Sons, Inc., Hoboken, NJ, USA.

218. Klonowski, D., and Gołębiowska-Tataj, D. (2008). *PESTEL Analysis of Challenges Ahead European Innovation and SME Development.* Working Note.

219. Kogut, B., and Zander, U. (2000). "What do firms do?," *American Sociological Review*, vol. 65 (2), pp. 169-190.

220. Kortum, S., and Lerner, J. (2000). "Assessing the Contribution of Venture Capital to Innovation," *The RAND Journal of Economics*, vol. 31, no. 4 (Winter 2000), pp. 674-692.

221. Kreijns, K., Kirschner, P.A., & Jochems, W. (2002). "The Sociability of Computer-supported Collaborative Learning Environments," *Journal of Education Technology & Society* 5(1), 822. Retrieved February 2, 2003 from http://ifets.ieee.org/periodical/vol_1_2002/v_1_2002.html.

222. Krugman, P. (1979). "A Model of Innovation, Technology Transfer, and the World Distribution of Income." *Journal of Political Economy*, vol. 87 (2), pp. 253-266.

223. Kwiatkowski, S. (2000). *Przedsiębiorczość intelektualna*. Warsaw: Wydawnictwo Naukowe PWN.

224. Kvale, S. (1996). *Interviews: An Introduction to Qualitative Research Interviewing*. Thousand Oaks (California): Sage Publication.

225. Lazonick, W. (2005). "The Innovation Firm," in J. Fagerberg, D.C. Mowery, R.R. Nelson (eds), *The Oxford Handbook of Innovation*. Oxford: Oxford University Press.

226. Lerner, J. (2010). "The future of public efforts to boost entrepreneurship and venture capital," Small Business Economics, October 2010, Volume 35, Issue 3.

227. LERU. (2006). Universities and Innovation: The Challenge for Europe. http://www.leru.org/files/general/Universities%20and%20Innovation%20The%20Challenge%20for%20Europe%20(November%202006).pdf/.

228. Levitt, T. (2003). "Creativity is Not Enough," in *Harvard Business Review on the Innovative Enterprise*. Boston: Harvard Business School Press.

229. *Lieberthal, K.,* and Prahalad, C.K. (2001). "The End of Corporate Imperialism," *Harvard Business Review*, vol. 81, no. 8 (August 2001).

230. Lindqvist G., and Sölvell, O. (2011). *Organising Clusters for Innovation: Lessons from City Regions in Europe – CLUSNET*, final report. http://www.clusnet.eu/fileadmin/user_upload/fichiers/documents/CLUSNET_Final_Report.PDF/

231. Liuhto, K. (2011). "Rosnano and Skolkovo are Russia's Best Innovation Promoting Measures, but They are Not Enough to Modernise Russia as a Whole," in E. Laaksonen (ed.), *Baltic Rim Economies Expert Articles 2010, Electronic Publications of Pan-European Institute,* vol. 2011/02.

232. London, T., and Anupindi, R. (2011). *Using the Base-of-the-pyramid Perspective to Catalyze Interdependence-based Collaborations*. P. Pingali, and Bill and Melinda Gates Foundation, (eds). Ann Arbor: William Davidson Institute and Ross School of Business, University of Michigan.

233. Lundvall, B.-Å., Johnson, B., Andersen, E.S., and Dalum, B. (2002). "National Systems of Production, Innovation, and Competence Building," *Research Policy*, vol. 31, pp. 213-231.

234. Lundvall, B.-Å. (1985). "Product Innovation and User-producer Interaction, Industrial Development," *Research Series, vol. 31*. Aalborg: Aalborg University Press.

235. Lundvall, B. (2002). *The University in the Learning Economy*. DRUID Working Paper, no. 02-06.

236. Meier zu Köcker, G., Müller, L., and Zombori, Z. (2011). *European Clusters Go International: Networks and Clusters as Instruments for the Initiation of International Business Cooperation*. http://www.tci-network. org/cluster/resources/.

237. Metcalfe, S. (1995). "The Economic Foundations of Technology Policy: Equilibrium and Evolutionary Perspectives," in P. Stoneman (ed.), *Handbook of the Economics of Innovation and Technological Change*. Oxford (UK) and Cambridge (US): Blackwell Publishers.

238. Metler, A., and Williams, A.D. (2001). "The Rise of the Micro-Multinational: How Freelancers and Technology Savvy Start-Ups Are Driving Growth," *Jobs and Innovation*, vol. 3. no. 3. Lisbon: Lisbon Council Policy Brief.

239. Mokyr, J. (1990). *The Lever of Riches: Technological Creativity and Economic Progress*. Oxford: Oxford University Press.

240. Monge, P.R., and Contractor, N. (2003). *Theories of Communication Networks*. New York and Oxford: Oxford University Press.

241. Mowery D.V., and Sampat, B.N. (2005). "Universities in National Innovation Systems," in J. Fagerberg, D.C. Mowery, and R.R. Nelson (eds), *The Oxford Handbook of Innovation*. Oxford: Oxford University Press, pp. 209-239.

242. Mueller, S.L., and Thomas, A.S. (2000). "Culture and Entrepreneurial Potential: A Nine Country Study of Locus of Control and Innovativeness," *Journal of Business Venturing*, vol. 16.

243. Mumford, M.D., and Gustafson, S.B. (1988). "Creativity Syndrome: Integration, Application, and Innovation," *Psychological Bulletin*, vol. 103, pp. 27-43.

244. Mumford, M.D., Hunter, S.T., and Bedell-Avers, K.E. (eds). (2008). *Multi-level Issues in Creativity and Innovation*. Elsevier JAI.

245. Nelson, R., and Winter, S. (1982). *An Evolutionary Theory of Economic Change*. Cambridge: Harvard University Press.

246. Nicolaou, N., and Shane, S. (2009). "Can Genetic Factors Influence the Likelihood of Engaging in Entrepreneurial Activity?," *Journal of Business Venturing*, vol. 24, pp. 1-22.

247. Nooteboom, B., and Stam, E. (2008). *Micro-foundations for Innovation Policy*. Amsterdam University Press.

248. Obloj, T., Obloj, K., and Pratt, M. G. (2010). "Dominant logic and entrepreneurial firms' performance in a transition economy," *Entrepreneurship Theory and Practice*, 34(1), 151-170.

249. OECD. (1996). *Oslo Manual, Guidelines for Collecting and Interpreting*

Data, 2nd Edition DSTI. Paris: OECD.

250. OECD. (2005). *Entrepreneurship Indicators Program*. OECD Statistics Directorate, 3rd edition. Paris: OECD.

251. OECD. (2007). *Science, Technology and Innovation Indicators in a Changing World—Responding to Policy Needs*. Paris: OECD.

252. OECD. (2008). *Compendium of Patent Statistics*. Paris: OECD.

253. OECD. (2008). *Open Innovation in Global Network*. Paris: OECD.

254. OECD. (2010). *Innovation Strategy: Getting a Head Start on Tomorrow*. Paris: OECD.

255. OECD. (2012). *Closing the Gender Gap*. Paris: Act Now, OECD.

256. OECD/European Union. (2012). *Policy Brief on Youth and Entrepreneurship: Entrepreneurial Activities in Europe*. http://www.oecd.org/regional/leed/Youth%20Policy%20Brief.pdf/.

257. Oldham, G.R., and Cummings, A. (1996). "Employee Creativity: Personal and Contextual Factors at Work," *Academy of Management Journal*, vol. 39, pp. 607-634.

258. Orłowski, W. (2011). "Post-accession Economic Development of Poland," *Eastern Journal of European Studies*.

259. Pain, H. (2009). *Innovation in Qualitative Research Methodology: Annotated Bibliography*. NCRM Working Paper. Southampton (UK): National Centre for Research Methods.

260. O'Reilley, C., and Chatman, J. (1996). "Culture as Social Control: Corporations, Cults, and Commitment," *Research in Organizational Behavior*, vol. 18, pp. 157-200.

261. O'Reilley, C., and Pfeffer, J. (2000). *Hidden Value: How Great Companies Achieve Extraordinary Results with Ordinary People*. Boston: Harvard Business School Press.

262. O'Sullivan, M. (2005). "Finance and innovation," in J. Fagerberg, D.C. Mowery, and R.R. Nelson (eds), *The Oxford Handbook of Innovation*. Oxford: Oxford University Press.

263. Patel, P., and Pavitt, K. (1994). "The Nature and Economic Importance of National Innovation Systems," *STI Review*, no. 14. Paris: OECD.

264. Parker, C.S., Storey, D.J., and van Witteloostuijn, A. (2010). "What Happens to Gazelles? The Importance of Dynamic Management Strategy," *Small Business Economics*, vol. 35, pp. 203-226.

265. Pavitt, K. (1984). "Sectorial Patterns of Technical Change: Towards a Taxonomy and a Theory," *Research Policy*, vol. 13.

266. Pavitt, K. (2005). "Innovation processes," in J. Fagerberg, D.C. Mowery, and R.R. Nelson (eds), *The Oxford Handbook of Innovation*. Oxford: Oxford University Press.

267. Pendelton-Jullian, A. (2009). *Design Education and Innovation Ecotones*. http://president.asu.edu/files/Design%20Innovation%20and%20Innovation%20Ecotones.pdf.

268. Phang, Ch.W., Kankanhalli, A., and Sabherwal, R. (2009). "Usability and Sociability in Online Communities: A Comparative Study of Knowledge Seeking and Contribution," *Journal of the Association for Information Systems* 10(10), 2.

269. Plucker, J.A., Beghetoo, R.A., and Dow, G.T. (2004). "Why isn't Creativity More Important to Educational Psychologists? Potentials, Pitfalls, and Future Directions in Creativity Research," *Educational Psychologist*, vol. 39, pp. 83-96.

270. Płoszajski, P. (2011). "Management on the Edge of Chaos: The Challenges of the Petbyte Age," *Journal of Management and Financial Sciences*, 4(5), pp. 65-67.

271. Polanyi, M. (1967). *The Tacit Dimension*. New York: Anchor/Doubleday.

272. Polanyi, M. (1974). *Scientific Thoughts and Social Reality: Essays*. Madison: International University Press.

273. Pollack, R. (1994). *Signs of Life: The Language and Meanings of DNA*. Houghton Mifflin Company.

274. Porter, M.E. (1998). *Clusters and Competition: New Agendas for Companies, Governments, and Institutions: On Competition*. Boston: Harvard Business School Press.

275. Potocnik, J. (2006). *Embedding European science into European society*. Vienna, 20 Jan 2006, Austrian Academy of Sciences.

276. Prahalad, C.K. (2005). *The Fortune at the Bottom of the Pyramid: Eradicating Poverty Through Profits*. New York (Upper Saddle River): Wharton School Publishing.

277. Prahalad, C.K., and Hammond, A. (2002). "Serving the World's Poor, Profitably," *Harvard Business Review*.

278. Prahalad, C.K., and Krishnan, M.S. (2008). *The New Age of Innovation*. Ann Arbor: University of Michigan Ross School of Business.

279. Pratt, A.C., and Jeffcutt, P. (eds). (2009). *Creativity, Innovation and the Cultural Economy*. Routledge.

280. Preece, J. (2001). "Sociability and Usability in Online Communities: Determining and Measuring Success," *Behaviour & Information Technology* 20(5), pp. 347-356.

281. Putnam, R. (1995). "Bowling Alone: America's Declining Social Capital," *Journal of Democracy*, vol. 6 (1).

282. *Regulation (EC) no 294/2008 of the European Parliament and of the Council establishing the European Institute of Innovation and Technology* (11 March 2008). Official Journal of the European Union.

283. Radiou, R., Prabhu, J., Ahuja, S., and Roberts, K. (2012). *Jugaad Innovation: Think Frugal, Be Flexible, Generate Breakthrough Growth*. San Francisco: Jossey-Brass. A Wiley Imprint.

284. Riddle, L., Hrivnak, G.A., and Nielsen, T.M. (2008). *Bridging Two Worlds: Incubating Transnational Business Ventures*. Paper presented at the Transnational Entrepreneurship and Global Reach conference at Wilfrid Laurier University and 4th Annual Research on Entrepreneurship Conference at George Mason University (USA).

285. Russo, E. (2003). "Special Report: The birth of biotechnology". *Nature*, 421(6921).

286. Salter, A., and Tether, B. (2006). *Innovation in Services: Through the Looking Glass of Innovation Studies*. Background Paper for AIM Grand Challenge on Services. Oxford: Oxford University.

287. Saxenian, A.L. (1990). "Regional Networks and the Resurgence of Silicon Valley," *California Management Review*.

288. Saxenian, A.L. (1996). *Regional Advantage: Culture and Competition in Silicon Valley and Route 128*. Boston, Cambridge and London: Harvard Business School Press.

289. Saxenian, A.L., and Hsu, J.Y. (2001). "The Silicon Valley-Hsinchu Connection: Technical Communities and Industrial Upgrading," *Industrial and Corporate Change*, Oxford University Press, Volume 10, Number 4, pp. 893-920.

290. Schumpeter, J. (1934). *The Theory of Economic Development*. Cambridge: Harvard University Press.

291. Schwab, K. (2011). *World Economic Forum: Competitiveness Report 2011-2012*. Geneva: World Economic Forum. http://www.slideshare.net/AdrJasonCates/competitive-economies-report/.

292. Scott, A. (2006). "Creative Cities: Conceptual Issues and Policy Questions," *Journal of Urban Affairs*, vol. 28 (1), pp. 1-17.

293. Senor, D., and Singer, S. (2009). *Start-up Nation: The Story of Israel's Economic Miracle*. New York: Twelve Hachette Book Group.

294. Shackel, B. (1991). "Usability—context, framework, definition, design and evaluation," in B. Shackel, S. Richardson (ed.), *Human Factors for Informatics Usability*. Cambridge (UK): Cambridge University Press, pp. 21-37.

295. Shalley, C.E., Zhou, J., and Oldham, G.R. (2004). "What Leaders Need to Know: A Review of Social and Contextual Factors that can Foster or Hinder Creativity," *Leadership Quarterly*, vol. 15, pp. 33-53.

296. Shane, S., and Venkataraman, S. (2000). "The Promise of Entrepreneurship as a Field of Research," *Academy of Management Review*, vol. 25 (1), pp. 217-226.

297. Shane, S. (2000). "Prior Knowledge and the Discovery of Entrepreneurial Opportunities," *Organization Science*, vol. 11 (4), pp. 448-469.

298. Shane, S. (2006). "Introduction to the Focused Issue on Entrepreneurship," *Management Science*, vol. 52 (2), pp. 155-159.

299. Shane, S., and Ulrich, K.T. (2004). "Technological Innovation, Product Development and Entrepreneurship in Management Science," *Management Science*, vol. 50 (2).

300. Shaver, K.G., and Scott, L.R. (1991). "Person, Process, Choice: The Psychology of New Venture Creation," *Entrepreneurship Theory and Practice*, vol. 15 (2), pp. 23-45.

301. Shenkar, O. (2010). *Copycats: How Smart Companies Use Imitation to Gain a Strategic Edge*. Boston: Harvard Business Press.

302. Shoemaker, P.J., and Reese, S.D. (1990). "Exposure to What? Integrating Media Content and Effects Studies," *Journalism Quarterly*, vol. 67.

303. Shook, C.L., Priem, R.L., and McGee, J.E. (2003). "Venture Creation and the Enterprising Individual: a Review and Synthesis," *Journal of Management*, vol. 29 (3).

304. Shrift, N. (1992). "Neo-Marshallian Nodes in Global Networks," *International Journal of Urban and Regional Research*, vol. 16, issue 4 (December

1992), pp. 571–587.

305. Simonton, D.K. (2000). "Creativity: Cognitive, Personal, Developmental, and Social Aspects," *American Psychologist*, vol. 55 (1) (January 2000).

306. Smits, A., Vissers, G., and de Wit, J. (2009). *Exploratory and Exploitative Market Learning in Discontinuous New Product Development.* The Netherlands: Institute for Science, Innovation and Society, Radboud University.

307. Storey, D.J. (1994). *Understanding the Small Business Sector.* London: Thomson.

308. Sun, A. Y. (1998). "From Pirate King to Jungle King: Transformation of Taiwan's Intellectual Property Protection". *Fordham Intell. Prop. Media & Ent. LJ, 9, 67.*

309. Sundbo, J., and Gallouj, F. (2000). "Innovation as a Loosely Coupled System in Services," in J.S. Metcalfe and I. Miles (eds), *Innovation Systems in the Service Economy: Measurements and Case Study Analysis.* Boston: Kluwer, pp. 43-68.

310. Taftie. (2009). *Internationalisation of National Innovation Agencies: Seizing Global Opportunities.* http://www.taftie.org.

311. Tagger, S. (2002). "Individual Creativity and Group Ability to Utilize Individual Creative Resources: A Multilevel Model," *Academy of Management Journal*, vol. 45.

312. Taleb, N. (2010). *The Black Swan: The Impact of the Highly Improbable.* Random House.

313. Tapscott, D., and Williams, A. (2006). *Wikinomics: How Mass Collaboration Changes Everything.* Portfolio.

314. Tapscott, D., and Williams, A. (2010). *Macrowikinomics: Rebooting Business and the World.* Penguin.

315. Technopolis. (2011). *Catalysing Innovation in the Knowledge Triangle: Practices from the EIT Knowledge and Innovation Communities.* http://eit.europa.eu/fileadmin/Content/Downloads/PDF/Key_documents/EIT_publication_Final.pdf/.

316. The Call for Proposals EIT-KICs. (2009). *Knowledge and Innovation Communities.* (2009). http://www.eit.europa.eu.

317. The Council of the European Union. (2009). *Conclusions on Developing the Role of Education in a Fully-functioning Knowledge Triangle.* 2009/C 302/03. http://eur-lex.europa.eu/LexUriServ/LexUriServ.do?uri=OJ:C:2009:302:0003:0005:EN:PDF/.

318. Thom, N. (2011). *Foresight in Innovation Networks: The EIT Innovation Radar Example.* Paper presented at 4th ISPIM Innovation Symposium.

319. Thompson, J. (2012). "The Metamorphosis of a Crisis," in M. Castells, J. Caraca, and G. Cardoso (ed.), *Aftermath: The Cultures of the Economic Crisis.* Oxford: Oxford University Press.

320. Thomas, D., and Brown, J.S. (2010). "Learning in/for a World of Constant Flux," in L.E. Weber and J. Duderstadt (ed.), *University Research for Innovation.* Economica.

321. Timmons, J.A., and Spinelli, S. (2009). *New Venture Creation, Entrepreneurship for the 21st Century*, 8th edition. McGraw-Hill Higher Educa-

tion.

322. Timmons, J.A., and Bygrave, W.D. (1986). *Venture Capital's Role in Financing Innovation for Economic Growth*. Babson College, Arthur M. Blank Center for Entrepreneurship.

323. Uppenberg, K. (2009). *R&D in Europe*. Brussels: Centre for European Policy Studies.

324. Utterback, J.M. (1994). *Mastering the Dynamics of Innovation: How Companies Can Seize Opportunities in the Face of Technological Change*. Boston: Harvard Business School Press.

325. Vernon, R. (1966). "International Investment and International Trade in the Product Cycle," *The Quarterly Journal of Economics*, pp. 190-207.

326. Von Hippel, E. (2005). *Democratizing Innovation*. The MIT Press.

327. Von Hippel, E. (1988). *The Sources of Innovation*. New York and Oxford: Oxford University Press.

328. Weiser, M., Gold, R., and Brown, J.S. (1999). "The Origins of Ubiquitous Computing Research at PARC in the late 1980s," *IBM Systems Journal*, vol. 38, no. 4.

329. Welbourne, J., and Andres, A. (1996). "Predicting Performance of Initial Public Offering Firms: Should HRM be in the Equation?," *Academy of Management Journal*, vol. 38 (645).

330. West, M., and Rickards, T. (1999). "Innovation," in M. Runco, S. Pritsker, (eds), *Encyclopaedia of Creativity*, vol. 2, San Diego, CA: Academic Press.

331. West, M.A. (2002). "Sparkling Fountains or Stagnant Ponds: An Integrative Model of Creativity and Innovation Implementation in Work Groups," *Applied Psychology: An International Review*, vol. 51.

332. Westhead, P., and Storey, D.J. (1995). "Links between Higher Education Institutions and High Technology Firms," *Omega*, vol. 23, pp. 345-360.

333. *Women of Tomorrow: A Study of Women Around the World*. (June 2011). A report by Nielsen.

334. World Bank. (2012). *World Development Indicators*. http://data.worldbank.org/about/country-classifications/country-and-lending-groups.

335. Wu, Y., Wang, Zh., Chang, K., & Xu, Y.J. (2010). *Why People Stick to Play Social Network Site Based Entertainment: Design Factors and Flow Theory Perspective*, http://www.pacis-net.org/file/2010/S24-02.pdf.

336. Yates, A.J. (2000). "The Knowledge Problem, Entrepreneurial Discovery and Austrian Market Process Theory," *Journal of Economic Theory*, vol. 91 (1).

337. Zhang, J. (2005). *Growing Silicon Valley on a Landscape: An Agent-based Approach to High-tech Industrial Clusters, Entrepreneurship, The New Economy and Policy*. pp. 71-90.

338. Zhongming Wang, Z., and Zang, Z. (2005). "Strategic Human Resources, Innovation and Entrepreneurship Fit: A Cross-regional Comparative Model," *International Journal of Manpower*, vol. 26, no. 6.

CPSIA information can be obtained at www.ICGtesting.com
Printed in the USA
BVOW02*0132151015

422399BV00002B/13/P